Power and Crisis in the City

SOCIOLOGY, POLITICS AND CITIES

Editor: JAMES SIMMIE

PUBLISHED

Manuel Castells: CITY, CLASS AND POWER
Patrick Dunleavy: URBAN POLITICAL ANALYSIS
Brian Elliott and David McCrone: THE CITY
Roger Friedland: POWER AND CRISIS IN THE CITY
John Lambert, Chris Paris and Bob Blackaby: HOUSING POLICY
   AND THE STATE
James Simmie: POWER, PROPERTY AND CORPORATISM

FORTHCOMING

Valdo Pons and Ray Francis: SLUMS AND SHANTY TOWNS
James Simmie and David Lovatt: MARXISM AND CITIES

Power and Crisis in the City

Corporations, unions and urban policy

ROGER FRIEDLAND

University of California, Santa Barbara

First published 1982 by
THE MACMILLAN PRESS LTD
London and Basingstoke
Companies and representatives throughout the world

ISBN 0 333 26075 9 (hard cover)
ISBN 0 333 26076 7 (paper cover)

Typeset in 11/12 Baskerville by
THE EASTERN PRESS LTD

Printed in Hong Kong

To my parents – Helen and Harry Friedland – at whose loving and quarrelsome dinner table I learned to think, I humbly dedicate this book

Contents

Editor's Preface

Sociology, Politics and Cities

Cities have been the focal points of economic, political and cultural life in all those countries experiencing the kind of rapid industrial and commercial evolution that was first seen in the early nineteenth century in Britain. To understand national economic and political forces was therefore to comprehend the development of cities. To follow culture required insight into urban life. Early appreciations of these links developed in the German works of Marx, Weber and Simmel.

This early appreciation of the importance of the relationships between national forces and cities was not emphasized in the American analyses of cities stimulated by the Chicago School. Although it was to some extent present in the work of Park, Burgess, McKenzie and Wirth, it was lost in subsequent work which tended to conceptualize cities as isolated and self-contained phenomena. The significance of the relationships between power and cities was, however, kept alive in the American community power study work. The Lynds, Hunter, Dahl and more recently Bachrach, Baratz and Crenson have all made important contributions to our understanding of cities.

The eruption of major urban-based conflicts on both sides of the Atlantic during the 1960s made it quite clear that cities could not be understood within the main American paradigms of the 1920s. They also demonstrated that both national economic forces and the concept of power were central to any comprehension of what was happening in cities at that time.

This intellectual challenge was first met in France in different ways by Lefebvre, Castells and Lojkine. Harvey also made a contribution in Britain. Much of this work was based either on neo-Marxist Althusserian structuralism or on extensions of Marxist political economy, particularly the concept of rent. Although this work provided a great stimulus to urban research, some elements of it have not proved as fruitful as was first hoped. It has suffered from ethnocentricity, circularity, inappropriateness in contemporary circumstances and a lack of comparative empiricism.

A different intellectual response to understanding cities was also started in the late 1960s, this time in Britain, by Rex, Moore and Pahl. They developed some Weberian themes to account for the observable distributions of urban resources by so-called 'gatekeepers'. This type of local work, although useful in understanding local processes, did not address the growing significance of national and international forces in shaping particular urban developments.

The series 'Sociology, Politics and Cities' provides a vehicle for the extension of these debates and for newer contemporary approaches to understanding cities. The series is trans-disciplinary, including not only sociological and political work but also interconnected economic and historical research. It includes analyses of both private and public intervention in cities and therefore encompasses an interest in public policy. The main aim of the series is to encourage and stimulate a continuing debate and analysis concerned with capitalist, socialist and underdeveloped cities. It is concerned to develop theoretical understanding of these phenomena based on empirical analyses. On the bases of such understanding the series is also concerned with the formulation and evaluation of significant and relevant urban policies.

London University   JAMES SIMMIE
January 1982

The Reasons Why Cities are
Ugly and Sad: A Foreword

Roger Friedland's *Power and Crisis in the City* deserves a wide
readership. Although the book is specifically concerned with
policy and politics in the central cities of the US, it also deals in
a fertile and original, not to say provocative, manner with
some issues of fundamental significance to social and political
science in general. The immediate subject-matter of the study
is the role and power of business corporations and trade unions
in American urban policy in the postwar period, especially
in so far as these organizations have influenced both the
formation of, and the impact of, urban policy on housing, the
poverty program, riots and civil disturbances, and most
recently of all, the urban fiscal crisis. These are all matters of
great importance in their own right, and specialists in
American studies and urban affairs will find Friedland's
discussion of them absorbing.

To study these issues, however, the author also has to
confront several of the central problems and issues which
bedevil a wide range of social science specialisms. Most
notably, he discusses the process of historical change in the
form of the dynamics of public policy – especially the
influences which help to create such policy in the first place,
and the influences which subsequently mould its impacts and
its unforeseen consequences. In order to deal with these
questions, the study, in turn, tackles one of the timeless
problems of political science, that of the relationship between
social, economic and political circumstances on the one hand,
and policy choices on the other. In other words, the book is a
case study of the essence of political science itself: Who gets
what, when, how? And in order to tackle this question,

Friedland has to face up to yet another long-running debate about how to define political power, and how to approach the study of its operation.

These are issues of such widespread interest that many readers outside the US, and many who are not specialists in either urban affairs or American studies, will want to examine its arguments and its conclusions. Therefore, I shall use this foreword to say something about the social and political background to the study which Friedland, being an American writing about America, quite naturally takes for granted. Those who are acquainted with the recent history, and with the special features of urban politics in the US, will do well to pass straight to the real business in hand which begins with Chapter 1, but those who feel some brief and general background information might be useful may prefer to read on.

Central cities and their suburbs. With the benefit of hindsight we can see that many of the central cities of the US were beginning to slide into serious social and economic trouble as early as the 1950s. Their problems were caused not by a combination of inflation, unemployment and economic slump, as we might well assume nowadays, for America was then the wealthiest nation in the world, and growing ever more affluent with every stock market report. On the contrary, urban disease was precipitated, paradoxically, by the booming affluence of the Eisenhower era, when the social and economic revolution that had begun to transform the cities at the turn of the century, and which was only temporarily halted by the Wall Street crash and the Second World War, picked up speed once again. It was economic growth, not economic decline, which put an impossible strain upon the central cities, and revealed the structural faults of the American system of urban government.

Why did peace and prosperity cause decay and dereliction? The answer is that the inner cities paid the price of growth, while the suburbs most generally reaped the benefits. In the social and economic accounts of the American nation, the suburbs took the lion's share of the gains, and the inner cities paid, almost exclusively, for the losses. They are still doing so.

During the swelling affluence of the postwar years the suburbs grew as weeds (like Topsy). New and spacious houses were built by the million for middle-class families who wanted to escape the city, and could afford the price. Their two-car garages were filled with the latest fin-tailed fashions from Detroit; for the children, new schools were constructed, lavishly supplied with equipment, and staffed with well-trained teachers; for the fathers, new expressways and beltways were built to carry them to their downtown offices; for the mothers, there were new suburban shopping malls where big department stores and specialist shops catered for suburban trade six days a week. And on the seventh day, there were immaculately maintained churches of every white, middle-class denomination. Doris Day's films may have caricatured suburban life, but like every good caricature, they simply played upon reality rather than inventing it.

On the other side of the tracks, or rather on the other side of the new urban beltways and expressways, parts of the central cities were beginning to decline and decay. Gradually they started to lose their more prosperous – usually white – population, as the suburban exodus picked up momentum. As people moved homes, so shops followed people, and as people and shops moved, so the small businesses which provide and service both followed suit. Some factories moved, too, in part because they were looking for newer, cheaper and larger premises, and also because it was convenient to follow their skilled and middle-class workforce.

The outward migration of population, shops, offices and factories to the city's rim left something of a vacuum where parts of the inner city had been. The central business district continued to thrive and to expand as the tempo of the economy increased, but just beyond the downtown department stores and high-rise office blocks, houses were abandoned and store fronts boarded up. Whole blocks began to decay, and were soon taken over by gangs of street kids, freaks and drop-outs, groups of down-and-outs and winos. Those who stayed in the inner-city residential areas found the job market tightening up, as some of their employers started to leave for the suburbs. Their children's schools grew worse and worse. Violence and crime became increasingly commonplace, poverty increasingly concentrated and visible. Slums, ghettos, unemployment, abandonment, violence, crime, poverty, ugliness; they all contributed to the suburban exodus, which, in turn, fed the vicious cycle through second and successive phases.

Within a stone's throw (almost literally) of the splendour of the White House in Washington, a rather elegant department store stood gutted and boarded up, looking for all the world like some transplanted relic of wartime Berlin. In Philadelphia abandoned houses started to collapse on the kids playing in them, fires broke out, and gas pipes started to leak dangerously. The city moved in with bulldozers to knock the danger flat. In Pittsburgh, a once handsome and friendly neighborhood, close to the city's central business district (aptly named the Golden Triangle), showed signs of deterioration, slow at first, but then with alarming speed. In Philadelphia another all-white, inner-city block was busted, and quickly transformed into an all-black slum, which then became just another block in the building of a modern ghetto. In Detroit . . . in Cleveland . . . in Chicago . . .

In each case the problems of the inner city grew in direct proportion to the growth, size and affluence of the suburbs, because both responded, though in opposite ways, to the growth of industry and commerce. Thus the central city and its suburbs are different aspects of the same process – neither more nor less than opposite sides of the same coin.

The effects of polarization were dramatically magnified by the strange political arrangements of the typical American metropolis, a set of arrangements which cannot be found in any other urban-industrial society in the west. The great majority of metropolitan areas in the US were – and still are – fragmented into many local government jurisdictions, with a large central city usually being surrounded by tens, hundreds or even thousands of politically autonomous suburban authorities. By judicious use of their building, zoning and tax laws the suburbs could maintain, or even improve upon, their exclusive middle-class status, thereby ensuring that their boundaries were virtually impervious to the social and economic problems of the central cities. As a result, as social problems became increasingly concentrated in the inner cities, so the resources necessary to deal with them were increasingly locked up in the suburbs. While the political structure of many urban areas in west Europe ensure that central cities can call upon at least some of the resources of the suburbs, the fragmented system of metropolitan government in the US makes this very difficult at best, and impossible at worst. Small wonder the suburbs became known as 'the white noose' which strangles the predominantly black residential areas of the inner cities.

In the words of a perceptive but anonymous social scientist and poet:

The reason why cities are ugly and sad,
Is not that the people who live in them are bad.
It's just that the people who really decide
What goes on in the city live somewhere outside.

This is true in the sense that the mere existence of autonomous suburbs has a profound effect on central cities, and often in the sense that politicians, businessmen and most community leaders with a powerful influence over central-city affairs live in the suburbs. They may make decisions for the central cities, but do not necessarily have to live with all the consequences.

By the early 1960s it was abundantly and painfully clear that something had to be done to help the central cities. And, indeed, something was done, mainly in the form of two federal programs known as Urban Renewal and the War on Poverty. And since these are the center of attention of the early chapters of Roger Friedland's book, they also require some background material for non-American readers.

(1) *Urban Renewal.* The term 'urban renewal' was added to popular usage in the US by the 1949 Housing Act, which turned the attention of the Federal Government away from public housing, which had a bad name, toward the idea of revitalizing the inner cities by demolishing slum property, and also by modernizing and rebuilding property which could be saved.[1] The costs of doing so were too high, it was argued, for the private sector, so the Federal Government stepped in with its own scheme. It would not actually lay one brick or glaze one window on its own, but it was prepared to encourage local urban renewal authorities to help others to do so by contributing handsomely to their costs. Specifically, the Federal Government paid two-thirds of the difference between

the costs of buying and clearing land, and the income received from selling it to private developers. The remaining third had to be found from local sources.

Although the main emphasis of the program was shifted in 1967, it was not so much concerned with building low-income housing or with the task of rehousing the poor, as with urban revitalization and restoring property and tax values in the central cities. Nevertheless, urban renewal authorities had a clear responsibility to find adequate housing for those displaced by their schemes, and the overall aim was certainly not to worsen the parlous state of low-income housing in the central cities. The aims of the scheme also included the wholesale rehabilitation and reconstruction of the areas worst affected by urban blight, and it was not intended to fatten the profits of private businesses, or to subsidize them to move into areas which were prime sites for redevelopment in the first place.

However, the eventual outcome of the program was different from its initial intentions. At the outset, in 1949, 10 per cent of the federal funds to any one urban renewal authority could be used for non-residential purposes, but this was increased to 20 per cent in 1959, and to 30 per cent two years later. However, throughout its history, from 1949 to its end in 1974, the scheme devoted less than 50 per cent of the annual total of cleared land to housing, and for long stretches of time (1956 to 1967) the figure hovered somewhere between 15 and 30 per cent. By 1965 it had resulted in a net loss of residential land, and a net gain in land used for commercial purposes, usually shops and offices. Nor were the worst slums and ghettos tackled. Rather, the need to find sites which were attractive to both private developers, and to local authorities with a watchful eye on property and tax values, resulted in the development of areas close to the central business district. Nor was much contributed to the low-income housing stock. On the contrary, because this was the least profitable use of land, it invariably gave way to middle- and high-income accommodation, or else to commercial property. There was therefore a considerable net loss of cheap housing.

Between 1950 and 1971 some 300 000 families and 150 000 single individuals were moved by urban renewal authorities.

Assuming each family had three members (a conservative assumption), over one million people were moved in all – equivalent to a good-sized city in almost any country. Of the families, approximately a third were white, and the rest were of black or other ethnic minorities. Of the individuals, about 60 per cent were white, and the rest blacks, or other ethnic minorities. Thus, in round figures, some 650 000 (almost two-thirds of the total) blacks and other minority group members were moved, providing ample evidence for the popular claim that 'urban renewal is negro removal'. To make matters worse, only 40 per cent of the housing units on renewal sites were made available to them, the rest being put at the disposal of a disproportionate member of white and middle-class citizens. The great majority of those displaced had incomes of less than $6000 in 1962, but rents on the renewal sites averaged $2300 a year. The net effect of urban renewal on the housing stock was to increase the supply of middle- and high-income accommodation (at a public subsidy), and to reduce the amount of low-income housing, thereby driving up its price.

In addition, a further 100 000 businesses were forced to move, many of these being small concerns employing a handful of people, and many (between a quarter and a third) going out of business as a result. Not infrequently, the land taken from small businesses was cleared for high-rise office blocks, which were then either occupied by, or rented by, relatively large and wealthy corporations. Once again, this was all done in the name of the public interest and at the price of a handsome subsidy from the public purse.

Urban renewal in the US is one of the more obvious examples of socialism for the rich – that is, of a policy which is designed to help the poor and the needy, but which ends up helping those who are so well able to help themselves that they help themselves to the benefits of others. There is nothing especially American about this perverse phenomenon, for it operates in both capitalist and mixed economies, as well, no doubt, as in the communist countries of eastern Europe. Nor is it a phenomenon of the modern state, for, as the Good Book says, 'Unto them that hath shall be given'. Nevertheless, Roger Friedland's account of urban renewal and the political and economic forces shaping its implementation throws a good deal of light upon the mysterious process, and thus upon the question: Who gets what, when and how?

(2) *The War on Poverty.* Urban renewal did not touch many of the major urban problems in the US, and nor, to be fair to it, was it ever intended to tackle anything other than land use and the local tax value of real estate. A broader attack on urban poverty commenced in August 1964, when President Johnson signed the Equal Opportunities Act and declared his administration's 'War on Poverty'.[2] There were at the time about thirty-five million Americans on or below the poverty line, and some experts firmly held the view that the line was drawn too high so as to exclude millions more in dire social and economic circumstances. Of those in official poverty, some sixteen million lived in urban areas, and another ten million lived in inner-city areas. While most of the poverty-stricken did not live in the cities, therefore, it was the big-city slums which contained the greatest concentration and the most visible array of social problems. For most Americans, the war on poverty was an urban program, especially a black urban program.

The origins of the war on poverty lay in a profound dissatisfaction with urban renewal on the part of the Ford Foundation, which set up a series of Gray Area Projects with the intention of creating community self-help organizations. This basic idea became the backbone of the War on Poverty, which was carried out at the local level by public and private non-profit-making agencies, with the financial backing of the Federal Government. In order to do this the Government set up the Office of Economic Opportunity (OEO) to coordinate a variety of different activities. In each case, the intention was to support promising local initiatives and experiments designed to deal, not with the symptoms of poverty, but with its causes. The poor and the unemployed were encouraged to help themselves become self-supporting, and since it was fully recognized that poverty and unemployment are not single problems, but whole bundles of them, many agencies were set up, each with a slightly different task:

- *The Job Corps.* The only part under the direct control of the

OEO, this provided education, training and work experience in rural camps for unemployed youths.

- *The Neighborhood Youth Corps*, providing education and work experience for youths living at home.
- *Volunteers in Service to America (VISTA)*, to provide volunteer workers for slums, hospitals, Indian reservations, labor camps, etc.
- *Head Start*, to provide a better education for children brought up in the slums.
- *Upward Bound*, to encourage older slum children in their educational attainments.
- *Legal Services*, to provide legal services for the poor in their dealings with public agencies.
- *The Community Action Program* – the most important part of the OEO's activity, and designed to develop and coordinate various local anti-poverty activities. The basic idea was to support new approaches and local initiatives, and to give community leaders, and above all the poor themselves, the chance to participate in these efforts.

The War on Poverty was shorter-lived than Urban Renewal, and was effectively killed off by Nixon, who cut funds and deflected much of what was left to the purchase of police equipment. However, during its peak years it involved thousands of millions of dollars of federal money – more than seven thousand million dollars from 1967 to 1970. At the height of its activity, there were more than a thousand community action agencies, and although most were in rural areas, most of the money (about two-thirds) was spent in the cities.

The special character of the whole program lay in its attempt to mobilize political activity. In the now famous statement, it aimed at 'maximum feasible participation of the residents of the areas and the members of the groups served'. The OEO's guide to applicants for funds added: 'The purpose of federal assistance to community action programs is to help urban and rural communities to mobilize their resources to combat poverty.' In practice this usually meant the formation of community pressure groups which would speak for, and act on behalf of, poor people in their dealings with public bodies of various kinds. The successes and failures of the whole scheme is hotly debated still, but in the view of Daniel Moynihan, 'Very possibly the most important long run impact of the community action programs of the 1960s will prove to have been the formation of an urban Negro leadership echelon at just the time when the Negro masses and other minorities were verging towards extensive commitments to urban politics.'[3] The relationship between the mobilization of urban blacks during the War on Poverty, Urban Renewal which preceded it, and the urban riots which followed it, constitutes one of the most important and fascinating aspects of Roger Friedland's analysis.

At the heart of this analysis there lies the long-debated problem of how to define, operationalize and measure political power. The nature of this debate is widely understood and discussed, so there is no need to waste words summarizing the state of play. Indeed, it is difficult to believe that anything fresh or original could be added to the recent work of Polsby, Lukes, Gaventa, Barry and Dunleavy on the general issue of how to treat the concept of political power.[4] Yet Friedland manages to do just that.

Starting from the position that the definition and treatment of political power has generally been too behavioral, in that it has concentrated almost exclusively on the ability of actors to get other actors to do things they do not wish to do, Friedland moves quickly to an exploration of the relationship between social and political structures, and political power. This is, potentially, at the very least, a highly promising line of development, if only because existing structures are, themselves, partly the outcome of past political battles, and have a decided influence on the outcome of current political struggles. To give only one example, one of the most vital of all political battles concerns not what decisions are to be made, but how they are to be made. In other words, who is to participate, in what issue-areas, under what conditions, and in which political arena? The 'game' of politics is not just about scoring goals; even more important are the questions of who controls the referee, who frames the rules of the game, how many should play, and what constitutes a goal. In politics the name of the game is to avoid playing for high stakes unless you have the referee in your pocket, or can frame the rules to suit your own game, or have twice as many players as the opposition, or can rule that the first ten goals scored by the opposition do not count.

Translated into the terms of American metropolitan politics, this means that if you can ensure the legal and governmental autonomy of the suburbs, and then use these powers to exclude the people and the problems of the inner city from your own territory, then you are more than half way home and dry when it comes to protecting your own social and economic interests. If, in addition, you can get others to believe, as you may believe yourself, that the system operates according to the normal rules of a free-market economy, then you have the added advantage that all the blame seems to lie with the wretched inhabitants of the inner city.[5]

This is the situation which Friedland analyzes in the pages that follow, and he does so using a strikingly original approach to the data. In this respect, however, he is not alone, for in the same week that I started the first draft of *Power and Crisis in the City*, I also proof-read an article by Tore Hansen, a Norwegian political scientist who lives and works halfway round the world from Roger Friedland's native California. Quite independently, they hit upon exactly the same method for studying urban power and decision-making, and justified it the same way. Compare the following:

How, then, are we to interpret the relationships between socio-economic variables and political factors? Rather than regarding socio-economic variables as causes of the decisions, it seems more reasonable to treat them as decision-making *criteria* upon which public authorities may act. It is important to notice the difference between a causal factor and a decision-making criterion. While a causal factor is automatically related to the effect variables, the relationship between a decision-making criterion and the decision has to be *established* by the decision-making body. In other words, the decision-makers select the criteria upon which the decision is going to be based, and this selection process will be determined by the political values of the decision-makers.

In other words, choice of decision-making criteria is a function of political perception, selection and ideology, not a problem of simple causal relationships. Another way of saying this is that socio-economic factors *interact* with political variables in determining the expenditures, or rather that the effect of one particular socio-economic factor on the level of expenditures is conditioned by political factors [Hansen].[6]

[T]he policy effect of local conditions will be contingent upon the local power of corporations and unions. In cities where corporations or unions are powerful, those local conditions that affect their interest will have a greater impact on policies intended to serve their interests than in cities where corporations or labor unions are not powerful. This model assumes that the local state does adopt policies in response to local conditions and the power of organizations outside the state. But it also assumes that policies are adopted in response to the extent that local conditions affect organizational interests. Corporate or union interests in local policy depend on the extent to which local conditions affect those interests. Thus the local state responds to local conditions that impinge upon corporate or union interests, but only where corporations or labor unions are locally powerful. If either local conditions do not affect corporate or union interests, or corporate or union power is lacking, policies are less likely to be adopted [Friedland, this book].

By pure coincidence these two passages elaborate basically the same theory and the same method for studying political power at the local level, one in Norway, and the other in the US. The theory and method can, however, be used anywhere in the world and at any level of a political system. It would not be the least bit surprising to find it used in all sorts of contexts and all sorts of countries in the years to come.

Dundee University, Scotland   KEN NEWTON
January 1982

Notes

1. For a good account of urban renewal and its impact see Robert L. Lineberry and Ira Sharkansky, *Urban Politics and Public Policy* (New York: Harper & Row, 1971) pp. 328–42. See also Thomas R. Dye, *Politics in States and Communities* (Englewood Cliffs, NJ: Prentice-Hall, 1969) pp. 434–9; Scott Greer, *Urban Renewal and American Cities* (Indianapolis: Bobbs-Merrill, 1965); Martin Anderson, *The Federal Bulldozer* (Cambridge, Mass.: MIT Press, 1964); Herbert J. Gans, *People and Plans* (Harmondsworth: Penguin, 1972) ch. 13 'The failure of urban renewal', pp. 239–61. For a recent attempt to defend the record of urban renewal see Heywood T. Sanders, 'Urban Renewal and the Revitalized City', in Donald B. Rosenthal (ed.), *Urban Revitalization*, Urban Affairs Annual Review, vol. 18 (Beverly Hills, Calif.: Sage, 1980) pp. 103–26.

2. For a general account of the War on Poverty written by a non-American see Edward James, *America Against Poverty* (London: Routledge & Kegan Paul, 1970). See also Lineberry and Sharkansky, *Urban Politics and Public Policy*, pp. 291–303; Thomas R. Dye, *Understanding Public Policy* (Englewood Cliffs, NJ: Prentice-Hall, 1972) pp. 111–29; Gans, *People and Plans*, pp. 262–83.

3. Daniel P. Moynihan, *Maximum Feasible Misunderstanding* (New York: The Free Press, 1969) p. 129.

4. Nelson Polsby, *Community Power and Political Theory: A Further Look at Problems of Evidence and Inference*, 2nd enlarged edn (New Haven: Yale University Press, 1980); Steven Lukes, *Power: A Radical View* (London: Macmillan, 1974); John Gaventa, *Power and Powerlessness* (Oxford: Clarendon Press, 1980); Brian Barry, 'Is it Better to be Powerful or Lucky?', parts I and II, *Political Studies*, 28 (June and September 1980) pp. 183–94 and 338–52; Patrick Dunleavy, 'An Issue Centred Approach to the Study of Power', *Political Studies*, 24 (December 1976) pp. 422–34.

5. For a discussion of the ways in which the political system hinders the working of a 'free-market' system, see Anthony Downs, *Opening up the Suburbs: An Urban Strategy for America* (New Haven: Yale University Press, 1973) esp. pp. 1–12.

6. Tore Hansen, 'Transforming Needs into Expenditure Decisions', in Kenneth Newton (ed.), *Urban Political Economy* (London: Frances Pinter, 1981) pp. 31–2.

Author's Preface

I am ambivalent about big cities. I experience a cinematic rush from the juxtaposition of girls with purple hair, silky black shorts on roller skates, against razor-cut, button-down executives. It also gives me headaches to spend too much time in Washington Square. The fleshy swelter of hands-on local political conflicts, complicated by histories of kinship, ethnic pride and neighborhood favor is vibrant. It is also trivial, parochial and irrelevant. The ping-pong conversation, the references to the latest movie and book, who won the regional elections in Italy and the real political suasion of the Korean rebels, this global voyeurism is scintillating. Yet the meat and potatoes production often goes on elsewhere. Knowing and doing have separate locations. But what do you expect from a two New Yorkers' son who grew up in a canyon suburb of Los Angeles.

As a social analyst of politics, particularly urban politics, I find it most comfortable to work in the erogenous zone between Weber and Marx. If politics are animated by class relations, they are structured by organizations – corporations and labor unions – whose interests and *modus operandi* are not explicable in terms of objective opposition. If urban policies have important consequences for capitalist growth, they cannot be explained by capitalism. If the structure of urban governance is vulnerable to contradictions between capitalism and democracy, these must be explained by the interplay of institutional interests of the state, capitalists and the electorate.

When I began to write this study, the opposition between critical neo-Marxism which called for a 'qualitative' analysis, and the more structural-functional social science which espoused a 'quantitative' analysis, was in its heat. I found this fusion of theoretical and technical conflict to be fundamentally unproductive and wasteful. The evolution of technique quickly evolved to make empiricism impossible, to incorporate time and to require a theory of observability. A strong commitment to causal structure, historical process and a theory of data became prerequisites to the appropriate roge of technique. I hope that the debates will increase over specification and conceptual meaning, and how to combine different techniques to answer particular questions. I have tried to use quantitative techniques to elucidate specific historical processes. This is not, then, a study of all cities. It is a study of certain aspects of US central cities between 1964 and 1975.

Finally, I take great pleasure from intellectual production, yet I often accord it very little meaning. For me it is the most exquisite of games, often played viciously and with great seriousness, because it is being played for reality. I happen to believe in truth. Because it is embarrassing, this grotesque alchemy, I like to poke fun at it.

With such an orientation I have complex debts to my mentors, Robert Alford and Michael Aiken, who kept me jumping between theory and data and to whom I owe my training. To my friends and colleagues – Sam Bacharach, Ken Newton, Erik Wright, Gosta Esping-Andersen, Bill Bielby, Frances Fox Piven, Herbert Wong, Maurice Zeitlin, Bill Domhoff, John Mollenkopf, Manuel Castells, Don Cressey, Hal Winsborough, Jim Baron, Alex Hicks, Harvey Molotch, Jack Biello, and Richard Child Hill – I am grateful for their support and their criticism. I am also beholden, with the usual absolution, for the close critical readings I received from Robert Alford, Erik Wright, Frances Fox Piven and Ken Newton. Finally I want to thank John Burke, Professor of History at UCLA, for introducing me personally to the passion and struggle of ideas.

Shaped by the sexual tempests of my generation, work on this manuscript has endured longer than any of the relationships that made writing it possible. The love of three women binds these pages: Jette Thy, Merrie Klapp, and Debra Friedland. The last shall bind my life. It is not that I am promiscuous. I have simply been working on this project for too long.

University of California, Santa Barbara
January 1982
ROGER FRIEDLAND

List of Figures

List of Tables

Introduction

The origins of urban power

This book is about urban political power in the US, the power of national corporations and labor unions, and how that power shaped central city policies designed to sustain economic growth and social control.

Power, especially the power of national corporations and labor unions, is difficult to define, and more difficult to measure. In classical democratic theory, rights of participation are the core of citizenship. Rights of participation, whether or not they are exercised, are necessary to the power of the citizenry in its relationship to the state. In the social sciences it has been assumed similarly that political participation is the most important source of political power, that there can be no power without participation – whether actual participation or the possibility of participation. Voice is both a source and all-important indicator of political power.

I wish to argue that the power of national economic organizations such as corporations and labor unions does not originate in the participation of businessmen or labor leaders. Rather, its origins lie in the organization's control over resources – private investment and an apparatus for mass mobilization – upon which local governance depends. The participation of corporate or union élites is more a consequence than a cause of such political power. Political power may be silent, voiceless.

But how to measure political power without relying on the volume of corporate and union élite participation in local decision-making? In this study I examine the policy impact of the local density of corporate and union organizational resources as a measure of corporate and union power.

Previous studies have relied on the identification of political participants – whether visible actors at city hall or relatively invisible members of an inner circle – to measure the power of different groups. This methodological decision masks a theoretical one – that participation is necessary to power. As a result, it has often been argued that national corporations, with their geographically vast network of plants and subsidiaries, are neither interested, nor powerful, actors in urban politics. Whether heralded for its democratizing effects or denounced for its diminution of local leadership, it is assumed that national corporate élites are no longer powerful political forces in the city. It is the more local businesses – retailers, newspapers, developers – whose fortunes are more closely tied to the city, who are the important urban actors. I wish to argue that national corporations have become the dominant economic organizations in the urban economy, that their decisions link the local economy into the most important national flows of capital and income. As a result, they are simultaneously less dependent upon any given locality and more important to the survival of a city's economy. The urban political power of the national corporation grows while depending less and less on political participation.

Previous students of the city have often assumed that the organizational structure of a city affects its ability to identify needs and solve problems. Such an approach assumes that the policy impact of local organizations can be analyzed without regard to the divergent interests and powers of different types of organizations – whether these are corporate firms, voluntary associations, or even city departments. Either organizational élites are publicly interested or they provide equivalent alliance partners for those who would like to promote any particular policy. If the interests of different organizations are not specified, power tends to be analyzed as a capacity of a reified system – the local government, for example – to attain 'public interests', to which public policy is a presumed response. I will argue that different types of organizations have different interests and different powers. National corporations and labor unions have different interests in local economic growth and social control and different sources of political power. While these interests did not conflict in any fundamental way – office growth versus employment expansion, and pacification versus Democratic electoral strength – their divergent interests should be observed in the policy impact of their local powers.

When students of urban power structure attempt to measure the policy impact of a powerful group, they first control for local economic or social conditions to which the policy is a presumed response. If you want to know the power of the poor in getting the city to build subsidized housing, you would first control to see how badly the poor were housed. If two cities have equally bad housing and the poor have greater political resources in the city which also builds more subsidized housing, you would attribute this incremental effect to their greater political power. On this basis, it became fashionable to conclude that politics did not matter. Local economic and social conditions typically had substantially greater impact in explaining the variation in local policy than did local politics. Again a theoretical position lurks behind a methodological choice. Such an approach assumes that local government is an apparatus for technical problem-solving, and that local conditions can be evaluated as 'needs' or 'problems'. Because it is also a democratic apparatus, local groups can push it further forward or backward in solving any given problem. Local governments will make similar technocratic responses to similar local conditions, responses which may be impeded or accelerated according to the local power of interested groups. Further, it assumes that locally powerful groups shape local policy, and not policy-making, I will argue that powerful groups are interested in local policies because of certain local conditions. Local economic or social conditions become social problems because of the power of interested groups. Local governments respond to different local conditions to the extent those conditions affect the interests of powerful groups. Thus national corporations and labor unions do not simply shape policy, they shape policy-making, by affecting which local conditions affect local policy and which do not. Politics matters in the conversion of local conditions into local policy. Chapter 1 outlines a theory and method for studying the local power of national corporations and labor unions. Chapter 2 reviews the accumulated controversy over the structure of urban power in the US.

The crisis of urban power

Analysts of urban policy and power structure typically study a particular policy – rent control, urban redevelopment, welfare, police – as an independent phenomena. If more than one policy is examined, it is to compare the power of different groups according to policies with different distributions of benefits and constituency alignments. The relationship between policies is rarely analyzed. Here I analyze the historical relationship between policies designed to stimulate local economic growth and sustain local social control in the decade between 1964 and 1975. I show how the consequences of one set of policies create costs – political, economic or fiscal – which later policies must try to absorb. Through such an approach it becomes possible to reveal the political relationship between groups as they are mediated through different policies which absorb their interest and energies. It is also possible to show the contradictions of a power structure.

There are always public costs to local economic growth, particularly when the structure of the local economy shifts. In the three decades after the Second World War, the economic structure of American cities was transformed, changing the location of jobs and residents. Municipal budgets registered the economic and social costs of these changes. City governments adopted new policies to manage the new economic growth and to control those populations which were its unintended victims.

From an industrial workplace geared to material production, the city increasingly became an office center managing production located elsewhere. From a city whose working hands touched metal, wood and concrete, it became a city where workers handled paper, computer tapes and other people. Once the primary locus of the industrial economy, the city became the site of an emerging managerial and service economy.

Transformation meant growth – of new office towers, hospitals, universities, rapid-transit, super-highways, super-parking garages and apartment complexes. New places to work, new ways to get to work, new places to live near work – all indicated the buoyancy of the new urban economy. But transformation also meant decline – of industrial jobs and low-skilled employment in general, of neighborhoods and of retail trade. People without work, without ways to get to what work existed and without money to maintain the neighborhood and its stores – all indicated the darker side of economic change. Chapter 3 traces the changing structure of the central city economy.

These changes in the structure of the city's economy incurred enormous private costs, costs which public policies were designed to absorb. The new office economy required changes in land-use: downtown expansion, transit connections between white-collar suburbs and office employment centers, new residential complexes for the city's growing white-collar labor force. These changes in urban land-use did not proceed smoothly through the market. Highly built-up patterns of land-use, fragmented land ownership, encroaching slums, and a paucity of fiscal resources necessary to finance complementary public infrastructure – all these constrained economic growth in the city. As a result, city governments were called upon to provide the public infrastructure of private growth, to absorb publicly the private costs of growth. To do so, they turned to higher levels of government for help.

Urban Renewal was a federally funded program adopted by many cities to overcome these constraints on urban economic growth. Armed with eminent domain powers and earmarked funds for public infrastructure, cities tried to stimulate private investments that might otherwise not take place. Chapters 4 and 5 analyze the impact of corporate and union power on urban renewal.

But the new urban economy increasingly failed to provide private sector jobs for the city's residents, particularly its rapidly growing, unskilled non-white residents. The new economic growth, and the policies designed to sustain it, accelerated the displacement of the low-skilled employment which historically had absorbed new immigrant populations. It also destroyed a substantial segment of the low-income housing stock that had housed them. These shrinkages in low-income employment and housing occurred at the time of one of the largest waves of cityward immigration in US history, a migration of rural southern blacks to the nation's cities. The absorption of this new population into the city's body politic did not occur naturally. Excluded by the changing structure of the city's economy, yet a growing proportion of the city's electoral base, urban blacks began to violate the rules of political representation to protest their deprived status. Growing black numbers and black violence threatened to overwhelm established routines of social control. As a result, cities were also called upon to provide new forms of social control.

City governments attempted to provide public services and public employment for those who could not obtain them in the private market. The cities also tried to control politically a community which traditionally had little access to the centers of urban power, and now refused to accept their deprived status in the new order. Again, the central government played a vital role. The War on Poverty was another federally funded program variously adopted by the cities to provide employment, services, and new forms of political participation for emerging black leadership. So, too, local public employment expanded rapidly – to provide services and jobs – particularly in the wake of black violence which erupted summer after summer in the late 1960s. Harsher methods of social control were also adopted as cities expanded their arsenals and the number of men who could use them. More public jobs, public services, public participation and public force – through these means, cities attempted to maintain social control.

Chapter 6 analyzes the impact of corporate and union power in shaping local War on Poverty policy. Chapter 7 analyzes the black riots of the 1960s, exemplary cases of breakdown of local social control. The riots have been argued to follow a national rhythm of black mobilization. When local social and economic conditions are examined, they are found to have little impact on the frequency or ferocity of local black violence. I find, in Chapter 7, that local public policies have a large impact on local black violence. The riots have a local political logic. For those outside the social structure of work, collective dissent is conditioned by state action, not by mean living conditions and injustice in the market. The subsequent chapter (Chapter 8), shows how corporate and union power shaped local patronage and repressive responses to these violent ruptures in the routines of democratic politics.

Managing the public budget is difficult in the best of times. After the Second World War it became increasingly difficult as the central city economies changed. The function and skyline of US cities were transformed. The transformation required large infusions of public spending to reshape land-use and infrastructure. According to public finance analysts, public expenditures which stimulate growth are not only self-financing, but self-legitimating. Local private investments generate local jobs, from which local incomes and the taxes for local public services are derived. Local private investments are expected to provide more tax revenues to the local community than they consume in public services. When cities lack the expected budgetary surplus, they are unable to finance services for those who contribute little in tax revenues.

Contrary to expectations, the central city's economic growth, and the programs intended to sustain it, were neither self-financing nor self-legitimating. Not only did cities subsidize private investment that may have taken place anyway, but the economic growth that did occur failed to provide a fiscal surplus. Importantly, the employment and income benefits from the city's economic growth were increasingly being captured by non-resident workers – both white-collar and blue. In response, the resident population made strident demands for the public services and jobs that the local private market was unable to provide. The public costs of urban growth ballooned, resulting in serious fiscal strains. Chapter 9 analyzes the origins of urban fiscal strains which emerged by the mid-1970s.

Contrary to those who heralded the revitalization of the central city as a solution to problems of maintaining mass support during a time of growing urban poverty and maintaining fiscal health in a period of declining tax base, the new urban growth and the policies to stimulate it failed at both tasks. Indeed growth and growth policies produced conflicts, intense and violent conflicts, as well as exacerbating fiscal strains. Fiscal strains appear to be as much a public cost of the new urban growth as it is a symptom of decline.

This study tries to close the theoretical circle between the causes and consequences or urban policy. But the circle rolls in historical time. Thus this study is a history of corporate and union power in the US central cities between 1964 and 1975, an idiosyncratic snippet of historical time.

Chapter 1

Corporate and Union Power: Theory and Method

There are always local constraints to economic growth and social control. I shall argue that corporate and union power shaped the impact of these constraints on local policy. Growth policies, like Urban Renewal, were not automatic responses to the difficulties of stimulating investment through the market. Social control policies, like the War on Poverty or expansions in local patronage and repression, did not inevitably follow local black violence or respond to a locally powerful black citizenry. Corporate and union power not only shaped what policies were adopted, but in response to which local conditions they were adopted.

The policy impact of corporate and union power: a model

How might corporate or union power affect urban policy? On the one hand these powerful organizations may try to push policies in a similar direction in all cities. Such an expectation assumes that corporate and labor union interests can be defined independently of the characteristics of the cities in which they are located, characteristics which vary between cities. On the other hand, corporations and labor unions may have no effect on city policies. City policies may be a technical response by local government to intractable problems of economic decline or social disorder. Because all cities must maintain their tax base and the quiescence of their citizens, the local power of corporations and labor unions may be irrelevant to the policies they adopt. Both are partial views. National corporations and labor unions affect local policy, but their impact on policy depends on the extent to which local conditions affect their interests. Local economic and social conditions also affect local policy, but their impact on policy depends on the local power of national corporations and labor unions.

Because conditions vary between cities, corporate and union interests in the adoption of local programs for economic growth or social control will also vary. Consequently, the impact of corporations and/or unions on local policy depends both on the extent to which local conditions affect their interests, *and* the level of their local power. The local power of corporations and/or unions selectively filters the policy impacts of local economic and social conditions.

The central empirical hypothesis of this book is that where national corporations or labor unions are locally powerful, local conditions that affect their interests will affect public policies intended to serve those interests. Where national corporations or labor unions are not locally powerful, such local conditions will not affect those policies. The coincidence of corporate or union power and local conditions affecting their interests shapes central city policy. Thus power not only shapes policy, but policy-making. The fusion of local corporate or union power and interest will produce different patterns of policy than either could produce alone.

A model of these relationships is shown in Figure 1.1. The top entry in each box refers to the observable empirical indicator. The bottom entry refers to the unobservable theoretical variable. The model has three observable elements: local conditions, the local presence of national corporations or labor unions, and local policies. Each is assumed to indicate something unobservable. Local conditions potentially indicate the extent to which corporate or union interests are at stake in the city. The local presence of national corporations or labor unions indicates their local power. Local policies indicate the level of city government commitment to an intended solution, a solution that can be analyzed in terms of corporate or union interests.

Referring to the figure, a technocratic model (a) would focus on the ways in which local economic or social conditions

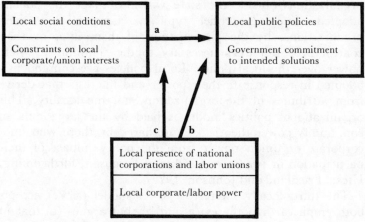

a   Technocratic model

b   Organizationally interested power model

c   Locally interested power model

FIGURE 1.1   *Local conditions, power and policy*

directly determine local policy by creating an environment to which all cities will react similarly. For example, all cities with a declining tax base will develop policies to encourage new taxable private investment. This model assumes that the local state is an autonomous problem-solver, such that governments endowed with similar authority will respond similarly to similar problems. This is a statist model used by post-industrial theorists who argue that economic development causes the policies of otherwise different polities to converge. It is also shared by structuralist neo-Marxists who suggest the existence of a state whose autonomy assures that policies will be developed in response to the general requirements of capitalist growth.

Other political models of local policy-making (b) focus on how corporate or union power directly determine local policy. For example, in all cities where corporations are powerful, they will try to minimize their tax burdens and maximize their public benefits. This model assumes that while the local state may adopt policies in response to local conditions, certain organizations outside the state will also shape the policies adopted. Such a model typically assumes that these organizations, by the participation of their élites or their control over resources necessary to the community, wield power over the local polity. Local policies are consequently adopted in response to their power and interests that derive from attributes of the organization, not the locality. This organizational politics model is held by the large bulk of community-power theorists. It is shared by those who infer corporate or union power from the policy impact of their participation or presence (Clark and Ferguson, forthcoming; Hicks, Friedland and Johnson, 1975).

The third locally interested power model (a/b/c) accepts both empirical hypotheses (a and b), but argues (c) that in addition, the policy effect of local conditions will be contingent upon the local power of corporations and unions. In cities where corporations or unions are powerful, those local conditions that affect their interests will have a greater impact on policies intended to serve their interests than in cities where corporations or labor unions are not powerful. This model assumes that the local state does adopt policies in response to local conditions and the power of organizations outside the state. But it also assumes that policies are adopted in response to organizational interests in local policy, interests which depend on local conditions. Thus the local state responds to local conditions that impinge upon corporate or union interests, but only where corporations or labor unions are locally powerful. If either local conditions do not affect corporate or union interests, or corporate or union power is lacking, policies are less likely to be adopted.

The central cities

To study the policy impact of corporate and union power, I will analyze the differences in policy and policy-making in large central cities. All central cities which had 100 000 or more population in 1960, 130 in all, will be studied. The criteria used by the US Census for designation of a central city are complex. Two major criteria are of concern here: city size and functional position in the larger metropolitan area.

Central cities must have a minimum population of 50 000 and must be employment centers within a larger metropolitan area, thus excluding residential suburbs.

Analyzing these central cities has advantages. First, the analysis included two federal urban programs, Urban Renewal and War on Poverty, for which local government had responsibility for local planning, funding application and implementation. Large central cities in particular responded to these federal program opportunities. By 1966, some 84 per cent of these cities had at least begun a federal Urban Renewal program. While county governments, with their frequent responsibility for welfare functions, received some War on Poverty funds, central cities were responsible for the bulk of the funds and new poverty programs. By 1966, these central cities accounted for 71 per cent of city *and* county War on Poverty expenditures, and for 72 per cent of all city *and* county programs authorized by the Federal Government. Second, use of *large* cities minimizes variation in two aspects of a city's administrative and political capacity: adequate personnel and fiscal resources to develop and implement new programs and visibility in the national political system. Small cities and townships, in contrast, have limited resources and are apt to lack their own Congressional representation. Because the policies analyzed here involve the development of new local administrative capacities and the securing of federal approval for local project plans, it is important to choose a population of cities with the necessary administrative capacity and national political significance to achieve that development.

Corporate and union power

The political power of any social group hinges upon its control of resources of importance to the state. Because there are different resources of importance, there are multiple sources of political power. Corporations and labor unions drew upon different sources of political power. Locally situated national corporations control the most productive investments whose output is most competitive in national markets. The multilocational structure of the national corporation makes it relatively easy to invest and disinvest selectively in response to local conditions, including local policies, that adversely affect the local profitability of the corporation. Equally important, the headquarters of the national corporations were the engines of downtown economic growth, a growth that was increasingly vital to central cities that were steadily losing their industrial functions to smaller towns and suburbs. Thus national corporations were locally dominant economic organizations. This dominance and the relative ease in capital movement gave the national corporations considerable local political power. In many ways, the participation of national corporate élites in urban politics only communicated their economic dominance, a participation which was actively solicited by city fathers anxious to sustain the local tax base, employment and economic growth.

The sources of labor union power were very different. The labor unions did not control the investment process. Concentrated in industrial production, the labor unions were unable to stem the tide of industrial decentralization and disinvestment from the central city as new industrial investments moved to places where wages were lower and the workers less organized. Further, while capital – particularly its more liquid forms – moved fast and far in response to locational variation in profitability, laborers moved less quickly and to less distant places. The friction of space affected labor much more than it did capital. Labor unions were unable to control the local economy or to adapt easily to local conditions by moving their members elsewhere. Corporations could start up production at new locations much more easily than unions could reorganize. If the corporation was placeless, the unions were more tied to places.

The labor unions were not locally dominant economic organizations. As a result, the unions had to rely upon their ability to mobilize their membership politically and to organize other mass constituencies within the city. If corporate power drew upon capital investment, union power drew upon political investment. The participation of union élites in urban politics communicated their control over a mass organization, a participation sought by local leaders desiring electoral support.

Corporate political power derived from their impact on the

local economy, while union political power derived from their potential ability to mobilize mass participation. The participation of corporate or union élites in local politics was a consequence of their political powers, not a cause.

Measuring corporate and union power

Corporations and labor unions have transformed the organization of the American economy. Today several hundred corporations control its mainsprings. These corporations typically control a large share of the national market for a product, invest in all stages of its production and distribution throughout the world, and make use of the most advanced technologies. They make decisions within the firm that used to be made by the market. Their capital intensity and large size makes potential competition difficult, and as a result they enjoy higher profits and easier access to capital markets for financing new investment (Averitt, 1968; O'Connor, 1973; Holland, 1976). In addition, these national corporations are interlocked with each other, and with the most important banks and financial institutions (Domhoff, 1967; Zeitlin, 1974). These interlocks increase their ability to control their markets, rather than be controlled by them.

The largest corporations control an increasing share of the nation's productive capacity. By 1964, the top 1000 industrials accounted for 70 per cent of all industrial output. Such corporations – their investment, production and location decisions – determine the economic conditions under which smaller firms must operate. Lesser firms are limited to more localized markets, use less productive technologies and face more stringent competition. As a result, their profits tend to be lower and more insecure, and consequently they have more difficulty expanding.

The development of large national corporations in the US made the development of national labor unions both necessary and possible. National unions were necessary because localized union opposition to wages and working conditions in the face of the geographically and industrially diversified corporation was impossible. National unions were possible because national corporations provided the organizational framework through, or against, which national unions could form; and because the national corporations had sufficient profitability and market power to absorb union demands. National corporations provided both the target and resources which made national union formation possible.

While it is predominantly the largest firms that are unionized, a small percentage of American workers are unionized compared to other advanced economies. In 1964, only 29.5 per cent of all non-agricultural workers were union members compared to the near universal unionization in Sweden, for example. The national labor unions are highly concentrated. In 1970 there were 189 national labor unions with twenty million members, of which sixteen million were members of the 120 AFL–CIO (American Federation of Labor–Congress of Industrial Organization) unions. In 1970, 44 per cent of all union membership was employed in manufacturing, 44.5 per cent in non-manufacturing, and 11.2 per cent in the public sector (*Statistical Abstract*, 1972). These national unions have over 45 000 locals spread across the country.

The number of *corporate headquarters* of the largest 1000 industrial corporations located within the central city as of 1964 (*Fortune*, 1965) was used to measure the local power of national corporations.[1] The presence of such headquarters indicates the presence of corporate élites, many of whom are resident in the same central city. It also indicates the presence of local plant investment within the city, often the largest and most innovative plants.[2] Finally it indicates the presence of a major corporate office complex, whose continued presence and growth is of vital importance to the central city economy. Thus the presence of national corporate headquarters indicates the organizational basis for the participation of corporate élites and their control over the local economy, particularly its growing office economy.

In 1964, 708 of the top 1000 industrial corporations had headquarters in the 130 central cities studied here. The geographic distribution of corporate headquarters was not even. The average city had over five national corporate headquarters, forty cities had none, and another thirty-one cities had only one.

The number of *national labor unions* in the central city as of 1960 (*Register of Reporting Labor Organizations*, 1960) was used to measure the local power of national unions. National labor unions are important units of local union political organization. Cities with a large number of such national unions also tend to have a larger number of national union headquarters and to have a large number of unionized manufacturing workers. The average central city in this study was located in a highly unionized metropolitan area. On average, 75 per cent of all plant workers in the metropolitan area were unionized in 1965. The 130 central cities had an average representation of fifty-two national labor unions. The smallest number of national unions represented in a city was six, while the largest was 120.

Just as the organizational structure of the economy is polarized into two worlds – the world of the giant corporation and the small firm, of the national labor union and the unorganized worker – so too are the cities in which they are located. Some cities are integrated into the national corporate and union structure, while others are not. To capture the two types of cities, the population of central cities studied here was split into those with high and low national corporate power, as well as those with high and low national labor union power. Cities with two or more corporate headquarters are considered high corporate power cities. Cities with fifty or more unions are considered high union power cities; those with six to forty-nine are considered low union power cities. The distribution of central cities among these types is indicated in Table 1.1.[3]

Measuring corporate and union power by these dichotomies makes some assumptions about the relationship between the number of corporate or union organizations in the city and the level of local corporate or union power. It assumes that the local power of national corporations need not increase regularly with each additional corporate headquarter located in a city, for example. Using the local presence of these organizations to indicate their local power is a very 'distant' operationalization. To assume that each additional organization adds a constant increment of power, that the difference between the presence of one and two headquarters is the same as that between forty-eight and forty-nine, would

TABLE 1.1 *Corporate and union power* in 130 central cities*

	Number and percentage of cities					
	Low corporate power		High corporate power		Total	
	no.	%	no.	%	no.	%
Low union power	48	36.9	13	10.0	61	46.9
High union power	23	17.7	46	35.4	69	53.1
Total	71	54.6	59	45.4	130	100.0

* Low corporate power = 0–1 headquarters per city; high corporate power = 2 or more; low union power = 6–49 national labor unions per city; high union power = 50 or more.

require tighter measurement, less distance between indicator and concept, than that available here.

The dichotomies are relatively arbitrary. The break-point for corporate power was chosen as two or more headquarters rather than one or more for various reasons. Case-study work indicated that the single dominant corporation was frequently overburdened politically, whereas in multicorporate cities, political divisions of labor were possible. In addition, in such cities, the indicator would suggest the power of a single firm, rather than a category of firms. The break-point for union power was the mean number of national unions represented in the city.

The presence of national corporate headquarters and labor unions indicates a variety of things about their host cities. These include the presence of national corporate and union élites who are available for local political participation; the size and diversity of organizational resources and the presence of organizations whose control over economic and political resources limits the range of feasible political coalitions and public policies.

Corporate and union interests

National corporations and labor unions both had interests in using city government authority and resources to foster *economic growth* and maintain *social control*. If their interests converged on similar policies, their interests were none the less different.

National corporations were interested in maintaining the value of their investments in the city, particularly their burgeoning headquarter operations, and hastening the growth of the city's office economy. While existent industrial investments were to be protected, the city was decreasingly important as a site for industrial production. The major corporations preferred suburbs and smaller towns as locations for new plant investments. The labor unions saw economic growth as a way to sustain local employment and wages, particularly for unionized workers. The unions were interested in stemming the decline in industrial employment in the cities.

In the post-1945 period, both corporate and union élites had coalesced into a political coalition supporting urban growth policies (Mollenkopf, 1976). Both viewed the growing numbers and growing organization of the urban blacks as a threat to that coalition and the policies it pursued. Even though the policies necessary for growth could be housed in agencies far from electoral control, the orchestration of urban growth ultimately depended upon mass electoral support for the city's political leadership, to which growing black numbers were crucial. Yet cities' non-white populations were particularly disadvantaged by the city's changing economy. Maintaining black electoral support through other means was therefore crucial. It was precisely the blacks' strategic position that provided the conditions under which black militancy could also emerge and be effective. This militancy also had to be contained.

For the corporations, social control was a matter of quiescence, of protecting local economic growth. For the unions, the city's poor and non-white populations had additional national political significance. The city's blacks had become important components of the national Democratic Party's electoral base, an electoral base which the unions had helped construct over several decades. Maintaining rising black protest within the confines of electoral routines, and hopefully within the Democratic Party, was important for the union's national political strategy. The sources of corporate and union political powers were not the same. National corporations linked the city into the national economy and thereby controlled the prospects for local economic growth. Their ability to move capital easily throughout the nation and their superior market power allowed them to control the gates of the municipal economy. This economic power was a most important source of political power. Corporate ability to exit, to disinvest selectively from any particular city, empowered local corporate voices. Labor unions, on the other hand, did not control local economic growth. They could only react to it. Union political power was consequently more dependent upon their ability to organize the voices of their members and to deliver mass electoral support of other urban constituencies. For the unions, maintaining social control and the electoral allegiance of the new urban masses was vital to their political power. For the corporations, in the absence of any programmatic challenge to their privileged position in the political economy, angry and recalcitrant masses did not threaten the roots of their political power.

Measuring corporate and union interests

Corporations and labor unions are not only locally powerful organizations, they are also locally interested organizations. Corporations and labor unions were both interested in maintaining local economic growth and social control, although for different reasons. This would suggest that they would have such interests in any city, and that policies intended to maintain local growth or social control would be adopted in all cities where they were powerful. This formulation derives corporate and union interests from an analysis of the organizations, not from attributes of the cities. If corporate power, for example, affects local policy irrespective of local conditions, these effects indicate the operation of such interests.

However, corporate and union interests in the use of public authority and public monies to achieve economic growth or social control are also affected by local conditions. Local conditions which potentially constrain economic growth or endanger social control vary between cities. It is the variation in such conditions which is the local source of corporate and union interest in local policy.

At the most general level, where corporations or unions are powerful locally, and local conditions affect their different interests in economic growth or social control, local policies intended to serve them are more likely to be adopted. Corporate and union interest will filter which conditions have policy impact, to which conditions local governments are responsive. Local policies are shaped by the intersection of local conditions which threaten organizational interests in economic growth or social control, and by organizations to whose power the local political system responds.

Corporate and union interests cannot be directly measured. Their existence is assumed, and their impact is observed in the patterning of local conditions which affect local policies where corporations and unions are powerful.

This specification has a number of limits. First, it neglects the variable characteristics of the organizations – corporations and labor unions – as a source of interest in local policy. Organizational interest in a given city should also be treated as a variable attribute of the organization, and not just the city. Thus some corporations' plants are concentrated in a particular city or metropolitan area, while others are spread across the country and the world. Some corporations' executives live in the headquarter city, while others live elsewhere. To the extent that interest in a city varies between corporations and affects the local power of the corporation, the model is not correctly specified.

Second, faced with constraints on local economic growth or social control, corporations in particular have another alternative besides reshaping local policies – to move. Between 1960 and 1975, hundreds of corporate headquarters changed location (Friedland and DuMont, forthcoming). To the extent corporations choose 'exit' rather than 'voice', when faced with local constraints on their interests, the model is not correctly specified. This is particularly problematic if corporate relocation is correlated with those local conditions likely to affect their interests in growth or social control policies. However, if corporations move in response to such local conditions, this should attenuate their expected policy impact in cities where corporations are presumed to be powerful.

Methodology

The policy difference between cities where corporations or labor unions are powerful and those where they are not can have many sources. I will take the case of corporate power and urban renewal as an example. First, cities where corporations are powerful may have different local economic or social characteristics than cities where corporations are not powerful. High corporate power cities may be cities with a more dilapidated housing stock and thus greater housing needs for urban renewal. As a result, high and low corporate power cities will have different levels of urban renewal activity. But the difference in urban renewal activity would not be due to corporate power. This will be measured as a *compositional* effect and is of no theoretical interest.

Second, corporate power may influence the way in which local economic conditions affect local urban renewal activity. In high corporate power cities, the effect of population density, for example, on the level of local urban renewal may be different than in low corporate power cities. Here the difference in urban renewal between high and low corporate power cities is due to the ways in which corporate power shapes the translation of local economic conditions into public policy. This can be measured as a *slope difference* effect, and is of central theoretical interest here.

Third, corporate power may itself have a direct effect on the level of local urban renewal activity. High corporate power cities may have more urban renewal, for example, regardless of the nature of local economic conditions. Here the difference in urban renewal activity is due to the local power of corporations to further local urban renewal. This kind of effect assumes that corporate interest in urban renewal is not dependent on local economic conditions. This can be measured as an *intercept effect* and is also of theoretical interest.

The population of central cities will be split into two groups: a group of high corporate power cities and a group of low

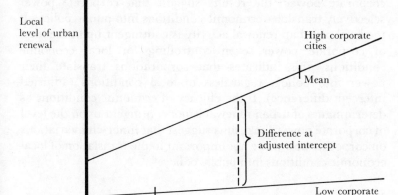

Local level of urban renewal

High corporate cities

Mean

Difference at adjusted intercept

Low corporate cities

Mean

Difference in two slopes

Local constraints on economic growth

FIGURE 1.2   *The impact of corporate power on the relationship between local economic conditions and urban renewal*

corporate power cities. The level of urban renewal activity will be regressed on local economic conditions within each group of central cities. These two sets of regression results will provide the evidence against which the types of corporate impact can be compared.

The differential pattern of significant regression coefficients in the two groups of cities indicates the effect of corporate power on the transmission of economic conditions into urban renewal policy. While the differential presence and absence of significant effects indicates where corporate power is necessary for a particular economic condition to have *any effect* on public policy, tests on the difference in the unstandardized regression coefficients indicate whether corporate power is necessary for economic conditions to have significantly *different effects* (slope difference).

If the efficacy of economic conditions as determinants of urban renewal activity is contingent upon the level of corporate power, the results suggest that corporate power selectively translates economic conditions into public policy. If the level of urban renewal activity is contingent upon the level of corporate power, even controlling for local economic conditions, this indicates that corporations translate their power into policy, regardless of local conditions (adjusted intercept difference). If the efficacy of economic conditions as determinants of urban renewal is not contingent upon the level of corporate power the results suggest that inner-city variations on corporate power are not important in the translation of local economic conditions into public policy.[4]

Notes

1. The absolute size of a group is an important determinant of its internal structure and its relationship to the local society. Simmel, for example, talks of the way in which group size becomes a symbol of the group and its relationship to the larger society. Thus the guild masters of Frankfurt were referred to by their number, 'the six' (1950:107). Simmel writes,

> The role of one millionaire who lives in a city of ten thousand middle-class people, and the general physiognomy which that city receives from his presence, are totally different from the significance which fifty millionaires, or, rather, each of them, have for a city of 500 000 population – in spite of the fact that the numerical relation between the millionaire and his fellow citizens which alone (it would seem) should determine that significance, has remained unchanged . . . The strange thing is that the *absolute* numbers of the total group and of its prominent elements so remarkably determine the relations within the group – in spite of the fact that their numerical ratio remains the same . . . [We see that] the relation of sociological elements depends not only on their relative but also on their absolute quantities [Simmel 1950:97–8].

I am grateful to Jim Baron for bringing Simmel to my attention.

2. Previous research (Friedland, 1977) indicates a strong relationship between the number of corporate headquarters situated in a central city and the number of locally owned plants in that city, as well as the number of large financial intermediaries. In addition, cities with a larger number of corporate headquarters were also more likely to have exclusive upper-class clubs, social registers and foundations, social institutions of importance to corporate power.

3. Phi, a measure of association which corrects for population size, is 0.45, which is highly comparable to the measure of association for the continuous variables (= 0.44).

4. In the analyses that follow, the impact of corporate and union power are measured separately. The analyses must assume, for these policies, that the impact of corporate and union power can be described additively, that the impact of corporate power is not contingent upon union power (or vice versa). Given the absence of corporate and union opposition on these policies, and the absence of conflict of interest, this is not an unreasonable assumption. For other policies, like unionization or wage rates, it would not be a reasonable assumption.

Chapter 2

The Local Economy of Political Power: Participation, Organization and Dominance

Corporations and labor unions have political power. What accounts for their political power, how that political power affects public policy, and how that power can be observed are questions that have puzzled researchers for most of this century. Group political power, including that of groups of economic organizations like corporations and labor unions, is affected by three attributes of the group: the political participation of its members, the organizational structure which composes it, and its control over local material conditions. Each of these attributes is a source of political power. Each has been studied, at least partially, in order to understand the power of a group. In this chapter I will review how these attributes of corporations and labor unions have been studied as sources of political power.

Business power and the city

Muckrakers often look for the political power of business in the flow of favors which firms dispense to politicians who do their bidding. Campaign finance, bribes and jobs – on these they can crack their teeth. Arguments then range over the magnitude of such flows and what they can buy in the political market place.

For social scientists, political power is a lightning rod for theoretical dissent. Social scientists argue over the amount of business political power and, more fundamentally, over the nature of that political power. In the resultant litter of scholarly literature, the conceptualization and measurement of business political power takes on ritual significance, demarcating lines of theoretical conflict for years at a time.

The unusual significance of local business power derives from the theoretical status of the locality in sociological theory. Durkheimian social theory suggested that the unmediated link between citizen and state would have consequences ranging from anomic political cultures to governmental policies ill adapted to the idiosyncratic character of individual lives. The city, with its small-scale and easier access, was seen as a point from which local associations could be formed, popular opinions and public policies autonomously articulated and independent political leadership cultivated. Together with the political associations which flourished there, it would protect both the citizen from the central state and the central state from the citizen. The city played a key role in the body politic.

These ideas were reinforced by the ideology of American federalism which viewed subnational units as a defense against a potentially autocratic central state, and as a source of both progressive movements and innovative political leaders. These views were also bolstered by the corresponding absence of centralized political parties in the US. The state, if not the city, was the territorial base for partisan organization in the US.

In addition, human ecology presented an organismic model of urban society in which the spatial organization of functions – production, coordination, services – within the city became integral to the operation of the social system itself. This insight was subsequently lost as technique was severed from theory in technical studies, ecological correlation and ethnographic studies of 'natural areas'. What remained from this tradition was the notion of the city as a bounded organism with a metabolism, a natural history. Ecological theory conceptualized power as an attribute of the city, deriving from its position in the national division of labor. Power was no longer a business capacity to realize parochial and private interests, but an urban system capacity to adapt, to identify needs and to act generally. Business organizations, particularly those linking the city to the national division of labor, were now agents by which this munificent energy was produced.

The first perspective legitimated the city as a democratic breeding ground, one whose successful operation at the local level might be necessary for the functioning of the national democracy. The second ecological perspective legitimated studying the city as a unit, a bounded system whose political capacities are determined by the economic functions it performs in the national economy. In political sociology, overweening business influence was seen as potentially dangerous, blocking channels for popular participation. In human ecology, business influence was seen as the benign, if not inevitable, outcome of its dominant economic function.

These conflicting theoretical assumptions have generated diverse methods of measuring business political power. The methods identify different attributes of business that are presumed to affect public policy. As these attributes become part of the stock and trade of social research, debates have increasingly centered on their theoretical meaning.

Three research traditions studied the local political power of business. Each identified a different attribute of business as the determinant of its political power. A first tradition focused on patterns of business political participation; the second on the local organizational structure of business; a third on the level and type of local business activity. Within each research tradition, these respective attributes were related empirically to urban public policy. These empirical relationships were then used to infer the political power of business.

Political participation and business power

In this first approach, the primary attribute of business, and the source of its political power, is the political participation of businessmen. The political power of business was observed in its successful attempts to influence urban policy. This approach identified political participants in policy formation by their business role and related their expressed policy preferences and the volume of their participation to policy outcomes. Neither the participation of business élites in urban politics nor their influence on urban policy was at issue. On both counts, all researchers were agreed. Munger (1961), for example, wrote:

> The only distinction that can in fact be observed among community power structures is that between systems in which only the business community exercises a significant power and systems in which the business community shares power with other groups.[1]

The empirical debate centered on the extent to which business élites influenced urban policy; other groups tempered that influence, and other kinds of participants were also able to affect urban policy. In short, researchers attempted to measure the relative volume and efficacy of business participation in the formation of local public policies.

Two seemingly conflicting research strategies emerged to measure the volume and efficacy of business participation in urban politics. The reputationalists (Hunter, 1953; Miller, 1958) asked key informants to identify the uncontested leaders on a variety of issues (e.g. attracting new industry, city development plans), while the decisionalists (Polsby, 1963; Dahl, 1961) asked informants to identify those who participated and those who prevailed in actual, controversial decisions taken by the city government (e.g. adoption of urban renewal, mayoral selection). The former researchers tended to find greater business influence – greater volume and less contested participation – than did the latter.

But on closer examination, the similarities between these two kinds of studies are more striking than the differences in their findings. Both strategies assumed that business political participation is at least necessary for business to have political power. Both examined the impact of that participation on the issues which had penetrated the public arena and on the subsequent decisions taken to resolve those issues. The extent of business influence in a particular city was inferred from the extent to which participants in political issues were drawn disproportionately from businessmen and the extent to which the positions articulated by businessmen prevailed. Dahl, for example, used three issues: urban redevelopment, public education, and party nomination. He found that business élites were not the predominant participants, that individual businessmen had specialized patterns of participation and divergent interests according to issue area, that the composition of participants changed across time and issue area, and that public officials had the most direct influence on urban policy (cf. also Pellegrin and Coates, 1956).

The empirical focus of these studies was on *individual* businessmen – whether retail, bank, or industrial owners or managers – and their participation. Individual businessmen have preferences and choose to use their political resources to realize them in the political arena. These studies assume it is possible to aggregate individual acts of business participation as if they were equal. Further, both kinds of studies focus on those concerns which had already become public issues (but see Crenson, 1971). The role of political participation in generating those issues is not systematically considered.

Beyond individual participation

The implicit assumption that the political power of business derives from their aggregated *individual* acts of participation has been challenged. Both the participation and power of individual businessmen are often determined by the organizational structures from which they are drawn. An individual's reputation for community leadership was found to be related to the pattern of participation of the organization to which he/she belonged (Freeman *et al.*, 1963). Individuals who are executives in many local organizations participate in more issues and have a greater reputation for power (Perrucci and Pilisuk, 1970). Their source of power derives not from individual political participation, but from their position in the structure of inter-organizational relations in a city.

If this is true, the political participation of individual businessmen is not the primary attribute which accounts for their influence. Rather, the local organizational structure of business is the primary determinant of business power. This shift towards an inter-organizational approach to urban power structures has been taken furthest in the study of local interorganizational networks. In this case, organizations – particularly corporations – are treated as actors, whose interests generate their participation in the network (Domhoff, 1978; Galaskiewicz, 1976). Organizations wield power to the extent that they have valued resources and are central in the network (Burt, 1977; Coleman, 1977; Galaskiewicz, 1976). Although organizations have replaced individual aggregations as units of analysis, organizational participation is still regarded as necessary to the exercise of power (Laumann, Galaskiewicz and Marsden, 1978).

Much of the individual political participation of corporate élites can be explained by their organizational affiliation. Corporations routinely encourage, if not mandate, the political participation of their top executives in central city politics. It is common practice for corporations to designate their executives to serve on various city commissions, working on company time, as a means to secure access to centers of public power. Corporations describe such executive participation as 'good corporate citizenship' (American Cyanimid, 1973; Magnavox, 1973).[2] According to a retired Mattel executive, headquartered in the Los Angeles area, executives were assigned to different voluntary associations and required to report back to the corporation on their activities. Beyond the creation of a good political image, this was considered a means to secure influence from political élites involved in the same voluntary associations. Corporations also loan executives to the city government to help in formulation of new programs, bolstering limited city personnel with corporate technical and managerial expertise. For example, Magnavox's director of corporate transportation was appointed to the Ft Wayne public transportation commission, while their head of data processing was assigned to a city task force to improve government efficiency (Magnavox, 1973). The local renewal agency made extensive use of Magnavox staff from personnel and accounting (Magnavox, 1973). In Houston, the local Model Cities and Planned Variations program relied on top executive support from Exxon (Exxon, 1973).

Executive involvement in city commissions, politically relevant voluntary associations and city-wide policy-making groups is often a form of organization as opposed to individual politics. For example, the Blythe–Zellerbach committee in San Francisco was a group of corporate executives critical in developing central city urban renewal. It was composed of representatives of the largest corporations and banks, many of which were headquartered in the city. According to *Business Week*, 'It is the corporations, really, rather than the executives that comprise the B–Z Committee' (Kessler, 1973). In Wilmington, Deleware, an important corporate-controlled policy organization is the Greater Wilmington Development Corporation (GWDC). In this organization, the corporation, rather than the executive, is the unit of participation.

When a representative on GWDC retires from a firm, he is replaced on GWDC by another high-level executive. For example, when Ed Crumm retired from his position in Hercules, he also quit as President of GWDC and appointed another Hercules executive to replace him (Phelan and Pozen, 1973: 180).

Locally situated corporations and banks are tied together by dense local networks of interlocking directorates and common director memberships in exclusive social clubs. In his study of the St Louis metropolitan area, Ratcliff (1980) found that the centrality of individual commercial bank directors within this network was a strong predictor of that director's participation in civic policy organizations. Thus an individual's role in the organizational network – both its economic and social aspects – determined his role in local politics. But more importantly, Ratcliff also found that the position of the organization as a whole, as indicated by the aggregate characteristics of all its directors, also had a strong effect on the political participation of individual directors from that organization.[3] This research indicates the relation between organizational centrality and political centrality (see also Useem, 1979, 1980).

More recent studies of business participation no longer take either the individual or the firm as a unit of analysis. Rather, individual participants are identified as representatives of self-conscious politically and socially organized business groups. These individuals, whether or not they are themselves businessmen, are assumed to speak for different segments of the city's business population. The boundaries of the group vary, from a downtown, corporate-based growth coalition (Mollenkopf, 1976), to a local grouping of growth-dependent businesses such as newspapers, realtors and banks (Molotch, 1976), to a socially integrated local component of a national ruling class (Domhoff, 1978; Whitt, 1981).

In his study of business participation in five different mass-transit ballot issues in California, Whitt (1979) found that the corporate community was sometimes in support and sometimes in opposition. In all cases, however, there were no major public conflicts within the business community on any issue. Those conflicts of interest within the business community, as for example between the oil and other downtown corporations over allocation of highway trust funds for fixed-rail mass transit, were settled privately within corporate political organizations. The resultant consensus was then the basis for individual corporate participation. Indeed, the pattern of organizational stratification within the corporate community was used to allocate participational responsibilities of each individual firm. For example, bank assets were used to determine bank contributions to the campaigns.

While the position of business organizations has been used to explain the participation and influence of individual businessmen, the structure of the network of business organizations has not been used to analyze the collective power of the network itself.

Organizational structure and business power

Parallel, but largely subsequent to the original concern with business political participation, there emerged a body of comparative urban research which converts what had been theoretically problematic – business political domination – into a politically neutral structural attribute of the urban political system. In this perspective, business domination of urban policy is rendered benign by its impact on the 'decentralization' of participation. It was observed that cities vary systematically in the number of different individuals who participate in policy issues and the extent to which the composition of those participants varies across issues. Clark

(1968), for example, asked a set of informants in comparable positions (e.g. mayor, president of the largest bank, largest newspaper editor) to name key political participants on four issues (urban renewal, mayoral election, air pollution, War on Poverty). He argued that the larger the number of participants and the less participants overlap between the issues, the more 'decentralized' is the structure of influence.

In this way the political power of business slipped from view as a theoretical concern. In its place rose the structure of 'community leadership' (see Grimes *et al.*, 1976, for a recent example). The city was viewed as a political system whose structure of political participation affects its policy outputs. In general, more decentralized leadership arrangements lead to higher levels of policy output, because there are more centers of power to which access may be had or by which needs may be identified (Clark, 1968; Aiken, 1970).

This new body of research treated the overall configuration of business participation as an outcome of the organizational structure of the local economy. The impact of business on local policy was seen to be contingent on the organizational structures from which business participants are drawn. In moving from individual business participation to the organizational structure of the local economy, the conceptualization of political power changed. Whereas, before, power was a relational concept, based on a Weberian conception – a probability that an individual or group can realize its will against opposition (see Polsby, 1963, for example) – here political power is an attribute of the political system, its capacity to identify needs, mobilize resources and attain goals. In this view, the organizational structure of the local economy determines the ability of the political system to execute policies of any kind.

The effects on local power structure of four organizational attributes of the local economy have received attention: differentiation, absentee ownership, extra-local linkage and coordinative dominance.

Organization differentiation

The theoretical importance of organizational differentiation of the local economy for political power derives from a democratic élitist political theory, which assumes that organization is necessary for political access and that political conflicts are primarily between organizational élites. Business organisations are assumed to compete for political influence, a competition which parallels their economic competition for factors of production and markets. From this perspective then, the existence of a single firm which dominates the local economy must have centralizing consequences for the local polity. Conversely, a multiplicity of firms will have decentralizing consequences. More organizations means more competing centers of power and thus more 'democracy' (Aiken, 1970).

In his comparative study of US cities, Aiken found that organizationally differentiated local economies have more diffuse power structures and higher levels of policy outputs that ostensibly benefit poor and unorganized residents: public housing, War on Poverty, and Model Cities (Aiken, 1970: 496, 508; Crenson, 1971; but see Clark, 1968). In a similar vein, Aiken and Alford (1970a) measured the organizational differentiation of the local economy by the number of manufacturing establishments with 100 or more employees and the number of independent banks with $50 million or more in deposits. They found that the organizational differentiation of the city's economy is positively associated with both the speed of innovation and the level of output in public housing, poverty programs and urban renewal. The large number of inter-organizational connections in such economies facilitates the formation of a 'minimum coalition'. Because it only takes a small number of interested organizations to adopt a policy, the multiplication of organizational units makes it easier to establish these 'minimum coalitions'.

Absentee ownership

A second organizational attribute of the local economy which received attention was absentee ownership – local plants controlled by firms headquartered elsewhere. Research on absentee-owned plants found that their executives tend to withdraw from the local political scene (Mills and Ulmer, 1970; Schulze, 1958; Noland, 1962; French, 1970). Typically, it was argued that the low level of political participation by corporate executives of non-headquarter plants decentralizes the local structure of influence. In cities whose economies are absentee owned, economic power is severed from political power. In his study of Ypsilanti, where Ford and General Motors' executives were found to have low levels of political involvement, Schulze argued that political and economic power had been 'bifurcated' (Schulze, 1958). In a similar study, French discovered the same pattern of non-participation by executives in absentee-controlled plants.[4] French (1970: 186) argues:

> Bifurcation limits the economic sanctions that local leaders can impose. Apparently, as lower ranking leaders realize that they need not fear reprisals from key influentials, they are less inclined to take secondary roles. In effect, bifurcation encourages democratization.

Comparative studies found that absentee ownership is associated with more diffuse local power structures (Aiken, 1970; Walton, 1967).[5]

That resident executives of absentee-owned firms have lower levels of political participation than those of local firms is not surprising. Executives of national firms have their eyes on career lines in the larger corporations. In addition, since social mobility within the firm also means movement to new firm locations, their interest in local politics is likely to be attenuated (Phelan and Pozen, 1973: 180).

Further, the political autonomy of branch-plant executives is likely to be circumscribed by policy decisions of the national office. Corporations frequently have corporate-wide urban policies for all their branch plants, policies determined at the national office. Mott (1970: 174) describes Ford's operation:

> Community relations at Ford Motors is located within a larger department which is concerned with political activity at the national, state, and local levels. It is a highly consolidated, complex, and well-financed operation. In each

locality where the company has one or more factories, it has a community relations committee. The committee is composed of management personnel from all of the local Ford factories. These committees meet once every other month for five or six hours in the evening. The agendas for the meetings are determined by the community relations department in Ford's central headquarters, not by their local committees. One-half of the agenda is devoted to national issues and the other half to local issues.

Interviews with corporate executives confirm that corporate headquarters typically determine their branch plants' political activity (Magnavox, Tenneco, Shell, 1973). Innovative corporate involvements in city politics are first tried in the headquarter city and, if successful, diffused to other cities.

Finally, branch-plant executives lack the political support provided by the large pool of corporate élites found in the national office, where the concentration of top-level executives facilitates formation of a 'management committee' through which corporate backing for a particular project can be secured. In the branch-plant city, the regional manager is isolated from this top executive structure. Consequently, not only is the absolute volume of executive participation lower in such cities, but it is confined to more parochial policy concerns such as tax assessments (Exxon, 1973).

Extra-local linkage

Given the theoretical importance of absentee ownership in comparative urban power structure research, and the growing recognition of the extra-local structures of which local establishments are a part (Walton, 1967; Warren, 1963), it is noteworthy that little empirical research has been done on the political impact of locally headquartered, national economic organizations. Research has been conducted on the political impact of absentee control of the economy by national firms, rather than on local control by such firms. This is not to mention the impact of integration into the national corporate economy.

Although not applying his insight to national *economic*

organizations, Turk (1970, 1973a, 1973b) was first to show that a concentration of national headquarters of voluntary associations has a positive effect on the ability of a city to attract federal funds. He argued that empirical associations between the number of national voluntary association headquarters and per capita War on Poverty funding levels were due to the headquarters' provision of 'extra-local linkages' which facilitate the flow of program information and promote national policy norms.

Turk argued that 'business' is not sufficiently visible and its participation would be too controversial to produce local coalitions around new, particularly federal, policies (Turk, 1973a: 33).

In fact, several students of the city suggested that large national corporations, with their eyes on Wall Street and their fingers spread around the world, had better things to do with their time than attend to city hall. Banfield and Wilson (1963: 263; see also Molotch, 1976) for example, argued:

> Companies that sell on a regional or national market often take little or no interest in local affairs. Having its headquarters or a plant in a city is not enough to give a business firm an interest in it . . . The Ford, Chrysler, and General Motors corporations, for example, are probably less important in the affairs of Detroit than the J. L. Hudson Company department store.

Such images of national corporate withdrawal from city politics are contradicted by a National Industrial Conference Board study in 1968 which found that of 1033 large firms surveyed, 93 per cent continuously review local legislation (Epstein, 1969: 98). The structure of 'business' influence clearly includes the executives of major corporations as well as those of small, downtown retailers (Morlock, 1974). But whether the local presence of national corporations has an impact on local policy formation has not received serious empirical attention.

Coordinative functions

Finally, an organizational attribute of the local economy argued to affect the city's power structure is the relative number of coordinative economic functions located in the city. Hawley (1963) argued that cities whose economies have relatively few people exercising coordinative or managerial roles have a higher level of 'systemic' power, or capacity to mobilize politically. He used the ratio of city employment in managerial, official or proprietor categories relative to the total employed labor force of the city (the 'MPO' ratio) as an indicator of systemic power. He argued that the higher this ratio, the greater the number of coordinative economic roles, and the less chance for community mobilization. Hawley found that cities with high systemic power (or low MPO ratios) have higher levels of urban renewal activity. Later studies, however, used the same approach and found that cities with low systemic power (a high MPO ratio) have centralized power structures, as measured by participation (Aiken, 1970).

These results are in conflict only if systemic power depends on a low level of political participation by occupants of coordinative roles. The relationship between the role structure of the local economy and patterns of political participation by the occupants of coordinative roles has not been empirically established. Later studies found that the impact of the MPO ratio was dependent on the policy studied (Smith, 1976). For areal policies – those affecting the entire jurisdiction (such as fluoridation, and Hill–Burton hospital construction) – cities with high MPO ratios have higher levels of policy output. For segmental policies – those affecting particular constituencies (urban renewal, public housing) – cities with high MPO ratios have lower levels of policy output.

In Hawley's terms, these results suggest that high levels of systemic power are positively associated with higher levels of policy output for segmental policy outputs, while low levels of systemic power are positively associated for areal policy outputs. In a path model where three policy variables (municipal expenditures, War on Poverty fundings and urban renewal) are used as indicators of unobserved 'mobilization' – the locality's capacity to achieve goals – Lincoln (1976) found that the MPO ratio has a net negative effect on mobilization, consistent with Hawley's interpretation of low systemic power.

In summary, four organizational attributes of the local economy have been related to public policy: organizational differentiation, absentee ownership, location of national headquarters and concentration of coordinative roles. Several criticisms of these studies can be made. First, these studies tend to neglect the differential power of the organizational units they are measuring. For example, the number of establishments is the unit of observation for constructing measures of differentiation in many studies (Aiken, 1970; Aiken and Alford, 1970a, 1970b; Clark, 1968). Similarly, the MPO ratio is assumed to measure the major coordinative or managerial roles in the local economy. (In fact, the average social status of MPO roles is relatively low, 47 on the Duncan SEI.) This operational approach neglects the differential power of the economic organizations which own and control these establishments and hire their managers. For example, an industrial establishment owned by a small local firm may have different political resources available to it than a plant or office owned by a national corporation whose sales are many times larger than the budget of the city. The simple adding together of organizational units assumes that such differentiated units are equally powerful in the determination of local policy.

Second, these studies treat political power as a capacity of the city to achieve goals, and not as the ability of business to secure its interests. As a result, the organizational structure of the local economy is analyzed as a neutral configuration of actors who organize access, provide coalition partners and diffuse national program information. The interests which these economic organizations have at stake in the city and the reasons their presence might affect patterns of political participation and public policy are not specified.[6] Without a specification of the interests which motivate business political participation or direct the political impact of business organization, the relationship between economic organization and public policy takes on a universalistic cast. Consistent with this oversight of local business interests, the actual or potential effects of public policies are also rarely mentioned. Spending levels for different programs are repeatedly related to the city's organizational structure without reference to the interests they serve. It is simply assumed, and the concept of 'mobilization' reveals this nicely, that the organization of the local economy affects the city's ability to solve its social problems. That policies may not be adopted for this reason, or that those adopted may not make any substantive impact on the social problem which legitimated their existence, is not subjected to empirical analysis.

The original pluralist–élitist debate was concerned with business political participation as an indicator of interest and power. The body of research reviewed above solved the sticky problem of interests by ignoring it.

Economic dominance and business political power

The human ecologists took the intellectual tools developed for studying the struggle for existence in the forest and the frog pond and applied them to human settlements. In the forest, the tallest trees capture most sunlight, forcing the nether ferns and shrubs to adapt to the dimmer light below. This control over the conditions of existence of other species, ecologists call *dominance*.

In urban settlements, human ecologists argued that certain activities and the units that execute them also control the conditions under which other activities must operate (Park, 1936; Bogue, 1949). As a result, the spatial structure of human activity takes definite forms, ordering activities within cities and the relationships among cities. Large industrial units are not dominant because of their ability to make political commands, but because of their control over the generation of income and employment in the local community, and over the flow of resources across city boundaries. With the rise of complex patterns of trade and production linking cities, large metropolitan centers come to dominate the lesser towns and rural areas whose production they organize (Lincoln and Friedland, 1978) and assume a coordinative role in the national territorial division of labor, specializing in administration and distribution, while routine production devolves to lesser towns and cities. As a result of rising interdependence, dominant economic units within a city are those which control the flow of resources with the outside economy (Hawley, 1971). This control enables them to set the conditions under which other units within the city operate and to outbid those units for key locations (Park, 1936).

Early ecological formulations focused on spatial units – cities, or zones within the city – and the functions they performed (administration, production, retail, residential). Increasingly, theorists have recognized that it makes more sense to analyze organizations rather than places or functions – as the units which organize the urban system (Lincoln, 1977). Cities are economically linked not simply by the functions they perform in the economy, but by the organizations which carry them out. Economic growth is now controlled by multilocational organizations, which generate the most important flows of goods, labor and capital (Pred, 1977; Holland, 1976). The position of a city within the national system of cities is determined by the economic functions it performs for the dominant economic firms located within its boundaries (Holland, 1976). The dominance of the multilocational firm derives from its market power, scale, productivity and ability to generate investment funds internally. As national economic conditions change, cities in which multilocational firms are located may benefit from the superior capacity of those firms to adapt to or produce such changes.

The political implications of the ecological approach in general, and of dominance hierarchies in particular, have not been spelled out. As noted above, the organization of dominant economic functions has been treated as an attribute of the local political system's capacity to act, not as a determinant of local firms' ability to shape public policy in their own interests.

Because they control the conditions of existence for other units, and determine the flow of income and employment and thus the tax dollars of the city, local success of dominant economic units is the unquestioned priority within which all policies are framed and debated. By their control over economic processes, they shape the material conditions necessary to the legitimacy and effectiveness of city government. The locational, production and investment decisions of major corporations affect not only the problems a city government must face, but also its capacity to deal with them. Under such conditions, business political participation is often a consequence of its political power, rather than a cause.

Because fiscal capacity and public spending depend on corporate growth, cities often encourage business political participation to assure policies which provide a good 'business climate'. The absence of political participation by business does not necessarily indicate a low level of business political power. Control over key economic processes allows dominant businesses to shape issues and limit the parameters within which political conflicts will take place. From this perspective, the political power of businesses, particularly of dominant economic units, derives more from their locational flexibility and control of the material base of the city, than from their present or potential political participation.

Inter-city competition and business power

In his celebrated study of New Haven, Dahl (1961: 250) found that local businessmen had become less active in the city's politics since the early twentieth century. Yet he was aware of this kind of business political power without participation. He wrote:

> Probably the most effective political action an employer can take is to threaten to depart from the community, thus removing his payroll and leaving behind a pocket of unemployed families. If the threat is interpreted seriously, political leaders are likely to make frantic attempts to make the local situation more attractive.

As a result, policies are often shaped and reshaped to increase the profitability of the city location for dominant firms. Dahl notes two cases where Urban Renewal programs were tailored to prevent corporate relocation from New Haven.

Banfield and Wilson (1963: 274) described Chicago as a city where the centralization of political control combined with a politically disorganized corporate community rendered business efforts to influence the Mayor ineffectual. While this may have been true with respect to various decisional conflicts, Mayor Daley's highly centralized political organization was not able to undo the economic bases of political power. His 1974 budget proposal, for example, included a city tax on all stock and commodity exchange transactions based on the broad home rule powers of the new Illinois constitution. Immediately, the Midwest Stock Exchange and the Chicago Board of Trade, the largest commodity brokerage in the US, threatened to move to the suburbs. Daley, one of the more renowned political 'bosses' still operating at that time in American urban politics, backed down.

In another case study, Phelan and Pozen (1973) documented the political power of the Greater Wilmington Development Corporation (GWDC), an organization controlled by national corporate élites, particularly those associated with DuPont. In Wilmington, a Democratic mayor, supported by lower-income ethnic groups, allowed this corporate group to develop blueprints for a downtown civic center which displaced a large number of poor ethnic residents and closed public streets for the benefit of DuPont Corporation with deleterious effects on local business (244–52). They write:

> The close cooperation between the Democratic mayor with an ethnic electoral base and the Republican-dominated corporate establishment may seem odd; but both stood to gain. The mayor wanted a financially viable city and he liked the ideal of large visible projects which would stand as monuments to his accomplishments. He also wished to avoid corporate dissatisfaction with his policies, which might lead to the locating of new buildings outside the city limits [244–5].

In capitalist societies, governments – including local governments – depend on taxes, ultimately drawn from incomes generated by the private sector. As long as local governments depend on taxes and do not have the authority to control corporate location decisions, they must avoid policies which undermine profitable investment. In the US, the decentralization of taxing, spending and implementation authority accentuates local government vulnerability to the vicissitudes of local economic activity. The rise of the multinational corporation and of new transportation and telecommunication technologies has made investment increasingly footloose.

While private investment decisions are centralized in the multilocational firm, local government taxing and spending decisions remain fragmented and decentralized. Consequently, firms can adjust or appear to adjust their production and locational decisions in order to squeeze the most favorable mix of taxes, public infrastructure and business-oriented services out of the public purse.[7] The market for economic infrastructure may be more competitive than that faced by the firms that use it.

Faced with threatened corporate flight and the continuous wooing of corporations by other localities, cities offer tax abatement, underassessment, cheap capital through industrial development bonds, free buildings, free land, reduced utility rates, flexible rezoning prerogatives, subsidized infrastructures and relaxed environmental standards (Hayes, 1972; Nader and Green, 1973; Gardiner and Olson, 1974). In this private market for public goods, the firms receiving public largesse are usually those that need it least, for it is the large, multilocational firms whose investment is often most important to the local economy and tax base.

It is the smaller, competitive firms whose profit margins and market power are low who would benefit most from the locational subsidies offered by localities and states. But such subsidies are not offered to them. The great bulk of industrial aid bonds and tax abatements are captured by the largest multilocational corporations (Bluestone and Harrison, 1980).

It is this economic power which explains how US Steel can refuse to provide Gary, Indiana – a city whose schools were millions in debt – with information on its local investments and depreciation and simply writes its own tax bill. According to the *Wall Street Journal*, the company was underassessed by $110 million in the early 1970s (Nader and Green, 1973). It also explains how Hallmark Cards, which has a $400 million complex in Kansas City, will pay no taxes for the first decade of its operation, and only 50 per cent for the next fifteen years

(Bluestone and Harrison, 1980: 223). Or how it is often the largest commercial and office properties downtown which are assessed most leniently.

Corporate bribery has not disappeared, but it is subsidiary to normal inter-city competition for corporate tax dollars and jobs. In 1973, I interviewed the president of an engineering firm that negotiates with cities on behalf of corporate clients seeking new locations. He indicated that the Chamber of Commerce is often the first point of contact. Frequently, the Chamber is the unofficial arm of the city government in its relations with the corporate community, and can negotiate more openly with prospective corporate residents than could city officials. In one case, for example, negotiations were conducted on behalf of one of the nation's largest paper companies which wanted to construct a mill for refining raw paper. The mill, a potential investment of over $10 million, would use a large volume of water and emit a large volume of pollutants into the water. Cities were played off against one another until the highest level of city subsidization and the lowest level of city control were obtained. The lucky city chosen for the investment offered no waste treatment requirements, no charge for sewer connections, highly preferential water rates and a secret promise to rezone land – purchased by the corporation as agricultural land at low prices – as industrial land some specified time after the corporation located in the city.

Corporations are able to use such inter-city competition to maximize public benefits and minimize their private costs. In the process the way is laid for a new form of bribery – advance information – which enables local officials to make inexpensive real estate investments in anticipation of the appreciation that comes with corporate location.

The end result is that cities offer sweeteners to firms that least need them, for investments that often would have occurred without them. For example, a study of US cities that issue bonds to subsidize industrial capital investment found that a majority of the projects subsidized and seven-tenths of the dollar value of the total investment would have occurred in the same cities without the public subsidy (Apilado, 1971). Given the miniscule percentage of total costs that inter-city variation in tax costs represent and the intense competition between localities and states for new investment, subsidy programs are ineffective in influencing the locational behavior of even the most mobile industries (Bluestone and Harrison, 1980). As a result, municipalities needlessly forgo millions in tax revenues, cut into the revenues available for public services and increase the costs of borrowing in the capital market for other purposes.

Economic activity and comparative local public policy

What is the relationship between the local economy and public policy? Comparative urban research has also examined the relationship between local business activity and public policy in US cities. Case studies indicate that city governments mold public expenditure and taxation policies to promote economic growth within their boundaries. Studies of city and state public expenditure variations, both in the US and Europe, have found that levels of economic development have large, significant effects, while electoral variables such as voter turnout and party competition have few significant effects (Alford and Friedland, 1975; Fried, 1975; Dye, 1972; Hofferbert, 1972). The fiscal impact of urban economic growth is not well understood. Studies show that public safety and transportation outlays are higher in cities with considerable commercial and industrial facilities, even when controlling for higher associated property values, indicating either increased costs or demands by such users (Muller, 1975b). Other studies indicate that local economic growth generates even faster public expenditure growth (Steiss, 1975; Heilbrun, 1974) and that development of open space on the edge of the city sometimes costs more in public expenditures than it produces in new taxes (Appelbaum *et al.*, 1976).

In the absence of a market for public services, it is difficult to establish empirically the level of demand for such services. Most empirical research on the economic impact of public spending has been developed in terms of the 'derived demand' of the residential household. Typically, this research assumes that residential properties contain a variety of consumption items, some of which are the public goods provided at the location. These consumption items (accessibility, public services, frontage, housing characteristics) are then regressed on property values or rents. The relationship between the consumption items and the property values or rents are argued to constitute price functions (or hedonic values), where the consumers' marginal valuation of the item equals its implicit marginal price (Deacon, 1977). While there is little evidence on the actual incidence of expenditure benefits (Henderson, 1977), these studies do indicate that increased public expenditures are capitalized in higher property values and rents (Yinger, 1977; Edel and Sclar, 1974; Oates, 1972). This research suggests that public benefits are reflected in private benefits.

In contrast to studies concerning residential consumer demand, little comparable research has been directed towards the derived demands for local public services by producers. According to Deacon (1977: 244–5):

Past efforts have focused upon consumers' evaluations and preferences, yet producing enterprises clearly have demands for services of roads and police and fire protection. The nature of these derived demands and the way in which they enter the collective choice process have received little attention from theoretical or empirical researchers.

While local spending and taxation may affect producer property values, the empirical evidence also suggests that the new locations of firms are relatively insensitive to the differential costs and benefits they impose (Brown, 1974; Morgan, 1967; Williams, 1967; Due, 1961). It implies that while businesses may benefit from public spending, variations in such benefits may not play an important role in determining where to locate. These studies do not speak of the impact of public spending on the more important locational decisions involved in routine investment, disinvestment, purchasing and marketing. In general, the impact of local public spending and taxation on local economic activity has not received empirical scrutiny. Until we understand the reciprocal relationship between local economic activity and local expenditure and revenue policies, the local political power of business cannot be fully understood. The political power of business should be inferred both from the effects of its activity on public policy, and from the ways in which local policy affects the costs and benefits of doing business in a particular locality, and thus its local activity.

The neglect of the impact of policy on business activity by all three research traditions is striking. Those who studied business political participation concluded it was necessary to reveal participant preferences, and that the local policy would deliver a substantive response to all groups who were successful in the use of their political resources. Those who studied the organizational structure of business made no effort to specify the potential congruence between the policies adopted, the benefits and costs they conferred, and the business organizations whose structures were described. This lacuna was partly because their concern was no longer with the power of business, but instead with the power of the local political system to attain goals or mobilize and the related implicit assumption that public policies served public interests. Those who studied the relationship between economic activity and public policy largely analyzed the economic causes of local policy, rather than its economic consequences. In part, this reflects the successful territorial claims of the economists coupled with the reluctance of the political scientists and sociologists to tread on apparently well-specified theoretical ground. But in part it derives from the assumptions of the urban economists who treat the relationship between economic activity and urban public expenditure as determined by resource and technocratic restraints. Preferences for public spending are the only political variables in a world dominated by fiscal capacity and market-adjunct government functions.

The neglect of policy consequences has obscured some important dimensions of the political power of business. To what extent does business's political participation mark the failure to obtain a given stream of policy benefits from the local policy? To what extent are local public policies necessary to the local private economic activity of business? To what extent are continuities in public policy the result of marginal adjustments made by investors and producers in the locality rather than the rules of administrative and legislative élites?

The relationship between economic structure and public policy has often been treated as though economic development were an exogenous and non-political determinant of public policy, often referred to as an 'environmental' effect. The impact of economic activity on public expenditure patterns can be interpreted as evidence of the political power of business, their ability to shape local public expenditure and taxation in ways which are most consistent with their own profitable operation. In this formulation, the political power of business is not inferred from participation in decision-making, nor from its contribution to community mobilization, but from its ability to secure a continuous stream of public goods contributing to the profitability of the urban location.

Only a few studies have examined the relationship between economic activity and public *policy* as an indicator of the political power of business. In an exemplary study, Friedman (1977a) examined water pollution control in 104 central cities and found that the more dependent the local economy was on high-polluting industries, the lower the city's participation in a federal matching-grant program administered by the Environment Protection Agency. A pollution control policy imposes specific costs on the affected industries. Beyond its direct monetary costs, a discharge abatement program interferes with the control of production (Friedman, 1977a: 333). Furthermore, it promotes public awareness of industrial wastes and thus increases the costs incurred in their disposal. In this case then, the city's dependence on industrial plants likely to be adversely affected by a particular policy impeded the development of that policy.

With the rise of the multilocational firm, economic dominance has come to be synonymous with locational flexibility. Such dominant economic units have become less dependent on political participation to secure the policies they want. Those economic units which remain locationally dependent are the most likely to participate in local politics. Thus current studies find banks, newspapers and major retail stores – less dominant economic units – to be key participants in city politics (Molotch, 1976; Banfield and Wilson, 1963). Their economic activities depend on the investment and location decisions of other, less locationally dependent economic units.[8] The celebrated 'withdrawal' of the executives of large corporations – both absentee and local – from local politics, and the bifurcation of political and economic élites, do not indicate declining corporate political power in the locality. They only indicate that the bases of power have shifted, that corporate participation is decreasingly important as a source of corporate political power.

The three research traditions reviewed above assessed the impact of selected attributes of local business on local public policy, inferring the power of business from that impact. The first measured the level of business participation in local decision-making processes, particularly those involving manifest political conflict. The second measured the organizational structure of the local economy and related that to aggregate levels of business political participation and to aggregate levels of policy outputs. The third measured the level and type of economic activity in a locality and related it to the level of policy outputs.

Thus corporate power does not depend on the participation of corporate élites. Rather corporate élite participation communicates the power of the corporate organizations which direct it, a power which derives increasingly from its control over the material life of the city and its locational freedom. Corporate power cannot therefore be inferred solely from the volume of corporate élite participation or the policy impact of that participation.

Union power and the city

The urban political power of the labor unions has received considerably less attention. The three attributes of business – the participation of élites, the organizational structure of the economy and their control over the local economy – can also be evaluated with respect to labor unions.

More often than not corporations and businessmen who shape public policy are regarded as benign, evidencing their civic leadership and the inevitable but fair-minded clout of those who determine the economic pulse of the community. The political power of labor unions presents a meaner public face. The general public and academics alike perceive corporate involvement as public spirited, and similar union activity as self-interested and parochial. These perceptions themselves constitute a political resource. But more importantly, they reflect the fact that labor unions and corporations have access to different sources of power.

Labor union participation

Like corporations, labor unions also participate in city politics. Labor involvement in local politics began in the early nineteenth century with the formation of labor parties pressing for free public education and abolition of licensed monopolies. Since its inception, the political power of labor unions has been based upon their capacity to move masses of people to the polls. When corporate executives speak, they communicate the power of the money, the investment, and hence the jobs and taxes their firms control. When labor union leaders speak, they communicate the electoral power of their union membership.

Labor union influence depends on its ability to mobilize electoral support or opposition for a candidate, political party or proposition. Since the early twentieth century, when the American Federation of Labor (AFL) started compiling information on how individual Congressmen voted on key issues and distributed this information to its membership, the US labor movement has used its mass membership as a political resource. As the Federal Government has become increasingly instrumental in the regulation of wage levels, social security, unemployment and union organization, the national labor unions have used access to their membership – to their votes, time and money – to help secure the kinds of representation that would support labor interests. The passage of anti-strike legislation in the 1940s led both the AFL and the CIO (Congress of Industrial Organizations) to form political organizations (AFL League for Political Education and Political Action Committee) which were subsequently merged into the AFL–CIO Committee on Political Education (COPE). These national political organizations are also organized locally.

Labor unions wield electoral power in a number of ways. They provide candidates with access to their membership, frequently endorse local candidates – usually Democrats – and attempt to influence their members' voting patterns. They cannot, however, dictate the political allegiance of their membership. Union members frequently disapprove of political activities of their unions as detracting from the meat-and-potatoes contract functions (Masters, 1962; Gannon, 1967; Banfield and Wilson, 1963). In the 1956 Presidential elections, United Auto Workers, one of the more political unions, could mobilize about two-thirds of its membership to vote, and of these, about three-quarters followed union endorsements (see, for example, Central Labor Council of Alameda County, 1965; Greenstein, 1963). For local issues and candidates, the ability of labor unions to get their members to vote and to vote according to union endorsements is certainly far more limited (Bok and Dunlop, 1970). In Detroit, for example, COPE constructed a party organization in a non-partisan city. Between 1946 and 1955, union endorsements won 91.2 per cent of all general partisan elections at the state level, but only 38 per cent in the city of Detroit (Banfield and Wilson, 1963: 287).

Labor unions are also able to raise money for political purposes. By 1968, union political contributions were more than $7 million (Bok and Dunlop, 1970: 393), and union contributions have totaled about 10 to 20 per cent of all contributions to the Democratic Party over the past twenty years (Bok and Dunlop, 1970: 414). This is probably less than that of business contributions.

One of the most important sources of union electoral power is its ability to provide political organization. In some cities, the labor unions supply much of the infrastructure – campaign workers, ward leaders, precinct captains – for the local Democratic Party. Through this infrastructure, the labor unions mobilize not only their own members, but also the low-income vote generally. Given that low-income families usually have lower levels of voter participation and that they tend to vote Democratic when they do vote, this strategy – and its selective use – strengthens union electoral power. Not surprisingly, labor union influence in local politics is correlated with that of local political parties, particularly the Democratic Party (Clark, 1974: 25a). Where labor unions are most politically powerful in local politics, it is as an adjunct of their partisan support of the Democratic Party in Congressional, state and local politics (Gray and Greenstone, 1961; Salisbury, 1960). Like corporations, national labor unions also encourage their local leadership to represent them on the city council, in civic associations, and on private welfare and social service boards such as the Community Chest (Form and Miller, 1960). In the 1960s about one-third of all United Fund and Community Chest contributions came from plants unionized by the AFL–CIO (Bok and Dunlop, 1970). Parallel to the contributions of their members, unions have consistently expanded their representation on community boards since the Second World War. By 1970 the AFL–CIO had more than 75 000 representatives on civic and welfare agency boards (Bok and Dunlop, 1970). This is usually seen as an accoutrement of status, rather than as a tool for political power.

Labor union influence in community decision-making is difficult to assess. In case studies, labor union representatives often constitute a small (5–20 per cent) but significant percentage of those reputed to influence the resolution of local issues (Form and Miller, 1960: 582; Freeman *et al.*, 1963). The significance of this influence is open to some question. Union leaders tend not to initiate political issues at a local level. Their participation in decision-making typically occurs at the later stages when issues are resolved and programs are implemented (McKee, 1953; Form and Miller, 1960). In the mid-1950s labor union leaders judged to be influential in East Lansing were asked about their role in local policy-making: one-half explicitly stated they were not brought in from the beginning when policies were initially formulated. Labor union leadership tends to react to agendas established by others and to legitimate programs over which it has little control.

None the less, comparative city surveys of informants (e.g. heads of Chamber of Commerce, and of local Democratic and Republican parties) repeatedly indicate that labor unions are influential in resolving local issues (e.g. mayoral elections, school board elections, municipal bond referendum). In each of fifty-one cities, seven such informants were interviewed on which actors in the community were essential for determining the outcome of five different issues (Clark, 1968). On the average, labor unions were judged to be essential on fewer issues by fewer informants than were industrial leaders (based on data reported by Burt, 1978). The differences, however, were not great. The average informant judged labor involvement to be essential in resolving the average issue about 45 per cent of the time, while the equivalent figure for industrialists was 51 per cent. Based on this measure of influence, labor unions were equally or more influential than local industrialists in twenty of the fifty-one cities, and less influential in thirty-one cities.

Labor union organization and political power

Labor unions, like corporations, are part of national organizational structures. The American Federation of Labor–Congress of Industrial Organization (AFL–CIO) is a national federation of diverse national unions, including both craft and industrial unions. Although the AFL–CIO is politically organized at all levels of government, local unions frequently take independent political action and do not formally affiliate with the state or local federation (Bok and Dunlop, 1970). The national unions, rather than the AFL–CIO federation, are typically the strongest local political organization. In many cities, for example, the AFL–CIO's COPE has been singularly ineffective in persuading local unions to build up COPE district organizations (Greenstone, 1970: 17).

As collective bargaining agents, the national unions successfully claim the allegiance of their rank and file (Greenstone, 1970: 177). Labor unions vary considerably in their local partisan involvement. Typically, industrial unions – whose contracts are negotiated nationally – are nationally integrated into the Democratic Party. Given their centralized nature, and the greater importance of federal legislation to their interests, national labor unions try to mobilize their locals along parallel partisan lines (Bok and Dunlop, 1970; Banfield and Wilson, 1963). For many craft unions (as in the building

trades) working and wage conditions depend on local
bargaining, frequently with local government interests. This
tends to make local unions shy of intense partisan
involvement, lest the party they support fails to carry the
elections (Banfield and Wilson, 1963). Whether the local
presence of different union organizational structures has an
effect on the city's power structure has not been studied.

The economy and union political power

While corporations wield considerable economic power *vis-à-
vis* the city, labor unions do not, and, like city governments,
cannot control corporate relocation. This ultimate sanction
constitutes a continuous constraint on union factory and urban
politics. Formally, unions may prevent relocation by proving
to the National Labor Relations Board that it is a 'runaway'
from legitimate union actions. According to a former
industrial relations executive for a major Los Angeles
manufacturer (interviewed in 1973), corporations can easily
justify plant relocations on technical criteria. According to this
informant, his corporation regularly chose new locations in
part based on 'which union location is most reasonable to deal
with'. As to the union posture, he said,

> Sometimes you get a protester, a misfit who is obstreperous,
> demanding. Sometimes the grievances are petulant,
> sometimes real. The tractability of employee groups is
> critical. Because of all the publicity given the black
> movement in the past four years, the black is more apt to
> stand up on his hind legs, more grievances, non-docile.

Given the dependency of employment and wages on
corporate investment, labor unions are likely to favor tax and
service subsidizations of corporate employers and oppose any
urban programs that would seriously jeopardize continued
corporate location in the city. In the fifty-one cities' study cited
above, for example, of all informants who listed air pollution
as an issue, only 4.6 per cent indicated that labor unions
supported air pollution control. Compared with 23.8 per cent

for the Chamber of Commerce and 27.5 per cent for
city/county agencies (Crenson, 1971: 89).

Labor unions may be hesitant to exert their political muscle
in the face of corporate locational flexibility. In Stinchcombe's
(1968: 158) study of Toledo, he notes:

> Some union leaders believe that an overt flexing of labor's
> muscles in city politics would hinder goals best advanced
> through the Toledo Area Development Corporations and
> good labor–management relations. The concept of a good
> local climate common to both labor and industry emphasizes
> an avoidance of disruptive issues and politics as such.

While the locational flexibility of labor may have increased, it
is far less spatially responsive to new job opportunities than is
corporate investment, particularly portfolio investment
(Holland, 1976). The high costs of movement, including the
irreplaceability of the family, friendship and community
network, makes labor less able to move than capital. This
attachment to place also undercuts the potential economic
bases of union political power. Thus local union power
depends on their political participation, their ability to
mobilize mass support, and their relative insulation from the
local labor market.

Corporations, labor unions and political power

To sum up, corporations and labor unions are powerful
organizations in the determination of urban policy. Yet the
bases of corporate and labor union power are not equivalent.
While corporations have an economic basis for their political
power by control over the economic processes which constrain
the fiscal capacity and policy success of urban government,
labor unions do not. While labor unions mobilize electoral
support or opposition as a mass organization and as an adjunct
of the Democratic Party, corporations do not. Thus whereas
corporations exercise power without mass participation, labor
unions cannot exercise power without it.

Corporation and labor union political participation are

therefore not equivalent. To aggregate patterns of individual participation into measures of local democracy (diffusion, decentralization of decision-making, access, or just plain participation) neglects the power of the organizations which condition the efficacy of individual political action, and ignores the different bases of power which such participation represents.

Labor unions may be the organizational base of a political coalition that pushes for high levels of public services and low residential tax burdens, but the resultant high business taxes or low level of economic infrastructure spending may stimulate corporations to disinvest from the city. As local employment and wages are threatened by the resultant decline in local investment, the political stage is dominated by the union anxious about their members' jobs. Those that participate may communicate their own power, or the power of others.

By and large, urban analyses of the policy impact of corporations or labor unions have analyzed only one source of political power. Studies have primarily relied upon the participation and policy preferences of corporations or unions to judge their local power. Study of the impact of their local organizational structure on local policy-making has barely begun. Further, there have been few attempts to specify the interests of corporations or labor unions, and to analyze how different local conditions might affect those interests and thereby shape their respective policy impacts. Corporate or union power need not be inferred from the consistency of public policy with their intentional participation, nor with their expressed preferences. Rather corporate and union power can also be inferred from the extent to which public policies are adopted in response to conditions which affect corporate or union interests. That the local organizational strength of corporations or labor unions will affect which local conditions affect local policies and which do not will be the subject of later chapters.

Notes

1. See also Walton (1970).

2. In 1973–4, I conducted a series of interviews with corporate officials, ranging from members of the board to middle-management personnel. These interviews, conducted in various cities around the US, are confidential. The references refer to the corporation from which the information was obtained.

3. There are a number of problems in deciding precisely what this correlation means. The study relies on commercial bank directors, members of organizations which are more tightly tied to a particular metropolitan area than are industrial corporations. Interlocks with local industrial corporations may only indicate the extent of local dependency and thus the interest in local participation. Banks whose operations are less locally dependent may participate less in local politics because their economic power is in fact *greater*. Further, there are always serious problems in estimating contextual effects and interpreting them, given the existence of complex processes of self- and organizational-selection, as well as organizational policy. Given the assertion that many directors join upper-class organizations as a *result* of their mobility into executive positions, its meaning for the organization still remains to be clearly specified.

4. In a four-city survey of 290 corporate executives, 169 of whom were located in firms employing 100 or more persons, Noland found that executives from larger firms were more likely to participate in city affairs (1962: 248) and were expected by other executives to participate more (1962: 236). Further, branch-plant executives were less likely to participate politically than executives from locally headquartered companies (1962: 250).

5. In one of the few recent empirical studies of the policy impact of absentee ownership, Lincoln (1976) found that external control over a city's manufacturing activity had a negative impact on the level of policy output. If this were interpreted as a reduced form coefficient, it suggests that the deleterious political effects of external economic control outweigh those of dispersion of influence.

6. Of course, the relationship between organizational and individual interests is problematic. Interests and preferences are not the same thing. The former are rooted in structured access to benefits, while the latter refer to expressions of political opinion. In an interesting study of thirty US cities, Williams and Zimmerman used the preferences of political leaders who reported business as sources of support to assess business 'interests' in redistribution. They found that such business 'interests' in redistribution varied significantly, often being more supportive of redistribution than the communities in which they were located. This study does not distinguish between types of business organizations, focusing instead on the local Chamber of Commerce. While it is a corrective to the assumption that preferences can be imputed to organizational types, it does not address the issue of the impact of business interests on preferences, or their joint relationship to public policy. To infer business preferences from the policy positions of political leaders who list business as sources of support is dangerous (Williams and Zimmerman, 1979). Finally, while businesses may support redistribution as an ideal, they may also be opposed to the reduction of public benefits which they receive and the expansion of public costs which they must bear in order to make such redistribution possible.

7. Max Weber (1968: 352) pointed out the dilemma of the decentralized local government faced with mobile economic activity:

Within compulsory associations, particularly political communities, all property utilization that is largely dependent on real estate is stationary, in contrast to personal property which is either monetary or easily exchangeable. If propertied families leave a community, those staying behind must pay more taxes; in a community dependent on a market economy, and particularly a labor market, the have-nots may find their economic opportunities so much reduced that they will abandon any reckless attempt at taxing the haves or will even deliberately favor them.

8. Downtown retail activity, for example, has been found to be dependent on the level of downtown office activity, even when controls are made for metropolitan size, city age and distance to nearest SMSA (Friedman, 1973; Kasarda, 1972).

Chapter 3

The Economics of Central City Change

Since the Second World War, both the economy and social composition of the US central city have been profoundly transformed. This transformation in urban employment and residence has changed the conditions necessary to maintain economic growth and social control.

Once a producer of material goods, the central city increasingly produced specialized business and professional services. Once economically dependent on the production of wealth, the central city has become tied to its management. Once a site where people both lived and worked, many central cities increasingly have failed to provide either homes or work for its people. As the central cities became more dependent on workers who did not live within their bounds, they became less able to provide private employment for those who did.

Industrial decline and office growth

In the postwar transformation of the central cities, industry declined while office work grew steadily. Skyscrapers supplanted smokestacks; offices replaced assembly lines as the economic backbone of the central city. Growth and decline were being charted by the same embryonic codes of corporate growth.

The rise of the office and the decline of industry as the economic base of the central city were both linked to the changing organizational structure of the US economy. As ownership was concentrated in the largest corporations, production was spread into a global skein of plants. Input–output relations were planned within the firm, instead of by the market. Accordingly, the tendencies to industrial agglomeration were reduced. Unitary corporate control made the geographic dispersion of production possible. It made the expansion and geographic centralization of management necessary.

Access to national markets, facilitated by declining transport costs, made corporate concentration easier. In turn, corporate concentration made geographic dispersion of plant activity possible, as the largest corporations entered new markets through new plant locations and firm acquisitions. The cycle of corporate concentration and geographic spread fed on itself. As a result, corporate investments were not localized within the central city nor did they radiate out into the metropolitan area and its proximate region. Rather, they were spread, almost randomly, across the nation. In a study of all large multilocational organizations (400 or more employees) in seven western US metropolitan areas in the early 1970s, Pred (1977: 128) found an average of only 27 per cent of their total employment was within the metropolitan area where the firm was headquartered. The largest firms' plant investments are not regionalized.

With growing scale, functional diversity and geographic spread, the corporation's organizational requirements also grew. As production decisions once coordinated through the market by the interaction of several firms were internalized within a single firm, the firm's planning requirements increased. As the number of input–output relationships which impinged upon corporate profitability expanded and their geographic distance widened, whether inside or outside the corporate shell, demands for research and development, prediction and control also grew. Thus, larger and more complex corporations had a larger percentage of their employees in office jobs than their smaller, less powerful counterparts (Child, 1973). High-salary office employment grew faster than clerical employment due to computerization of routine functions (Pred, 1977: 25). What had previously been the unplanned outcome of the market, now became the conscious decision of the firm.

The changing organizational structure of corporate production stimulated the growth of producer services, such as banking, engineering, accounting and legal services. Between 1950 and 1970, producer services increased from 4.8 per cent to 9.3 per cent of the total US labor force (Singelmann, 1978: 1229). Most of this growth was concentrated in the large metropolitan areas, particularly their central cities. Also through mergers and acquisitions, the subsidiary company's top personnel were transferred to the new headquarters, and the corporation's acquired demand for local business services cut back (see Udell, 1969; Mueller, 1972). As a result, corporate office activity and specialized business services expanded in the largest central cities.

Corporate concentration facilitated the physical separation of production and administration. The former pushed its way out of the central city; the latter pushed its way up. Office construction could take advantage of the air space above costly metropolitan real estate; factory construction could not. Once glued to the central city by the critical importance of central rail junctions and ports, industry became increasingly footloose. The rise of intra-metropolitan highway grids, with the radial spokes to the downtown and beltways connecting the suburbs, decreased the advantage of central city location for maximum accessibility to both the metropolitan consumer and labor markets. Coupled with mass auto ownership, workers could go farther and faster to work than ever before. The rise of the interstate highway and inter-city air system increased the ease with which managers, technicians, buyers and sellers could reach small-town and rural plants (Stanback and Knight, 1976: 30). As products reached the later stages of their life cycle, when production techniques were routinized, less skilled labor required and accessibility to high-level managers and technicians were less important, production was likely to be spun off to small-town locations (Krumme and Hayter, 1975; Stanback and Knight, 1976: 30; Thompson, 1965).

Changing industrial technologies also influenced siting needs and location. The new continuous-process technologies required linear horizontal space. The high costs of property acquisition for large city parcels pushed industrial plants outwards where land assembly was cheaper and easier (Noll,

1970; Birch, 1970). Combined with high central city property taxes and lower industrial service benefits, the high cost of centrally located land proved a potent repellant (Williams, 1967; Due, 1961). In addition to central city pushes, there were also suburban pulls. Protected, pre-packaged and planned industrial parks proliferated. In the 1950s there were less than 100 in the US. By 1970, there were 2400 (Liston, 1970). Due to the ease of municipal incorporation, these tax-rich, non-populated industrial suburbs multiplied.

Industrial plants were also relocated to secure a more pliant, less unionized, lower-wage labor force. In the large central city, wages were higher and labor more unionized than in rural areas and small cities and towns (Fuchs, 1967; Hoch, 1972). Industry moved in search of a cheaper, less fractious labor force (Stuart, 1968). Suburban workers, while highly paid, are more likely to own their own homes with a consequent need to support a continuous stream of mortgage payments. As a result, suburban plants have lower labor turnover, less absenteeism, fewer labor disputes and higher productivity (Mollenkopf, 1976: 270).[1]

All of the preceding factors contributed to the decline in the central city's *share* and *level* of metropolitan industrial employment. By the 1960s, in the largest 130 central cities, the average city accounted for only 50 per cent of all industrial activity in its metropolitan area. The largest-scale, most capital-intensive and best-paid industrial employment were most suburbanized. By 1964, the 130 central cities accounted for only 35 per cent of all metropolitan plants employing 1000 or more owned by the '*Fortune* 1000' largest US industrial corporations. Suburban industrial wages, and value-added per worker, also tended to be higher than in the corresponding central cities (Stanback and Knight, 1976: 68–9). This meant that lower-wage, less productive industrial employment was being left in the central city. As a result, business-cycle downturns were most likely to affect central city industry as firms shut down their least productive units in lean times (Cohen and Noll, 1968).

The central city's *level* of industrial activity also declined. In his study of forty large cities, Kain (1968) found a loss of over one million industrial jobs between 1954 and 1968 in the central cities and a gain of an equal number of jobs in their suburban rings.[2] More recent analysis of ten large metropolitan areas between 1950 and 1970 showed an annual average rate of decline in industrial employment of over 1 per cent in the 1950s and no growth in the 1960s (Stanback and Knight, 1976: 56).

As industrial investment slowed in the central city, the level of office activity grew rapidly. New production was increasingly located in suburbs, small towns and countryside. The burgeoning task of corporate management and the specialized services it required were taking its place in the central city; white collar was taking over for blue.

The central city, particularly the central business district, is an attractive location for office activity – especially corporate office activity. A single corporation might produce things as diverse as mattresses and movie stars, in places as distant as Los Angeles and London. While operating responsibility for production is largely decentralized to regional offices, the largest parameters for corporate operation are studied and set in the headquarters. There, strategies are mapped out, long-term capital allocation decided and coordination of the corporate network achieved. Central corporate offices make intensive use of available specialized services which many find more expensive to produce themselves. Business, legal, financial and technical services are concentrated in the central city. As these services became more specialized, corporations were less likely to provide them internally and the services were more likely to agglomerate in large central cities where corporate demand was extensive. This in turn maintained the attraction of the central city location for corporate offices wanting to ensure ready access to a maximum range of such services (Pred, 1977). Because use of such specialized business services often required quick, non-routine, face-to-face interaction, corporate proximity is important (Goddard, 1973 and 1975).

The informational appetite of corporate headquarters has been insatiable. As the organizational structure of the economy became more complex and more concentrated, and its technologies and markets more unstable, the potential benefits of environmental information increased. Many top corporate office employees spend half their working week exchanging information (Stewart, 1967). As the profitability of information increases, corporate offices become more sensitive to its locational costs.

With increasing frequency, informational spatial biases are also affecting explicit locational decisions in the sense that place-to-place variations in the availability and accessibility – or *cost* – of information are deliberately considered as a factor of location for administrative headquarters, advertising agencies, banks and other financial intermediaries, law firms, public relations firms, management consultants, data-processing service centers, and office and business service activities in general [Pred, 1977: 24].

Corporate office access to information cannot be entirely purposive. Due to the random nature of change in a market economy, investment opportunity, marketing and technological developments require that corporate executives continuously monitor information flows. The volume of potentially relevant public information is too enormous for corporate offices to monitor comprehensively. Corporate executives therefore rely on face-to-face inter-organizational networks to alert them to potentially relevant public or private information. Because it cannot be purposive, this monitoring of informational flows depends on continuous, face-to-face personal contacts. This may be the organizational interest in social-class formation, a formation which is often local in nature.

The central city continues to offer a location where channels carrying information of potential relevance to corporate offices are concentrated. This information is produced, stored and exchanged through a dense inter-organizational network. Corporate planning depends on its linkages into this network through service contracts, interlocking directorates and social contacts.

Specialized business services – such as investment banking, accounting, law offices – have become increasingly important to the large corporation. As Cohen (forthcoming) has forcefully argued, corporate management can no longer be left to the managers. As corporations have diversified into different industries and different countries, banks have become important sources of investment advice. With the rise of complex production and marketing structures, accounting firms have become important sources of management consulting. With the growing role of the state in the economy, legal firms have become increasingly important sources of legal and legislative information (Cohen, forthcoming). These 'advanced corporate services' are highly specialized, highly concentrated in the largest central cities, and an increasingly important source of corporate growth.

The largest corporations are most capital intensive and thus most dependent upon external financing (Fitch and Oppenheimer, 1970). Further, they frequently have to raise short-term capital to meet unpredictable needs. Thus, the largest corporations were most interlocked with financial institutions (Allen, 1974). Such corporate–bank interlocks, which are often localized in the central city, provide important information (McLaughlin, 1975). The commercial banks are increasingly able to control the flow and direction of capital investment in the US. In addition, the large central city commercial banks control local investment funds and hold mortgages on major parcels of central city real estate. Commercial banks thus control the rate and structure of local economic development. Locally headquartered corporations interested in potential competition for space, workers and markets tend to be well represented on the commercial bank boards.[3] Finally, the central city also provided the network of clubs, restaurants and cultural institutions where executives keep a local finger on the pulse of corporate America – that is, each other.

Corporate headquarter offices continued to find the central city an attractive location. Of the fifty largest banks and fifty largest life insurance companies, 95 per cent were headquartered in central cities in both 1960 and 1970. Of the 500 largest industrials, 83 per cent had headquarters in central cities in 1960 and 78 per cent in 1970 (Burns, 1977: 211).[4] For corporations which changed the location of their head office between 1960 and 1975, over three-quarters chose a central city location (Friedland and DuMont, forthcoming). Between

1954 and 1965, 73 per cent of all *new* private office construction took place in central cities (Harrison, 1974: 13). In ten metropolitan areas studied in 1960 and 1970, business services accounted for a larger proportion of employment in the central city than in the suburbs, and their proportion of central city employment was increasing (Stanback and Knight, 1976: 58–67). Those offices which moved out of the central city were those whose demands for information were lower and more routine, particularly divisional and regional offices (Armstrong, 1972; Pred, 1977).

The growth of corporate and financial intermediary office activity in the central city also induced related office growth in business and professional services. Not only were the large corporations themselves clients for such services (Gottmann, 1961), but they generated their own flow of buyers, sellers, investors, consultants, thereby providing a further potential market for the same services.

TABLE 3.1 *Central city business service activity, 1963–72*

	Average number of establishments		
	1963	1967	1972
Other business services	106 (107)*	377 (112)	427 (112)
Advertising	65 (107)	85 (112)	105 (112)
Management-consulting	107 (107)	146 (112)	251 (112)

* Numbers in parentheses refer to the number of cities upon which the mean is based. Changes in classification may affect some of the changes in number.
SOURCE: *Census of Selected Service Industries* (Washington, D.C.: US Government Printing Office, 1963, 1967 and 1972).

The growth of office-related business services is evident in Table 3.1, which indicates the average number of such establishments for cities above 100 000. Between 1963 and 1972, the office economy was clearly expanding. By 1970, fully one-third of all central city employment was either managerial or clerical (US Census, 1970). If the small town expanded by taking in each other's wash, the central city grew by taking out each other's paper.

Suburban development and the retail drain

Office growth produced high-income employment downtown. Industrial decentralization pushed the highest-income industrial jobs into the suburbs. Together they helped accelerate the post-1945 home-owner exodus to suburbs. Americans translated higher income into demands for more space (Alonso, 1971: 437–41). In the residential economics of *Lebensraum*, even wage-earners who worked in the central city gave up access in exchange for a patch of suburban green. Alonso (1971: 440) writes:

> the nature of the demand for space in this country seems to be a deeply ingrained cultural value, associated not only with such functional needs as play space for children, but also with basic attitudes towards nature, privacy, and the meaning of the family. A preference so deeply rooted in a culture is not likely to change suddenly.

Higher incomes meant a bigger appetite for and a capacity to purchase space. Since intensity of land-use, and thus land prices, declined steeply with distance from downtown, the relatively high costs of close-in locations pushed the upwardly mobile family out to the suburbs.

The growth of high-skilled white-collar employment downtown provided the higher incomes necessary for suburban residential location. As incomes increased, distance between house and work also increased (Kain, 1962). The decentralization of capital-intensive industry lowered commuting costs, while providing the higher wages necessary to purchase suburban space (Brown and Kain, 1970). By the mid-1960s, 50 per cent of all union members and 75 per cent of all union members under thirty lived in the suburbs (COPE, 1967).

The postwar flood of women into the labor force also

contributed substantially to the family incomes necessary for down payments on suburban homes. Between 1950 and 1970, the number of working women doubled (9 to 20 million), raising the percentage of employed women from 25 per cent to 40 per cent (Stanback and Knight 1976: 184). Women's wages contributed to the family income in half the households earning $15 000 or more in 1970 (Stanback and Knight, 1976: 184).

Attributing the suburban migration solely to an American penchant for space and backyard privacy would neglect the government's role in underwriting suburban preferences. This took many forms. First, postwar federal and state financing greatly increased the mileage of intra-metropolitan highways. This paving of America pre-empted public mass transit and radically extended the locational range of the suburban commuter. Second, in the aftermath of the Depression, the Federal Government created an institutional mortgage market designed to finance mass ownership of single-family homes. Before the 1929 crash, the typical home mortgage required large down payments, high interest payments and relatively short repayment periods (US House of Representatives, 1973: 8). During the 1930s, the Federal Government created a set of institutions which revolutionized the home mortgage system. The Federal Home Loan Bank Board and Bank System and Federal Savings and Loan Insurance Corporation permitted savings and loan institutions to use insured savings to finance long-term mortgages at low interest rates. The Federal Housing Administration provided mortgage insurance for long-term (twenty-year) low-down-payment (20 per cent) fully amortized mortgages. The Federal National Mortgage Association developed a new secondary mortgage market, increasing the liquidity of mortgage investments by allowing their sale on short-term securities markets and insulating the mortgage market from cyclical variation in other securities' markets.

Third, the Federal Government's income tax subsidies have been particularly favorable to single-family home-owners. Not only can they deduct mortgage interest and local property taxes, but they can also defer capital gains realized from sale of their homes. In general, the size of this subsidy increased with the value of the home and the level of taxable family incomes

(Aaron, 1975; Struyk, 1977).[5] By the mid-1970s the tax subsidy to home-owners was costing the Federal Government some $12 billion a year (Struyk, 1977; Harvey, 1975).

Finally, the American metropolis evolved a peculiar market for public goods, with municipalities bearing a relatively high share of total public expenditure and tax collection when compared to other Western countries. Combined with easy municipal incorporation, this produces a byzantine mosaic of jealous municipalities each trying to maximize its property tax base and minimize its expenditure costs.

In this context of municipal fragmentation and local financing of social services, there were strong incentives for suburbanization. Public finance economists treat the fragmented metropolis as a marketplace for public goods. Under this 'voluntary exchange theory', individuals seek out localities which offer their preferred bundle of service benefits and tax burdens (Tiebout, 1956). The citizens then vote with moving vans and mortgages. Tying the tax base to real estate values, and service provision to fragmented municipalities, causes the geography of need and fiscal capacity to diverge.[6] The higher the percentage of poor people in a municipality, the lower the per capita level of taxable resources, but at the same time the greater the demands for social services (Bradford and Kelejian, 1973).

For higher-income families, eager to maximize their public service benefits while minimizing their tax costs, living in a relatively homogenous suburban town makes sense. Homogenous upper-income suburbs may emerge 'naturally' through the housing market. But the barriers to suburban entry were not left to chance. The suburbs had their own enclosure acts in the form of zoning laws. A variety of exclusionary measures were used to wall out the less affluent: large lot and non-multiple unit zoning, strict building codes and lack of public transit to non-central employment centers.

As a result of rising family incomes and the emergence of public policies which reinforce the preference of higher-income families for suburban space, the central city's residential share of metropolitan population has slid consistently downwards since the Second World War (Campbell and Sacks, 1967: 17). This was particularly true where the suburbs effectively resisted central city efforts at annexation. The suburban frontiers have absorbed the bulk of new residential construction. Not only did the central city's share of metropolitan population decline, but its growth rate also slowed. In many of the largest central cities, it went into reverse in the 1950s and 1960s.[7]

Retail trade was pushed out by rising central city land prices associated with high density use, and pulled out by the home-owner retail dollar receding across the horizon. Suburbanites took their purchasing power out of the central city and the retail sector followed its best customers to the suburbs. Retail decentralization was intensified by the explosion of regional shopping centers since 1960. Of the 422 centers constructed in 151 metropolitan areas between 1946 and 1968, three-quarters were built since 1960 (Masotti, 1974). Financed by the largest department store and retail chains, the centers draw on a vast freeway-borne market.

Increasingly, retail corporations buy large suburban sites in advance of residential development, thereby reaping large profits from appreciation of peripheral land (Breckenfeld, 1972). The new shopping centers not only provide access to the dispersed suburban market, but also the retail chain to control the type and price of merchandise sold in the lesser stores in the complex.[8] As a result of retail suburbanization, the central city's share of metropolitan retail trade and its total level of retail trade both declined. In the ten metropolitan areas studied by Stanback and Knight (1976: 56–7), the average annual growth rate in retail employment between 1950 and 1970 was negative in the central cities and strongly positive in the suburbs.

Loss of the central city shopper hit the central business district particularly hard. As downtown land values increased and the high-income residential population decreased, the central business district's retail function eroded (Smith, 1961). Downtown department stores cut back shopping hours and low-prestige discount stores invaded the main avenues, and the *downtown* lost its prominence as a central city, or metropolitan, retail center.

The poverty trap

At the same time that industrial production was being increasingly organized by large-scale corporations who owned plants throughout the nation, agricultural production was also fast coming under the management of large firms employing capital-intensive techniques. Since the 1930s, mechanization and land concentration have transformed American agriculture and displaced millions of farm owners and workers. The small farmers' unpaid family labor was insufficient to keep them competitive. Tenant farmers and agricultural workers were displaced by the use of capital-intensive technologies on vast landholdings. Both went streaming to the cities. Between 1950 and 1965, 20 million people left the land, 4 million of them black. When the dust settled, agricultural employment had been cut by two-thirds (Piven and Cloward, 1971: 214) and American cities had absorbed the largest internal migration of unskilled labor in the nation's history.

In the 130 large central cities studied here, the average central city non-white population jumped from 31 472 to 73 445 between 1940 and 1960, thus an average absolute increase of over 40 000 blacks. By 1960, non-whites constituted an average of 16 per cent of these central cities' populations. Between 1960 and 1970, the central city black population continued to grow through natural increase and migration. In those central cities in SMSAs (metropolitan areas) with populations of 200 000 or more (148 such areas in 1970), the non-white population increased by 36.8 per cent between 1960 and 1970, rising to an average of 24 per cent of the 1970 central city population (US Department of Commerce, 1972: 839). Blacks approached numerical dominance in many cities. Net white out-migration from the central cities continued during the 1950s and 1960s.

The central city economy faced a vast increase in the supply of strong hands, particularly black hands, just when demand for them was waning. The largest, most capital-intensive, and best-paying industrial plants were being constructed in dispersed suburban locations (Vernon, 1967; Stanback and Knight, 1976; Harrison, 1974). Central city manufacturing employment had been slow growing or declining, and the jobs that remained tended to be labor-intensive, low-wage employment in the small, highly competitive firms which moved into locations abandoned by larger corporations looking for linear space and lower taxes.

New York City's industrial base, for example, is dominated by

industries producing unstandardized goods, continually changing their process and product, and assiduously avoiding commitments in machinery, buildings and other fixed capital. These are industries that are most restricted in opportunities to expand productivity. For such industries, continued growth of demand does not bring much increase in output per worker; it simply means the employment of more workers . . .

These are industries where entry is easy. Where entry is easy, profit margins and wage levels are constantly under pressure. As a result, even when productivity increases occur in such industries, such increases are not allowed to find their reflection in higher profits or higher wages per unit of output; instead they are squeezed out of the value-added measure by the onslaught of competition [Vernon, 1967: 110].

Together with the older, less capital-intensive plants of the largest corporations, this industrial base was highly vulnerable to the cyclical winds of the national economy. Thus not only did wages remain low in central city industry, but economic downturns generated massive unemployment.

The consumer service sector has been another traditional entry point for low-skilled labor. But like industry, consumer service employment was growing in the suburbs, not in the central cities. The suburban service sector provided low wages and thus insufficient incentive to offset the high costs and increased time to travel to work for central city residents. In addition, these jobs were being taken by a secondary labor market of wives and children of employed suburban males, who were willing to accept low wages and were closer to work (Stanback and Knight, 1976, 106–8).

As industrial and consumer service employment declined in the central city, specialized business and social services expanded. Between 1950 and 1967, eleven cities studied by Ganz lost 0.4 million manufacturing and trade jobs, while gaining one million government, business, finance and professional service jobs (Ganz, 1972). In ten large metropolitan areas, Stanback and Knight (1976: 86) found that central city employment growth was concentrated in professional-technical and clerical occupations associated with the new office economy. These jobs required both social and intellectual skills which low-income central city residents frequently lacked. Black employment in particular has been concentrated in those sectors of the economy – unskilled production and service jobs – which the central city is losing.

Not only did unskilled central city residents have to compete for this slow-growing pool of local jobs for which they were qualified, but they also faced increasing competition for these jobs from suburban residents. In the above ten central cities, suburban commuters accounted for about 50 per cent of male white-collar jobs and 40 per cent of male blue-collar jobs in 1970 (Stanback and Knight, 1976: 91; Kalachek and Goering, 1970; Kain, 1962). By 1970, over one-third of all central city jobs were taken by non-central city residents.

The changing structure of central city employment and competition for the remaining unskilled, low-wage jobs translated into high levels of unemployment and poverty. This was particularly the case for the black population, who in 1960 accounted for over 40 per cent of the 'official' poor. According to official definitions, there were 9.5 million poor people in the central cities in 1960 (Downs, 1971). While the largest group of metropolitan poor were economically unproductive children and elderly, fully one-third of all poor people were poor because their work paid so little (Downs, 1971: 237). Central city unemployment and low wages made for a bleak situation. In a 1970 survey of fifty-one central city neighborhoods, official unemployment was 9.6 per cent. Adding those workers who had been discouraged from job hunting by the poor prospects of finding acceptable work and those employed part-time but searching for full-time work, the subemployment rate rose to 13.3 per cent, 20.5 per cent if those earning $2.00 per hour or less are included. And based on a maximum wage of $3.50 per hour, the total of those unemployed or earning low wages amounted to 61.2 per cent (US Senate, 1973: 93–4). Thus manpower training and employment service programs could only funnel their clients into low-wage work (US Senate, 1973: 94). They could do nothing to change the structure of demand for labor.

Dilemmas of economic change

The central city was changing both as a place of employment and a place of residence. The combination of these changes in its economic and social structure posed serious problems of how urban government would simultaneously manage local economic growth and social control. The city was losing its function as an industrial employer, a center for blue-collar employment. With the suburbanization of the predominantly white middle class, the city was also losing its more routine retail trade and consumer services. Decreasingly a site for the production and distribution of things, its future economy relied on the production and exchange of symbols. The city economy's demand for low-skilled labor was either declining or growing very slowly.

At the same time the central city was losing its low-skilled employment and its white middle-class residents. Thus the city's economy was increasingly making demands for workers who did not live in the city, while gaining residents who needed jobs the city's private economy could not provide.

The public sector was accordingly torn in two. The rise of the office economy required both public purse and public authority to reorder land-uses. New economic infrastructure had to be built, land ownership had to be transferred and land-use patterns had to shift. All this was expensive and not immediately fiscally productive. Yet ultimately, it was the city's residents – many of whom did not benefit or might even suffer from the new economic growth – who held the votes necessary to maintain the local political leadership which this program of economic growth required. A growing percentage of the city's residents were poor, precisely because of the city's new economic structure. As a result of their poverty, they provided few public revenues and made many demands for public services and public employment to compensate for their inability to obtain them in the private market. That a large percentage of the urban poor were non-white made their poverty more visible, and their ability to organize against it more effective.

Thus the central city budget was hit on both sides of the line – capital expenditures to foster the new economic growth, and current expenditures to finance the services and jobs to maintain the quiescence of the new urban residents. If the city failed to provide the public infrastructure, it would risk losing its share of the new private investment and the public tax revenues it promised. If the city failed to provide new public services and employment, it would risk political instability, if not a breakdown in urban order.

In the following chapters, I shall examine central city attempts to manage economic growth and social control, and the ways in which national corporations and labor unions shaped city policy responses to the constraints on economic growth and social control.

Notes

1. The relationship may be that higher-productivity firms tend to locate in the suburbs, allowing the higher incomes which make home purchase possible. Regardless of whether workers have followed plant activity into the suburbs (Brown and Kain, 1970), home ownership is more likely in the suburbs than in the central city.

2. There has been considerable debate as to whether these effects were specific to the period studied by Kain. See Harrison (1974) for the argument that the late 1960s reversed this absolute industrial decline.

3. The commercial banks themselves are geographically constrained to the central city location as the location of clearing houses for cheques, as the point of maximum access to other banks for which the large banks are correspondents and 'joint' their loans, and for its access to corporate depositors, investors and borrowers.

4. Burns and Pang (1977) found some thirty-eight corporate headquarters relocated between 1960 and 1970. Of these, sixteen moved between central cities and twenty-two moved from central city to suburban locations. These results are potentially in conflict with Friedland and DuMont (forthcoming). There has been a tendency for both inter-regional dispersion and intra-regional concentration of corporate headquarter location (Semple, 1973).

5. This is so because the value of tax deductions and deferrals depends on the marginal tax rate, which increases with taxable income until the maximum tax rate is reached.

6. In a study of 2619 municipalities within 127 metropolitan areas outside the New England area, Richard Child Hill (1974) analyzed the variation in municipal median income. Hill found that the variation in median income across municipalities was positively related to the relative size of the non-white population, the relative size of families with $10 000 or more annual income, the number of municipalities in the metropolitan area, and the level of family income inequality.

7. Of the 130 largest central cities, the annual growth rate was 1.1 per cent between 1940 and 1960, and 0.6 per cent between 1960 and 1970. Between 1950 and 1960, 42 central cities suffered a population decline (see also Department of Commerce, 1972: 16).

8. Montgomery Ward, Allied Stores and Broadway Hale all derived more than half of their annual sales from shopping centers (Masotti, 1974).

Chapter 4

Urban Renewal: Interests, Actors, Structure

As the central city's downtown office economy grew, central city land-uses changed. In the world of urban economics, most of the upward and outward movement of the new downtown economy takes place quietly through the market. Firms and households weigh the benefits of downtown accessibility against their demands for space. Those who expect to benefit most from accessibility and who can make most intensive use of the relatively small downtown locations will tend to outbid others for the privilege of a central location. This power to command central locations is granted by the market, a noiseless outcome of one's income and the relative benefits of downtown accessibility versus non-downtown space.

But urban land was not allocated by the market alone. In the economic transformation of the central city, those firms which economic theory suggested would bid highest did not rely entirely on the market to secure their downtown locations. They frequently used the powers of government to facilitate land-use changes, changes which were often difficult to achieve through costly haggling over patchwork land assembly. They also used the powers of government to construct the complementary public infrastructure that made their investments profitable. Of all the urban programs that put public authority at the service of private investment, Urban Renewal was most visible, most explicit and most controversial.

What were the consequences of urban renewal – who benefited and which economic processes did the program reinforce? Who supported and who opposed urban renewal?

How was government authority for urban renewal organized? These are elemental questions – the role of the policy in the local economy, the political friends and foes of the policy, and the governmental structure charged with the policy's execution. It is against this backdrop that its relation to corporate and union power and interest can be analyzed.

Urban renewal: the program

The Federal Government's Urban Renewal program, initiated by the 1949 Housing Act, evolved from a skein of divergent interests. Liberal Democrats and labor leaders wanted to expand the supply of low-income housing.[1] The largest downtown corporations and financial intermediaries, however, were interested in the economic reconstruction of the central city, and the prevention of another depression in the wake of the Second World War (Keith, 1973; Straus, 1944; Lowe, 1967; Domhoff, 1978). What united these two groups was the desire to use eminent domain powers for new development, and the need to supplant the city's meager financial resources to finance the costs of land acquisition, clearance and reconstruction. What tore them apart was whether the new development should be public housing, or even residential construction. In time, the resultant legislation appeared to give both groups what they wanted.

While political liberals and labor leaders wanted to replace slums by providing new low-income housing, the corporate and financial interests wanted to replace them with new commercial and high-rent residential construction. Both groups wanted public authority to eliminate the slums. With the 1949 legislation, the city and Federal Government began to act as brokers for private developers. City governments were empowered to purchase large areas of central city land through eminent domain in accordance with a federally approved plan. Federal approval had to be secured on a project by project basis.[2] The local agency would then clear the land, provide complementary public infrastructure, and re-sell it to private developers or construct public housing on it. The Federal Government if it approved the local plan, would pay for up to two-thirds of the difference between the city's costs of land acquisition and preparation, and the city's revenues from resale of the land to private developers.

While corporate interests fought for broad non-residential and non-public housing re-uses of renewed land, the pro-housing interests hoped that new housing, particularly low-income housing, would be built as a result of redevelopment. The housing activists supported the redevelopment bill, which lacked strong provisions for low-income housing, but they hoped that redevelopment would have positive effects on the central city's housing conditions. First, renewal projects had to be 'predominantly residential in character' either before or after reconstruction. Second, the bill required that equivalent housing be provided to all displaced families (Douglas, 1968). Third, in anticipation that renewed land would be used for low-income housing, the Act authorised federal subsidies to private developers to make such construction more profitable. Finally, the same housing interests pushed through another bill which authorized the yearly construction of 135 000 units of public housing for six years, anticipating that four million people would be rehoused in public housing by 1955 (Douglas, 1968: 110).

In the initial years of the Urban Renewal program, relatively few projects were initiated. Local corporate and downtown real estate interests were not politically responsive to the prospects of low-rent residential construction around the downtown, and the limited profitability of such investments made it difficult to line up the requisite developers and financial backers. Of the six-year public housing authorization, only one-quarter was actually built. And so subsequent federal legislation consistently loosened the residential requirements of the original 1949 Act. A larger and larger percentage of the federal capital grant could be used for non-residential purposes (1954 – 10 per cent; 1959 – 30 per cent; 1965 – 35 per cent). Renewal sites no longer needed to be in the most severe slum areas.

The authorized level of federal public housing was severely cut back (1954). Urban renewal areas could be used for expansion of universities, hospitals and cultural centers (1959, 1961, 1966). To counteract the declining low-rent housing emphasis of renewal legislation, new federal programs were instituted: special FHA mortgage insurance (1954), low-interest loans for low-income construction (1961) and rent supplements (1965). But these programs were not legally tied to a city's Urban Renewal program and were not particularly effective. As the low-income housing policies were weakened as well as severed from the Urban Renewal program, central city urban renewal started to roll. Local agencies began to find both private developers and local political support to move their projects off the planning boards.

TABLE 4.1   *Number of central city urban renewal projects by historical period*

| Years | Total number of projects | | |
	Planned (land area/use)	Executed (demolition clearance)	Completed (private development)
1949–55	76	32	2
1956–60	157	11	28
1961–66	294	225	119
1967–72	422	582	800

Number of cities (n) = 123
SOURCE: US Department of Housing and Urban Renewal, *Urban Renewal Directory*, 30 June 1972 (Washington DC: US Government Printing Office).

Table 4.1 indicates the total number of projects planned, executed (actual clearance), and completed (re-sold to and

TABLE 4.2   *Planned local uses of central city urban renewal lands, 1949–66*

Type of re-use	Average percentage
Residential	19.3
Commercial	12.2
Industrial	12.7
Public-institutional	19.8
Streets, alleys and public rights of way	36.0

n = 111
SOURCE: US Department of Housing and Urban Development, *Urban Renewal Project Characteristics, 1966*, (Washington, DC: US Government Printing Office).

constructed by private developers) in different periods for the cities studied here. Table 4.2 indicates the average percentage of urban renewal acreage in each city planned for different uses.

For the majority of cities, residential re-use was not prominent. On the contrary, public sector and private commercial/industrial investment were far more important.

Once under way the magnitude of the renewal program was staggering. By 1972, $9 billion in federal grants had been approved for over 2000 projects. Almost half of these projects took place in the central cities studied here. This massive infusion of federal funds did not serve all equally well.

Urban renewal: the beneficiaries

The growth of the office economy required new land, lands difficult to assemble because of fragmented ownership, large-scale deterioration, and the persistence of small proprietors who survived on family labor and a loyal neighborhood clientele. Urban renewal pushed a bulldozer through all these obstacles.

Interviews with developers indicated that powers of eminent domain were the most important feature of urban renewal. Since vacant space was decreasingly available and central city land ownership highly fragmented, the assembly of a large parcel remained cumbersome and costly, as small owners held out for high prices or refused to sell altogether (Northam, 1971; Smith, 1961; Bourne, 1967; Edel, 1972). The average parcel acquired through urban renewal during 1962–3 was only 0.17 acres (Edel, 1972: 141). While public renewal was time consuming, private renewal without eminent domain powers often took even longer (Adde, 1969).

The expansion of the office economy concentrated downtown was also constrained by the concentration of the poor, non-white population around its borders. Table 4.3 indicates the characteristics of the core – all the census tracts in and around the city's central business district – relative to the central city as a whole.

The central city's core has a distinctive social and physical composition. The typical core is disproportionately non-white

TABLE 4.3   *Characteristics of the core and the central city, 1960*

	Core* %	Central city %
Non-white population	24	16
Families under $4000 annual income	44	18
Housing units owner-occupied	24	56
Housing units built before 1939	87	64
Sound housing units with all plumbing	58	78

n = 130
* Residential census tracts surrounding central business district (includes CBD).
SOURCE: *Census of Population and Housing*, 1960. Central Business District boundaries are based on 1963 tract boundaries given in *Census of Business, Retail Trade*, 1963.

and poor, and its housing stock consists of older, lower quality rental units. Redeveloping these areas parcel by parcel through the market proceeds slowly. It is here, on the central business district's rim, that prisoner's dilemmas are endemic. The profitability of each single investment is dependent on simultaneous investments in the surrounding area. Without concerted investments on many sites, the single investor is left holding the bill without a corresponding increase in market value. Urban renewal facilitated large-scale land assembly by substituting political authority for the marginal mandate of the market. Urban renewal projects cleared a large area for simultaneous new private and public investment.

Downtown expansion is also constricted by the extraordinary staying power of small businesses. Able to rely on family labor and cheap wage labor, dependent on neighborhood clientele, small proprietors cling tenaciously to their central locations. Again urban renewal provided the legal means to force small businesses out. The predominant form of enterprise displaced by urban renewal was the small merchant with a localized, often ethnically distinct, clientele, and a small production shop. By 1959, over 100 000 businesses had already been displaced from 650 urban renewal sites (Anderson, 1964: 68). Unable to move back to the renewed area, unable to replace their clientele, unable to absorb the costs of moving, the dislocated firms either folded or their sales declined in new locations, often outside the central city altogether (Anderson, 1964; Zimmer, 1964).

The growth of the new economy also required large amounts of public expenditure, particularly capital for roads, parking structures, public transit, sewerage and other public works (Steiss, 1975; Manners, 1974). Office growth pushed up current municipal expenditures of all types, especially transportation and police, in part to manage the enormous inflow of workers who commute downtown daily (Kasarda, 1972; Muller, 1975b). Urban renewal was legitimated on the basis of its munificent effects on the local public purse. For all renewal projects committed to developers by 1971, related tax revenues from the areas increased by 348 per cent compared to pre-renewal levels. This occurred despite a drop in taxable land area due to increased public facilities (US Senate, 1973: 64). Based on the assumption that *all* private investment that occurred on renewal sites would otherwise have taken place outside the central city, urban renewal was a profitable investment of local public funds (Weicher, 1976). Given the dubious nature of this assumption and the other public costs of growth, estimates certainly overstate urban renewal's fiscal productivity (Hartman, 1974; see also Chapter 9). But tax revenues were not the most important fiscal effect of urban renewal.

More importantly, urban renewal stimulated local public spending for private economic growth, and did so above and beyond the expenditures required by law (US Senate 1973; Gramlich and Galper, 1973; Bingham, 1975). A very large percentage of the increased tax revenues were required to pay for urban renewal itself. This was frequently made explicit by legally tying the increased tax revenues to finance the renewal bonds (referred to as tax-increment financing). By 1971, local governments had invested $3.9 billion on public construction related to urban renewal, or 21 per cent of the total public and private investment on renewal sites (US Senate, 1973). Thus urban renewal not only offered a means to change land-uses by force and to subsidize their private redevelopment; it also allowed considerable leverage over the composition and location of local public investment.

Finally, office expansion drew more and more on the whiter, better-educated suburban labor market. It is the suburbs that provide its professionals, secretaries and managers (Earsy and Colton, 1974; Hartman, 1974). Not only must the downtown increasingly compete with suburban centers where more routine office functions are concentrated, but it must pay its workers more to compensate for the increased congestion and long journey to work (Richardson, 1978). The growth of a housing market accessible to downtown employment was a means to ease the downtown labor supply problem. Urban renewal facilitated the growth of a central city housing market for downtown workers, at the same time that it displaced those who were increasingly redundant to the central city economy.

In those areas most accessible to the central business district, private developers have been able to nurture profitably the emerging market for high-rent, high-rise apartment units. Because local and federal officials are eager to maximize the fiscal productivity of their public investment, they are anxious to get the highest price for their renewal sites (Bellush and Hausknecht, 1969; Kessler and Hartman, 1973). The developers of such high-rise, high-cost apartments bid highest.

Consequently, urban renewal both destroyed large amounts of low-income housing and constructed housing which only the more affluent could afford. Through 1967, urban renewal had destroyed 404 000 dwelling units, the bulk of which were inhabited by low-income residents (Fried, 1971: 88–9; US Senate, 1973). Yet during the same time only 41 580 units were constructed through urban renewal that could be afforded by low- or moderate-income families (26 per cent of these were in public housing). Thus 90 per cent of the low-income housing stock destroyed by urban renewal was not replaced.

By destroying a large amount of low-income housing without replacement, urban renewal increased demand while cutting supply. For non-whites facing racially restricted markets, the situation was particularly severe. As a result, those displaced by urban renewal were pushed into tighter markets where rents and overcrowding increased (Hartman, 1967; Abrams, 1965). The low-income housing intent of many of the supporters of the original 1949 legislation was never fulfilled.

Not surprisingly much of the opposition to urban renewal came from the neighborhoods, particularly the low-income and non-white neighborhoods, which were the logical targets for displacement.

In sum, urban renewal put public powers – eminent domain, public subsidy and public investment – at the service of the city's office economy, an economy in which the corporate headquarters played a critical role. It did not provide housing, public services, fiscal relief or even much private employment for the city's poorer residents. For the unions, urban renewal could be used to try to stem the drain of industrial investment and stimulate local construction, but these were subsidiary benefits. Accordingly the unions' power and interests in urban renewal were not dominant. Next, I will review the local politics of its birth and the structure in which it grew.

Urban renewal: the participants

After the Second World War the nation's major corporations were fully integrated in a national network of urban policy formation and diffusion. This network of organizations grew out of efforts to plan the conversion of the American economy to peacetime pursuits, a task in which federal urban policy was instrumental (Domhoff, 1978). Such organizations as the Committee for Economic Development, the National Planning Association and the Urban Land Institute sought to use federal powers to prevent a postwar depression and rationalize the American economy. This network not only shaped federal renewal legislation, but sped its adoption and directed its use in America's major cities.

The Urban Land Institute

The Urban Land Institute was established by the National Association of Real Estate Boards in 1939 as an

> independent fact-finding agency for study of trends affecting real property values and to provide an advisory service for

cities interested in replanning and rebuilding their blighted or poorly planned central business districts [*New York Times*, 10 March 1940].

Representing the interests of the largest central city property owners and developers, the Institute wanted both to protect the value of downtown properties and to generate new downtown construction through redevelopment. Well before 1949 the Institute's strategy was to consolidate property through eminent domain for subsidized resale to private developers, link the downtown to the burgeoning suburbs through metropolitan highways, and provide subsidized off-street parking for suburban office and shopper commuters (Adde, 1969). The Urban Land Institute was not only concerned about the difficulty of consolidating large downtown sites, but also fearful of what might happen to the financial intermediaries – banks, insurance companies, savings and loans – who held the mortgages, as slum property values continued to slide (Domhoff, 1978). Many of the mortgages for slum properties around the downtown were uninsured. While economic theory suggested that the conversion of downtown sites would begin as property values fell low enough, the major real estate interests were not interested in waiting that long. The Urban Land Institute therefore developed a legislative proposal for a separate federal agency which would subsidize most of the difference between the costs of site acquisition and clearance and the resale price the city received from private developers.

The Urban Land Institute, which wanted to mobilize the legitimacy of wartime planning for postwar city reconstruction, lent its support to national and local efforts for postwar economic planning. According to a survey by the National Association of Real Estate Boards, 51 per cent of cities of 200 000 or more had established organizations to plan for postwar city reconstruction (Urban Land Institute, June 1942). These organizations included major corporate and financial interests. The Urban Land Institute was frequently in contact with these organizations, if not represented in them.

After the 1949 Housing Act was passed, supported by both the National Association of Real Estate Boards and the Urban

Land Institute, the Institute developed a consulting service for the study of central city redevelopment, transportation, parking and tax problems. It provided small groups of corporate, financial and real estate executives to make 'panel studies' of a particular city. These studies were initiated and financed by local sponsors, usually local corporate organizations. By 1967, over seventy-five such 'panel studies' had been carried out. According to a ULI study, 'A major benefit of most ULI Panel Studies is that they frequently serve as catalysts for urban and economic development efforts in the communities in which they are conducted' (Adde, 1969). The studies almost always recommended the use of urban renewal, the development of transportation networks between suburbs and downtown combined with off-street parking, and the use of a small, exclusive corporate political organization to formulate and initiate such policies (Adde, 1969). The Urban Land Institute was critical in establishing a common program, both locally and nationally, between real estate interests who owned downtown properties and the corporate interests who used them. If the first produced the central place, the latter consumed it.

Chambers of Commerce

The US Chamber of Commerce was also involved in the national diffusion of urban renewal. In 1947, Earl Shreve, President of the US Chamber of Commerce, suggested that local Chambers should sponsor 'a non-official community planning group, composed of business and civic leaders' to study city conditions and find means for the 'rebuilding of blighted areas' (*American City*, October 1947). The national Chamber of Commerce had originally opposed the 1949 legislation because of its emphasis on public housing construction and its use of federal funds (Domhoff, 1978). After passage, the Chamber held a national Businessmen's Conference on Urban Problems in 1950. Its sessions on urban redevelopment included such men as Paul Martin, director of the Mellon-controlled Allegheny Conference, General Nelson from the New York Life Insurance Company and Max Wehrly, Paul McCord and Seward Mott from the Urban Land

Institute (Domhoff, 1978). All of these men stressed the ways in which urban redevelopment need not be used for housing, let alone low-income public housing. McCord, for example, suggested:

> I should like to emphasize at this point that redevelopment does not necessarily mean clearing slums for housing. Proper land use should be the keynote of any redevelopment program. I cannot emphasize that too much. It seems to be the general concept around . . . the country that urban redevelopment means housing. It certainly does not. More often it means anything but housing [US Chamber of Commerce, 1951: 159–60].

In 1952, the national Chamber of Commerce appointed a committee from the American Institute of Planners to write a guide to the city's uses of urban redevelopment (Domhoff, 1978). The pamphlet essentially stated the Urban Land Institute's position, stressing the need for separation of the local redevelopment agency from the public housing authority and for a 'citizen's group' to assist in the formulation and implementation of local redevelopment policy (Domhoff, 1978). In 1960, another Chamber pamphlet, *Planning Urban Renewal Projects*, was distributed to local chapters.

The national Chamber of Commerce has generally not been viewed as a national corporate political organization (Domhoff, 1970). However, its membership includes both very small, local firms as well as the largest multinational corporations. It is within the Chamber that a broader consensus of the local business community can be formed (see Whitt, 1981). The Chamber also acts as a transmission belt for urban policies generated by other national corporate organizations. Urban renewal was such a policy. In the national Chamber of Commerce, the largest corporations oversee this diffusion process. In the national Chamber of Commerce's 1971 Urban and Regional Affairs Committee, for example, executives from the largest corporations and banks are clearly dominant. Members of the Committee include executives from North American Rockwell, Metropolitan Life Insurance Co., American Airlines, Boise Cascade, General

Motors, General Electric, Exxon, Shell Oil, American Telephone and Telegraph, Ford Motor, etc.

Local Chambers perform a multitude of functions in central city politics: tax research to promote low taxes and government efficiency, development of policy proposals or positions, management and performance evaluation of city government programs, political brokering among business interests, financing of local development corporations and relocation assistance to new corporations (Crncich, 1973).

In large cities, local Chamber political influence is part and parcel of the general influence of all segments of the local business community (Crncich, 1973). Whatever divisions may exist between big and small business, or between retail and industrial enterprises, they are not expressed through local Chambers of Commerce. The local Chambers have participated heavily in the planning and implementation of urban renewal. In a survey of 347 local chambers in 1971, over three-quarters reported Chamber of Commerce involvement in urban renewal politics. Not only have local Chambers participated, but local informants tend to judge their participation to be important to the success of urban renewal (Crncich, 1973).

These are but two of the national corporate-dominated political organizations that link the cities, in which national corporations are located, into a network of urban policy dissemination, a network which helped catalyze local action on federal Urban Renewal. National corporations linked the cities into this network in other ways as well: as clients and contractors for federal agencies, particularly HUD; as representatives on Presidential advisory committees; as Washington lobbyists and as key backers to Congressional representatives.

These national policy organizations contradict the autonomy of local actors assumed by studies of the local power structure. Local patterns of business participation were not locally determined. Rather organizations like the national Chamber of Commerce and the Urban Land Institute tried to influence the political strategies and program preferences of their local corporate constituencies. Local corporations do respond to local problems, but the ways in which they do so are patterned by larger national political organizations.

Local corporate politics and urban renewal

National corporate political organizations were concerned with mobilizing local corporate support for local urban renewal. City receipt of federal renewal funds required local formulation of a program which was acceptable to the city council, as well as to those corporate financial interests who owned downtown property and mortgages, controlled local investment capital and generated central city employment. Local corporate political organization was often necessary to move urban renewal forward. Particularly in their headquarter cities, corporations provided essential political support for urban renewal through original stimulation and financing of central business district studies, the provision of seed money for project proposals, the loaning of corporate executives to redevelopment agencies and sometimes the provision of support as legislative and electoral allies in the more visible mobilizations surrounding urban renewal.

During the post-1945 period, major corporations in many central cities formed policy groups concerned with the direction of central city and metropolitan area economic development. The purpose of these corporate-financed and controlled organizations was to assure the rationalization of the metropolitan economy through the regional planning of economic infrastructure and the continued viability of the central city through central business district development. The policy tool for the redevelopment of the central city which interested them most was urban renewal. In San Francisco, the corporate-sponsored policy organization was the Bay Area Council and its Blythe–Zellerbach Committee; in Oakland, OCCUR; in Los Angeles, the Downtown Businessman's Association; in Chicago, the Central Area Committee; in St Louis, Civic Progress; in Pittsburgh, the Allegheny Conference; in Boston, the Civic Conference; In Philadelphia, the Greater Philadelphia Movement; in Wilmington, the

Greater Wilmington Delaware Committee, etc. According to Banfield and Wilson (1963: 267–8):

> The business élite of the city met privately, agreed upon more or less comprehensive plans for the redevelopment of the central city, and presented the plans to the press, the politicians and the public as their contribution to civic welfare . . . The new committees were different in that they consisted of a few 'big men' whose only concern was with the central business district.

These new corporate political groups went on to align themselves with strong, often Democratic, big city mayors who could deliver the votes and provide the legitimacy to push urban renewal through (Mollenkopf, 1976).

Pittsburgh – an example

In some major cities, downtown redevelopment began before passage of the 1949 federal renewal legislation. Pittsburgh was such a city and in many ways provided the prototype for corporate political organization that later emerged in other cities. After the Second World War, Pittsburgh faced a declining industrial base. With the growth of the Mellon fortune, Pittsburgh had become a major corporate headquarter city with twenty-one of the top 500 industrials in 1960. Corporations acquired or financed by Mellon interests were required to locate their headquarters in Pittsburgh (Lowe, 1967: 123). None the less, the downtown Golden Triangle, which provided one-quarter of all city revenues, suffered a decline in assessed valuation with the decentralization of upper-income families and retail trade, and the encroachment of residential slums (Lowe, 1967: 112).

Already in 1943, Mellon brought together the city's corporate, labor and institutional leadership to form the Allegheny Conference to study the region's problems, develop projects and stimulate private or public organizations to implement them (Lowe, 1967: 127–8). Their strategy for redevelopment of the central city stressed the reconstruction of the downtown, the first commercial use of redevelopment (Weiss, 1980). Using eminent domain powers, they hoped to construct office towers, new cultural institutions, high-rise, high-rent apartment complexes on the one hand, and transit systems linking downtown to the suburbs with metropolitan expressways and subsidized off-street parking structures on the other. This strategy for central city growth, also promoted by the Urban Land Institute, was later adopted in most major central cities in the US.

Through the Allegheny Conference and its program for central city redevelopment, the largely Republican corporate community forged an electoral coalition with the city's Democratic political organization. While the city's corporate élite could secure the passage of state-enabling legislation and approval of intra-metropolital highway funding from a Republican state legislature, Democratic Mayor Lawrence could deliver the working-class votes and the legitimacy necessary for central city redevelopment (Lowe, 1967: 133).

Although Pittsburgh's corporate élite originated and initiated much of Pittsburgh's redevelopment program, they also wanted Democratic Party participation in its execution and implementation. Mellon's personal legal counsel, Van Buskirk, went to Mayor Lawrence to suggest the establishment of a redevelopment agency with eminent domain powers to be chaired by Lawrence (Lowe, 1967: 133). The Democratic Mayor balked at the suggestion because,

> he thought that the banks, the insurance companies, and other private investors that Pittsburgh needed for its redevelopment would be frightened off by his own political stamp. And he knew that he, personally, and even in his elected role, lacked the entree to the moneymen ... Further, he was concerned that if a Democratic administration were to take private property for a redevelopment, local business people would label the program 'socialistic' and state Republicans would block the needed new legislation [Lowe, 1967: 133–4].

Van Buskirk, Mellon's representative, argued successfully,

> If we condemned people's properties, it was better for the

Mayor with his popular following to be responsible, rather than someone with the Mellon or U.S. Steel nameplate [Lowe, 1967: 134].

This pattern of corporate support for urban renewal was later replicated in other central cities (see also Hartman, 1974; Hayes, 1972; Kaplan, 1966; Adde, 1969; Phelan and Pozen, 1973; Edgar, 1970; Domhoff, 1978).

Corporate political strategy was to dominate the origins of local urban renewal planning, while political élites – especially Democratic mayors – were highly visible in the execution and implementation of the specific urban renewal program. Corporate organizations had already set the parameters – often through corporate-financed redevelopment plans – within which later urban renewal controversies would rage (Hartman, 1974; Phelan and Pozen, 1973). This suggests the difficulty of choosing important decisions upon which an image of the local power structure can be built. Because corporate élites may be less visible in the legislative and implementation stages, studies which rely on these issues may underestimate corporate influence.[4]

Corporate groups also linked the cities into a national network through which renewal policy ideas were transmitted. In Oakland, for example, not only did the local corporate group – OCCUR, dominated by locally headquartered Kaiser – bring in dozens of federal officials to promote redevelopment, but the corporations chartered private airplanes to take the entire city council and mayor to visit urban renewal sites in several eastern cities (Hayes, 1972: 115; Phelan and Pozen, 1973: 180–5). National corporations were primary catalysts for local urban renewal program development. Without them, local urban renewal might not have got off the ground. And if it did, it would certainly have looked very different.

Union politics and urban renewal

At the national level, labor unions have historically supported urban renewal. Their interests in doing so were an amalgam of economic interest in the construction jobs which renewal stimulates, and political interest in expansion of moderate-income housing supply (Keith, 1973; Foard and Fefferman, 1966; Friedman, 1968). Thus nationally the unions opposed the cutback in the residential component of urban renewal, including its original public housing emphasis.

At the local level, labor unions have taken a subordinate role to corporate leadership. Lured by the promise of unionized construction jobs, new industrial employment and the prospect of property tax relief for their home-owning membership, union leadership has been easily brought behind the pro-renewal political coalition, a coalition frequently led by Democratic mayors.

In San Fancisco, the city's union leadership had initially opposed the downtown Yerba Buena center because it displaced unionized blue-collar jobs. According to a statement issued by the AFL–CIO and Teamsters, 'It may suit the purpose of some to make San Francisco a financial and service center, but it destroys the jobs of working people and weakens the City's foundations' (Hartman, 1974: 65). San Francisco Central Labor Council therefore hired an organizer to attempt to establish a coalition of residents and union locals around blue-collar jobs and low- and moderate-income housing. According to Hartman (1974: 107),

> The core of this coalition was to be union locals whose members would be losing their jobs as a result of YBC (Yerba Buena Center) – garment workers, longshoremen . . . The locals would then try to ally with the building trades unions to create a massive program of construction work, stressing light industrial plants, the rehabilitation and conservation of existing housing and construction of new units and supportive community facilities . . . The union coalition would then develop linkages with organizations representing the aged and with Black, Mexican-American and other minority organizations in need of jobs and housing.

The unions associated with construction, tourism and hotels, however, gave support to Yerba Buena (Hartman, 1974:

66–7). Labor leadership's political support of the pro-renewal Mayor Joseph Alioto also facilitated labor's turnaround. Finally, labor leadership was coopted through appointment to positions on the renewal agency's board and staff (Hartman, 1974: 62). Union opposition to downtown renewal turned to support. According to the *San Francisco Chronicle*'s labor reporter:

> union leaders usually agree to whatever projects are proposed by business – just as long as the projects provide jobs . . . Unions merely react to the doings of others, occasionally forcing them to alter their plans after they have been unveiled but usually playing only the role of important supporter [Hartman, 1974: 67].

This pattern of labor union absorption by pro-renewal political forces was played out in other cities (Edgar, 1970; Kaplan, 1966; Stinchcombe, 1968; Dahl, 1961; Williams and Adrian, 1963). Union presence on renewal advisory boards helped legitimate the renewal program to the city's residents (Domhoff, 1978). Frequently, renewal was used to prevent industrial relocation and under these conditions, union support was easy to obtain. In Pittsburgh, for example, a redevelopment project for the Jones and Laughlin steel plant, the city's second largest tax-payer, would have dislocated 235 working-class families, many of whom were home-owners. According to Lowe (1967: 146):

> Mayor Lawrence asked fellow Democrat Philip Murray, president of the United Steelworkers, to explain to the residents and property owners, many of whom worked for J. and L., the importance of this holding operation – if J. and L. stayed, so would their jobs.

Given the fiscal and employment losses that would result from plant relocation, the steel unions diffused resident opposition to the renewal project.

In sum, national corporations linked the central cities to national networks of urban renewal policy formation and diffusion. This network provided the information, the impetus, and the models for local corporate political mobilization behind local urban renewal. Corporate political organizations managed the local political birth of central city urban renewal – outlining future land-uses, planning specific renewal sites, locating investors and pressing for the requisite political backing to bring their ideas before the body politic. Labor unions, on the other hand, tended to be willing, but less powerful, partners to the urban renewal coalition.

Urban renewal: the structure

While central city corporations were both beneficiaries and supporters of the Urban Renewal program, other groups were its victims and opponents. Lower-income, particularly non-white neighborhoods were destroyed in the bulldozer *blitzkrieg*. Low-income housing markets tightened. Small businesses were displaced. As the city's demand for unskilled labor declined, urban renewal did little to provide new employment for its growing pool of poor immigrants. As the city's tax rates increased, urban renewal did little to alleviate the fiscal strain on its residents' pocketbooks. The city's growth program was vulnerable to political challenge which rose at the polls, in the neighborhoods and eventually in the streets.

For its supporters, the problem was how to insulate urban renewal from popular opposition. While Democratic mayoral support lent legitimacy to urban renewal, it also made it vulnerable to the poor, non-white, and neighborhood constituencies upon which these mayors increasingly had to depend (Mollenkopf, 1976). A tension remained between the policy requirements of economic growth and those of electoral survival.

Urban renewal was organized locally to insulate it from political challenge. Local urban renewal policy formation was structured to make it very difficult for political opposition to block the program, delineate alternatives, or even to organize. State organization is rarely politically neutral. Its structure tends to affect which social groups have political access and which do not, which policies are vulnerable to political challenge and which are not. In this sense, the structure of government is a source of political power.

Urban renewal policy formation was structured so as to minimize the influence of elected officials, the neighborhoods targeted for clearance and other city agencies. There were many sources of autonomy for the local renewal agencies: their direct relationship to the Federal Government; the inferior resources of oversight agencies; their formal severance from public housing agencies; and their direct dependency on private developers.

Direct federal–local agency links

The local renewal agency had direct relationships with the Federal Government through the national or regional Housing and Urban Development (HUD) offices. Federal bureaucratic procedures, upon which the approval of a local project for funding was contingent, were complex and lengthy. The average renewal application was two and one-half feet thick and weighed fifty-three pounds (LeGates, 1972: 14). A HUD management study indicated that there were approximately 4000 discrete 'steps' in the processes of completing an urban renewal project (LeGates, 1972: 15). A local renewal agency acted as the primary interpreter of this labyrinth of federal regulation in its negotiation with other city officials (Kaplan, 1966), and could usually count on the support of HUD officials eager for success.

Until 1970, regional authority for local renewal projects was vested in an Assistant Regional Administrator for Renewal Assistance (ARARA). The effectiveness of the regional and local renewal directors are interdependent. LeGates (1972: 21–2) notes:

> Effectiveness of the ARARAs depends upon their continued popularity with their constituency: LPAs (the local planning agency) and development interests which work with them. To, in effect, side with displacees or another dissident group attacking a renewal program would undermine their credibility with their constituency. Accordingly, the ARARAs have 'backed up' the LPA director and other defendants against plaintiff groups and resisted compromise and change . . . The ARARAs in the San Francisco office

have been highly sympathetic to the commercial development aspects of their programs, or to architectural and design problems, and relatively unsympathetic to the low-income housing, relocation, and social aspects of their programs.

Not only do federal officials back up the objectives of local agency officials, but the local agencies use this support to avoid scrutiny or amendment by local elected officials (Kaplan, 1966).

Relative agency resources

Central city renewal agencies also had superior technical and administrative resources when compared to the federal and local agencies with oversight responsibilities. In all the phases of federal Urban Renewal organization (HUD only became a cabinet department in 1965), federal regional administrators lacked the staff capacity to do either long-range planning or adequately monitor local renewal projects (LeGates, 1972). With a tiny professional staff and high turnover, the regional offices were unable to keep tabs on a growing volume of renewal activity.

Local urban renewal agencies grew in proportion to their local political support. This growth allowed them to internalize as much of the planning, execution and evaluation of their projects as possible. As a result, they were able to get more projects off the drawing boards and into concrete.[5] In San Francisco, for example, this strategy of self-reliance allowed the redevelopment agency to avoid relying on staff studies done by the Planning Commission, which was not necessarily supportive of its plans for the Yerba Buena downtown expansion project. Although California state law required that the City Planning Commission determine renewal project boundaries, the Commission only saw the major downtown Yerba Buena plan *after* it was completed. As the San Francisco Redevelopment Agency told an irate Planning Commission, 'I respectfully suggest that you leave the decision to the Board of Supervisors. I doubt that Mr McCarthy (Director of Planning) could find a staff capable of evaluating our planning' (Hartman, 1974: 77).

The Board of Supervisors was in no better position to evaluate or control the San Francisco Redevelopment Agency. Thus a controversial plan for lease revenue bond and tax-increment financing was devised by the local agency to avoid general obligation bonding which would require a two-third voter approval in referendum (Hartman, 1974: 160–83). If renewal project financing is not to impose major new tax burdens on city residents, agency projections of the project's future fiscal productivity are critical. Yet the Board of Supervisors approved the plan after a 'perfunctory' hearing. As one supervisor explained:

> Once a project reaches the financial stage, it becomes almost unstoppable . . . I am not at all confident in the projections.

Another said,

> If you really want me to tell you, we have very little control over the Redevelopment Agency . . . Most people in this city don't know much about Yerba Buena Center (Kessler and Hartman, 1973: 35–6)

According to New Jersey state law, Newark Central Planning Board (CPB) had the formal authority to determine whether blight existed on a development site and whether a local project was in accord with the city's master plan, as well as to approve many tasks critical to urban renewal such as street closings, subdivisions and zoning variances. Yet the Newark Housing Authority (NHA), the agency responsible for the city's urban renewal, insisted that project proposals would be submitted to the Planning Board *after* negotiations with the Federal Government. They were able to present this to the Planning Board because the latter had no staff and little expertise in urban redevelopment while NHA did (Kaplan, 1966: 116). As a result, the Newark Central Planning Board was reduced to a judicial tribunal and the City Planning Office achieved only consultative status on selected projects. In contrast, local redevelopment agencies' superior resources provided them with considerable autonomy from both the federal and local agencies who were formally entrusted with their supervision.

Separation of urban renewal and housing agencies

In most central cities, the provision of public housing and the execution of urban renewal were carried out by separate local agencies. Public housing agencies generally had little authority over the renewal agencies and their powers were even dependent upon the renewal agency's supply of public housing sites. Given the political conflict over the public housing emphasis of urban renewal, this organizational split of the two agencies was neither politically accidental, nor neutral in its effects. By separating the two agencies, effective political organization by displaced residents and other low-income groups concerned with the provision of adequate housing was made more difficult. Political mobilization *against* clearance and displacement could not easily be fused with mobilization *for* the provision of alternative low-cost housing, on the urban renewal site or elsewhere in the city.[6]

In San Francisco, residents of the proposed Yerba Buena site were able, through court litigation, to force the San Francisco Redevelopment Agency to construct some 1500 to 1800 replacement low-income housing units. To minimize the net new low-income housing to be constructed, the San Franciso Housing Authority had been pressured into admitting Yerba Buena displacees on a super-priority basis. Later, the Authority refused. The Housing Authority's Executive Director sent the following affidavit to the court:

> we are not in a position to make our units available strictly and solely as a relocation resource for the Redevelopment Agency. In addition to the several hundred persons facing displacement from Yerba Buena . . . the Housing Authority has a constituency – persons on the waiting list. This constituency includes large numbers of persons already displaced by government action [Hartman, 1974: 143].

While this action undermined the court and federal administration requirements for an adequate relocation plan, it also eventually forced the construction of new low-cost replacement housing units on the renewal site. This outcome, however, was only achieved after more than a decade of political organization, resident refusal to move and court litigation. The administrative separation of the renewal and public housing agencies had increased the political costs of achieving adequate rehousing for residents displaced by renewal.

The bureaucratic split between urban renewal and public housing agencies was a structural source of power for those groups who did not want urban renewal to be used to rehouse the poor. And it was the corporate political organizations who fought successfully to hive off redevelopment from housing.

The Urban Land Institute had forcefully presented the view in Congressional hearings that urban redevelopment be used for non-residential reconstruction of the central city's core. To the Urban Land Institute, administrative separation of urban renewal from public housing was a means to avoid confusing redevelopment with public housing. The ULI lobbied for state-enabling acts before the 1949 Housing Act was passed which did not make the public housing authority the redevelopment agency. Regarding state legislation, which made the public housing authority responsible for redevelopment, the ULI (1945: 2) noted:

> It is a housing bill, not an urban redevelopment bill. The emphasis is on the construction of public housing for the low-income group. The redevelopment of the area for the benefit of the city as a whole is largely incidental . . . Placing the administrative control in the hands of a public housing authority would tend to discourage the participation of private enterprise in urban redevelopment . . . A development program should not be under the control of any special interest group whether they be public housing officials or a manufacturers' association.

Further, the Institute's principles for redevelopment stated clearly: 'The redevelopment agency should not be required to provide for the rehousing of displaced tenants. The redevelopment bill should not be a housing bill' (Urban Land Institute, 1945: 4).

The national Chamber of Commerce held similar views. In a 1950 'Businessmen's Conference on Urban Problems', the

Chamber stressed that public housing need not be part of a local renewal program and that a city's housing agency would be too partisan to their low-income housing constituency to be entrusted with commercial and industrial redevelopment (Domhoff, 1978).

To use urban renewal for economic growth rather than low-income housing required structural insulation of the city's redevelopment agency from those agencies which might represent alternative constituencies. The campaign for autonomous redevelopment agencies was relatively successful. In a sample of the large cities studied here, in only 9 per cent was the public housing agency formally responsible for urban renewal (*Municipal Year Book*, 1959).

Private developer dependency

The 1949 Housing Act expressly forbade the local redevelopment agencies to engage in potentially marketable construction. The local agency had to rely on its eminent domain and subsidy powers to attract private developers. Site location, resale prices of land, land-use and building design had to be accommodated to developer profitability objectives. Exclusion of the public sector from production made local agency success dependent on private developers. This structural feature of the program accentuated the economic power of the largest corporations and real estate interests, for it was these groups which could make most profitable use of the land.

The redevelopment agency's dependency on private developers both required the local agency to be relatively autonomous from other segments of the municipal bureaucracy and provided the means to secure the autonomy. In order to assure developer investment, the local agencies would negotiate site selection, land prices, and land-uses with their private clients before renewal plans would be announced to the targeted communities or to city officials (Lowe, 1967).[7] These private negotiations between developer and redevelopment agency allowed project design to be accommodated to the requirements of investor profitability before groups likely to be hurt by the project could mobilize

(Bellush and Hausknecht, 1969). The insulation of private investor–public agency negotiations from public scrutiny also allowed the avoidance of competitive bidding and changes in investor plans due to market shifts (Bellush and Hausknecht, 1969; Kaplan, 1966). In turn, the agency's direct relationship to private developers allowed it to resist public efforts to modify its plans on the grounds they would compromise delicate negotiations with private investors.

To sum up, the bureaucratic autonomy of the city's redevelopment agency derived from its direct relationship to the federal bureaucracy; its large resource base which allowed it to minimize dependency upon other agencies; its bureaucratic separation from the city's housing agency; and its dependency on private developers and investors.

The organization of public authority is not politically neutral. If a program is bureaucratically insulated and remote from electoral influence, the program's beneficiaries are more powerful. Because those segments of the municipal government which might serve their interests – public housing agencies, city councils, planning commissions – are structurally subordinate, the victims of such programs are less powerful. Thus the overall structure of public authority is a political lens through which the demands and interests of different groups are differentially refracted into policy. The structure of government crystallizes the organization of power in society, such that some groups cast a powerful light, while others glimmer weakly.[8]

Conclusion

The central city was becoming an office economy, a site whose income came more from the management of wealth than its production. Corporate headquarters appeared to be a driving force behind this new economic growth. Urban renewal was locally designed and adopted primarily to increase the profitability of new private investments, particularly those investments essential to the office growth of the city. For the national corporations, urban renewal offered a means to restructure the downtown, to facilitate office growth, to provide housing for the city's white-collar workers. Urban renewal offered a means to clear out deteriorated housing that brushed up against the edges of the central business district, thereby deterring its expansion and appreciation in value, to acquire subsidized locations for new construction through eminent domain powers, to stimulate public capital spending required for economic growth. Urban renewal served corporate interests, and they were thus key participants in urban renewal politics. But corporate participation derived from the dependency of the urban economy upon their continued presence in the city. Corporate élites spoke with organizational voices, organizations the central city could ill afford to lose.

The central city's new role also involved its de-industrialization. The labor unions, unlike the corporations, did not control the economic future of the central city. Indeed, they were concentrated in the city's declining sectors. The urban strength of the labor unions had itself contributed to the industrial decline of the central city. Beyond the short-lived construction boom, urban renewal could be used to stem the outflow and depreciation of industrial investment, and thus slow the decline in unionized industrial employment. Urban renewal could also serve union interests, and they were also subsidiary participants in urban renewal politics. But labor union participation did not result from its control over the urban economy, rather from the lack of it. Union élites also spoke with organizational voices, but organizations whose power was political in a more narrow sense.

Notes

1. Certain real estate interests were of course concerned to protect the profitability of their slum investments.

2. Project grants, which give the Federal Government great discretion over the substance of local policy, steadily increased in the postwar period. Urban Renewal, the War on Poverty, and Model Cities are all project grants.

3. Given their frequent ownership of central city real estate, locally headquartered national corporations also benefited from the appreciation of their properties which urban renewal facilitated.

4. So, too, these organizations often attempted to minimize their visibility (Adde, 1969; Hartman, 1974).

5. To validate that larger local renewal agencies were able to push their programs through more easily, a regression analysis was done for the fifty-six cities with complete data. The number of urban renewal projects planned between 1949 and 1960 which were not completed as of 1972 was used as a measure of successful political opposition. Given that the average time from planning to completion for urban renewal projects in these cities was 4.27 years, this indicator taps the number of urban renewal projects which have become embroiled in political controversy, resident opposition, court litigation or failures to secure private developers. The number of urban renewal projects which had gone into planning between 1949 and 1966 was used as a control variable, for the political and administrative load of the renewal agency would increase the potential number of failures. The regression results are presented in Table 4.4. The size of the urban renewal agency has a net negative effect on the number of such 'stalled' urban renewal projects. The data indicate that the size of the urban renewal agency is a good indicator of its ability to weather political opposition and to effectively execute its urban renewal program.

TABLE 4.4   *Renewal agency size and political success: dependent variable the number of urban renewal projects planned between 1949 and 1960 which were not completed as of 1972*

Independent variable	b	beta	st. error	F
Number of urban renewal employees	—0.006	—0.16	0.003	2.64
Number of renewal projects planned 1949–66	0.63	0.97	0.065	93.72

$n = 56$ $r^2 = 0.743$ adjusted $r^2 = 0.733$ $F = 76.7$

6. Castells has documented the difficulties of political organization in the case of Parisian urban renewal (Castells, 1972). Demands for staged rehousing for residents on renewal sites or elsewhere in Paris were administratively impossible because the Office des Habitations à Loyer Modéré (HLM), the public housing authority, allocated public housing on the basis of a department-wide waiting list (Castells, 1972: 113, 116). Castells refers to this as an 'incompatibility between the basis for mobilization and the possible response to the claims' (1972: 113).

7. Securing private investment commitments before federal approval of a project was eventually institutionalized in the Housing and Community Development Act of 1977, which authorized $1200 million over three years to be spent on Urban Development Action Grants to leverage private investments.

8. In a study which I have not had time to read with the care it deserves, Clarence N. Stone (*Economic Growth and Neighborhood Discontent*, 1976) has analyzed the process by which urban renewal demands were converted into public policy in Atlanta over a twenty-year period. Stone divides demand conversion into three stages: mobilization to bring proposals up for formal consideration, official approval or disapproval and implementation. Demands fell roughly into business-supported proposals for CBD expansion, often involving considerable low-income displacement, and residentially supported proposals for moderate-income neighborhood renewal. Stone found that at those stages least accessible to public view – mobilization and implementation – CBD proposals were likely to be more successful than residential proposals. These differences do not reflect relative levels of controversy, intensity of interest or consensus. Indeed public officials were most likely to further business proposals, even though they provoked public controversy and to oppose residential proposals even

though they did not. This was particularly the case at the implementation stage. Thus conflict does not direct public policy formation, as suggested by pluralism, but is an indirect consequence of the ways in which policies are formed. Stone (1976: 212) writes:

> As indicators of influence, the outcomes of particular controversies are thus less important than the efforts made to contain and direct controversy. System bias comes about through the concrete actions that officials take to build coalitions, orchestrate proposals, and isolate opposition forces in order to move a policy forward in the face of resistance.

The orientations and stratagems of top officials can in part be explained by the biases of urban renewal structure described above, and in part by the importance of the CBD economy to the future growth and fiscal capacity of the city.

Chapter 5

Power and Policy:
The Two Urban Renewals

Economics, policy and political power

Economic characteristics are often seen as non-political constraints on public policy. In empirical research, they are treated as external, 'natural' determinants of a city's policy. Such an approach argues that because political units share common ecological structures or similar levels of economic development, they face similar constraints affecting public policy in similar ways. Such a view assumes that the transmission of economic conditions into public policy is a politically neutral, technical process (Hollingsworth, 1973; Dye, 1972).

A technical definition of urban problems reflects the political power of those who stand to benefit from such a definition. Technical definitions of problems assure that the populace is neither competent nor necessary to make a policy decision. Where dominant interests fear opposition, such definitions may protect their ability to establish public policy privately.

Different problems may all have technical solutions. However, which problems engender a policy response is a political issue. Not only are problems politically defined, they are also politically selected. Any given policy can be responsive to a variety of intractable economic problems. For example, urban renewal may be variously responsive to the quality of the city's housing stock, its fiscal capacity, or to the performance of its central business district. Urban renewal was certainly advertised to have effects on all these conditions. Which economic constraint affects public policy is a political question. The political system selects which economic problems affect government policy and which do not. This selectivity is an indicator of political power.

The policy impact of corporate and union power

In central cities where corporations or unions are powerful, a different set of economic conditions will determine urban renewal activity than in central cities where they are not powerful. These differences will not be random, but will reflect corporate or union interest in economic growth. Where corporations or unions are powerful, economic conditions that affect their interest in economic growth will have a greater impact on policies designed to serve those interests than in cities where they lack such power.

But corporate and union interest in economic growth, and thus in urban renewal, were not the same. For the major corporations, urban renewal was a means to restructure the downtown area, to facilitate office growth in the central city, to provide housing for the city's white-collar workers and to protect the value of real estate investments. Urban renewal offered a means to clear out deteriorated housing that brushed up against the central business district, deterring its expansion to acquire subsidized locations for new construction through powers of eminent domain, and to stimulate the infrastructural spending required for economic growth. Urban renewal was a way to use both the power and the purse of the local government to stimulate the growth of the central city's office economy.

The central city's office economy grew as its industrial base declined. For the labor unions, urban renewal could be used to try to stem the outflow of industrial investment by providing new and less expensive central city sites for plant investment. To the extent that urban renewal stimulated new industrial investment, it sustained industrial employment, the core of union strength in the city.

Corporations and unions had different interests in central city economic growth – the former to stimulate office growth and the latter to sustain employment, and industrial employment in particular. Not all urban renewal projects were equally responsive to these interests. Commercial, institutional and residential renewal were more likely to be conducive to a growing office economy. Industrial urban renewal was oriented specifically to the expansion of the city's industrial economic base.

Corporate and union interests in office-serving and industrial urban renewal were not the same. For the locally headquartered corporations, the use of urban renewal to support the growing office economy served common organizational interests. As long as they stayed in the central cities, corporate headquarters shared interests in promoting the agglomeration of central offices, ancillary services and housing for office workers. They were not equally interested in industrial urban renewal, however. The central city was no longer a desirable location for industrial investment for most of the nation's largest firms. New plants could be built more cheaply and operate more efficiently in peripheral locations. Locally headquartered corporations did not share common interests in industrial renewal. Rather, it was likely to be used to subsidize the location of a particular corporate plant. If the use of urban renewal to stimulate the office economy was a common, even a 'class' interest, its use to subsidize industrial investment was not.[1] The local office economy was agglomerative and thus its expansion involved a high level of positive externalities. Stimulating the local office economy would be likely to benefit all central offices, although not to the same degree. Given the multilocational nature of corporate production, industrial investment was decreasingly agglomerative. Isolated plants were increasingly viable operations, given the role of corporate management in integrating input–output relationships across vast expanses of space. Subsidization of industrial investment through urban renewal was likely to benefit only the particular corporation which located in the cleared space. Indeed, to the extent that labor mobility was less elastic, an expansion in local industrial investment might mean a tightening of the labor market and thus higher wages and greater union militance for all local corporations. It is not uncommon for corporations to try to control new plant investment in those localities where they have large concentrations of industrial employment in order to avoid these consequences.

For the labor unions, their interests in office-serving and industrial urban renewal were exactly the converse. The use of urban renewal to support industrial investment was a means to try to stem the decline of industrial employment in the central city. The unions were concentrated in the industrial sector, and maintaining industrial employment was necessary in order to sustain the wages, working conditions and ultimately unionization that had been achieved over the previous decades. Thus the use of industrial urban renewal to sustain local industrial investment was a potential strategy to serve the material and political interests of the unions as a whole. Further, industrial investment was necessary to maintain those interests over the long term. Office-serving urban renewal did not serve common union interests. While it unquestionably stimulated construction, which benefited the construction unions, this was a parochial interest and one that would only be served on a short-term basis by such measures. Further the office economy was largely non-unionized. The locally situated national labor unions did not share common interests in office-serving urban renewal. They were more likely to share common interests in industrial urban renewal.

The impact of corporate and union power can best be analyzed by studying its impact on the determinants of those policies which best serve their respective group interests. The impact of corporate power on renewal policy-making can best be studied by analyzing office-serving urban renewal; and that of union power, by analyzing industrial urban renewal.

If office-serving urban renewal was of greater interest to corporations and industrial urban renewal to the unions, corporate and union power in the determination of urban renewal policy was not likely to be equal.

National corporations controlled the mainsprings of local economic growth, upon which local income and fiscal capacity were dependent. The city's economic relationship to the larger economy was organized by these corporations. Most importantly, the central city was becoming an office economy, a site whose income came more from the management of wealth than its production. The central offices of the corporations were a dominant force driving this new form of economic growth. Urban Renewal was designed and adopted primarily in order to increase the profitability of those investments essential to this office growth.

The unions lacked this economic power, a power encoded into the very logic of the Urban Renewal program. As a result I would expect that the impact of corporate power upon urban renewal policy-making would be greater than that of union power, regardless of their greater or lesser interest in its specific components.

Measurement

Urban renewal policy will be measured by the total number of acres for office-serving and industrial renewal in projects executed between 1961 and 1966 (US Department of Housing and Urban Development, 1966). These data were submitted by local redevelopment agencies as estimates of the re-uses to which land cleared by renewal were put. The acreage for each project executed during this period was aggregated to form a total central city acreage figure. The renewed acreage figure is a gross estimate of the scale of public land-use changes and subsidization oriented to particular uses.

Office-serving urban renewal is measured as the total number of such acres for commercial, residential and institutional renewal. The bulk of commercial and institutional acreage was oriented to stimulating the new service economy of the city, much of it downtown (National Commission on Urban Problems, 1968). Institutional projects were used strategically to anchor land-use changes. Residential urban renewal in the main constructed high-income apartments likely to be occupied by higher-income clerical, managerial and professional workers.

Central cities with populations of 100 000 or more as of 1960 that had state legislation authorizing local urban renewal as of 1958 were used for data analysis. This eliminated central cities located in states that did not permit cities to respond to federal urban renewal grant opportunities. This provides a maximum data base of 118 central cities. Because of missing data for certain variables, however, the analysis is based on fewer cases.

A number of *local conditions* may constrain local economic growth – whether office growth or industrial growth – which were also the object of government intervention through Urban Renewal. Specifically such limits to local economic growth lay in the problem of changing land-use through the market given the existence of slums, the highly built-up nature of urban land and the inability to provide the complementary public infrastructure that private investment required.

In the following analyses of urban renewal, the cost and built-up nature of central city land will be measured by population density, or the number of persons per square mile in 1960 (*County and City Data Book*, 1962). Population density indicates both the costs of purchasing or renting land, the dearth of vacant land and the difficulty of parcel assembly.

The central city's fiscal burden is measured by the per capita level of property taxes. High property taxes not only represent a site cost to central city businesses, but they indicate the city's fiscal difficulty in providing additional economic infrastructure required by private investment.

The existence of city slums is measured by the percentage of all dwelling units in the central city that were considered sound with all plumbing by the *Census of Housing* in 1960. Sound housing consists of those units that are not dilapidated and have private toilets, bath and hot running water. The absence of sound housing indicates the general need for physical replacement and improvement of the city's residential structures. In the analysis of office-serving urban renewal, another spatially specific measure of poverty is used. The residential poverty of the central city's core is measured by the percentage of resident families having an annual income below $4000 as of 1960. The core includes all census tracts that are contiguous with the central business district, including the central business district itself (*Census of Population and Housing*, 1960). Downtowns surrounded by poor residential districts presumably had difficulty expanding, due to the likelihood of prisoner's dilemmas. While land was cheap, it was likely to remain a poor place to invest unless many invested simultaneously. Further, a large poor population was likely to deter shoppers and potential office workers from coming downtown, whether from physical fear or social discomfort.

Finally, I have, in each analysis, tried to control for the actual level of economic activity which each component of urban renewal was intended to stimulate. In the analysis of office-serving urban renewal, I control for the level of office activity by measuring the number of corporate headquarters, which is a direct measure of corporate office activity. Further, because of the prominence of downtown retail decline as a supposed motivation for urban renewal, I also included the level of retail performance of the central business district. This was measured by the percentage of change in central business district retail sales between 1958 and 1963 (*Census of Business*, 1963). Many central cities were experiencing declining downtown retail trade and downtown retailers were ardent supporters of urban renewal (Banfield and Wilson, 1963). Finally, in analyzing industrial urban renewal, I used the new capital expenditures per industrial establishment in 1963 (*Census of Manufacture*, 1963). This measures the extent to which firms are expanding and/or replacing industrial plants within the city, although not the aggregate volume of such investment.

Data analysis: corporate power and office-serving urban renewal

The first analysis of corporate power and office-serving urban renewal is presented in Table 5.1. Are the relationships between central city economic conditions and office-serving renewal contingent upon the level of corporate power? There is a strikingly different pattern of significant effects in high as opposed to low corporate power cities.[2]

In high corporate power cities, downtown retail growth, the level of poverty in the city's core, population density and the city fiscal burden, all have significant positive effects on urban renewal. In low corporate power cities, only downtown retail growth has a significant positive effect. In neither group of cities does the quality of the city's housing stock have a significant impact on the level of urban renewal.[3] In general,

TABLE 5.1 *The determinants of office-serving urban renewal in high and low corporate power central cities: dependent variable the number of commercial, residential and institutional urban renewal acres cleared by the central city, 1961–6*

Independent variables	High corporate power		Low corporate power		Statistical significance of difference of b_1-b_2
	b_1	t-ratio	b_2	t-ratio	t-ratio
Retail performance of central business district	3.58	2.1*	1.66	2.4*	1.47
Core poverty	333.10	2.0**	96.30	1.2	2.33**
Population density	6.98	1.8**	−0.19	−0.1	1.85*
City fiscal burden	0.69	1.8**	0.21	0.5	1.18
Quality of city housing stock	−63.20	−0.4	−52.40	−0.51	—
	$r^2 = 0.53$		$r^2 = 0.16$		
	$n = 50$		$n = 50$		

* significant at 0.05 level (two-tailed test).
** significant at 0.05 level (one-tailed test).
b = estimated net effect of independent variables on dependent variable.
t-ratio = a statistic used to assess significance of estimated effect, or differences in effects.
r^2 = Percentage of dependent variable variation explained.

the effect of economic conditions is greater in high corporate power cities than in low corporate power cities. Core poverty and population density in particular have significantly larger positive effects in high corporate power cities.

The analysis indicates that such urban renewal was not a response to the decline of the city's economy, but to the nature and constraints upon its growth. Urban renewal was not a retail merchants' program to combat declining downtown trade (see also Friedman, 1973). The corporate office economy enabled the downtown retailers to tap a new market created by the inflow of daily commuters, visitors and, perhaps, high-rise apartment residents (Kasarda, 1972; Masotti, 1974). Where a strong corporate office economy provided the basis for downtown retail growth, urban renewal was more likely.

In high corporate power cities, such urban renewal was

responsive to the difficulties of downtown growth. First, the poor at the downtown's rim impeded central business district expansion, were irrelevant as a labor supply and legitimized state intervention to 'eliminate slums'. Urban renewal could be used to clear such 'blighted' areas without replacing the low-income housing it destroyed. However, urban renewal was not a response to poor housing in general. If slums were a legitimation for clearance, it was their location around the downtown that was most likely to bring in the bulldozers.

Second, densely settled cities were heavily built up and their land prices promised large profits to those who could put a new development together. Urban renewal provided the public authority and financial means to supplant the real estate market and the fixity of its use patterns (Bingham, 1975). While eminent domain powers expropriated potentially attractive sites, urban renewal subsidized site acquisition and preparation.

Third, the fiscal strain of the central city cut into the flow of funds necessary to sustain the growing economy. Downtown development requires massive city expenditures to complement land-use changes (Manners, 1974; Steiss, 1975; SPUR, 1975). If urban renewal was oversold as a means to increase the tax base and lower tax rates (Weicher, 1976; US Senate, 1973), it did stimulate and structure the flow of public capital expenditure to support economic growth (Gramlich and Galper, 1973). Urban renewal was a means to organize city expenditure to support the office economy in those cities where fiscal resources were scarce and property taxes bit deep.

The data indicate that corporate power, as measured by corporate headquarter location, affects the city's responsiveness to local economic conditions. Corporate interest in local urban renewal was contingent upon local economic conditions. The policy impact of local economic conditions was contingent upon local corporate power. But does corporate power have an effect on the level of urban renewal, independently of local economic conditions?

High corporate power cities had higher levels of such urban renewal than low corporate cities (means = 76.9 acres *v.* 32.5 acres). But this difference in urban renewal acreage between high and low corporate power cities can have many sources.

First, it may be because, as we have seen, high corporate power cities are more responsive to local economic conditions than low corporate power cities. Second, it may be because cities in which corporations are powerful tend also to be cities with local economic conditions, such as higher population density, that are conducive to city adoption of urban renewal. Third, it may be because corporate power influences local urban renewal independently of local conditions. This would suggest that the impact of corporate power on local renewal policy was not entirely contingent upon the local economic conditions that would affect corporate interests in local urban renewal.

Did corporate power have an additive effect upon local urban renewal, as opposed to the interactive effect demonstrated above? In order to find out, it is also necessary to control for the differences in local economic conditions that may be associated with high and low corporate power. To assess whether corporate power had such an additive effect, intercepts were compared in high and low corporate power cities, intercepts that are adjusted for differences in local economic conditions in the two types of cities. To make the comparison, the expected level of urban renewal is assessed at the average economic conditions experienced in *both* kinds of central cities. The difference in urban renewal activity between high and low corporate power cities, when adjusted for differences in local economic conditions between the two kinds of cities, is much larger, 155 acres, than the gross mean difference reported above, 44.4 acres. While not statistically significant,[4] this suggests that corporate power increases the local level of urban renewal, net of local economic conditions, or that corporate headquarter activity is itself a local stimulant of such urban renewal.

Part of the reason for high levels of urban renewal activity in high corporate power cities may be that they are different kinds of cities with greater population density and greater fiscal strain. Such cities may not only respond differently to local economic conditions, they may also face different conditions. The total difference in urban renewal activity between high corporate power and low corporate power cities can be decomposed to see how much of the difference is due to slope differences as opposed to composition differences (see the appendix for the formulae). The results are presented in Table 5.2.

TABLE 5.2   *Decomposition of the difference in office-serving urban renewal activity between high and low corporate power cities*

Source of difference	Increase in urban renewal activity in low corporate power cities	
	Acres	Percentage increase
Total difference between high and low corporate power cities	44.6	
Difference due to differences in composition	4.9	11.2
Difference due to differences in slope	137.6	309

Office-serving renewal was designed to stimulate central city economic growth, a growth that was increasingly tied to the office functions of the city. The results suggest that cities adopted urban renewal not simply in response to the local difficulties in stimulating growth – whether physical, fiscal or economic – but in response to the power of the corporations headquartered there. Corporations were powerful in shaping local renewal policy both because they were prime participants in its adoption and execution and their local operations were critical to the continued growth of the central city and thus to the success of local urban renewal. Corporate power affected local urban renewal decision-making in two ways. On the one hand, cities with powerful corporations had more extensive renewal programs. On the other, cities with powerful corporations were more responsive in their policy-making to local economic conditions likely to constrain such urban growth.

In the public mind, urban renewal was a policy response to urban decline and housing deterioration. The data indicate that, on the contrary, urban renewal was a response to the problems of urban *growth*. Urban renewal was adopted in cities whose downtown economies were not only alive, but growing.

Urban renewal was adopted where the downtown corporate office and retail economies were strong, not weak.

The presence of corporate headquarters affected the way in which central cities responded to local economic conditions. This impact reflects corporate power – a power based on participation in local urban renewal policy formation, a privileged position in the structure of policy-making, and an increasingly dominant role in the central city economy. The corporations provided the power to push urban renewal forward; local economic conditions affected corporate interests in the use of that power, interests to which urban renewal could be made to correspond.

Data analysis: union power and industrial urban renewal

Are the relationships between central city economic conditions and industrial urban renewal contingent upon the level of union power? The second analysis of union power and industrial urban renewal is presented in Table 5.3. In contrast with the previous analysis of corporate power and office-serving urban renewal, the pattern of significant effects of local economic conditions upon industrial urban renewal is not different in high as opposed to low union power cities. Indeed, in neither group of cities do any of the policy-relevant constraints on new industrial investment have a significant impact on industrial renewal. In low union power cities, only the quality of the city's housing stock has a significant negative effect on the level of industrial renewal. Cities without a large quantity of slum housing perhaps also lacked the kinds of sites which were sufficiently inexpensive for industrial investment to take place.

The labor unions appear to be relatively powerless to shape industrial urban renewal in response to land-use constraints on new investment: high land costs, lack of suitable sites, high tax burdens, failures to provide complementary economic infrastructure. Indeed, industrial urban renewal does not seem to be adopted in response to land-use constraints on new industrial investment at all.

When the expected level of industrial urban renewal is

TABLE 5.3   *The determinants of industrial urban renewal in high and low union power central cities: dependent variable the number of industrial urban renewal acres cleared by the central city, 1961–6*

Independent variables	High union power		Low union power		Statistical significance of difference, b_1-b_2
	b_1	t-ratio	b_2	t-ratio	t-ratio
Population density	0.75	0.7	0.02	0.01	(None
City fiscal burden	0.003	0.03	0.05	0.5	are
Quality of city housing stock	10.5	0.2	−101.6	1.8*	statistically significant)
New industrial investment	0.0015	0.8	0.0009	0.9	
	$r^2 = 0.03$		$r^2 = 0.12$		
	$n = 54$		$n = 43$		

* significant at 0.05 level (two-tail test).

b = estimated net effect of independent variables on dependent variable.

t-ratio = a statistic used to assess significance of estimated effect, or difference in effects.

r^2 = percentage of dependent variable variation explained.

measured by comparing intercepts which assume high and low union power cities experiencing the same local conditions, high union power cities have higher levels of industrial urban renewal than low union power cities (a difference of about 55 acres). While not statistically significant, the difference suggests that cities where unions were powerful adopted higher levels of industrial urban renewal regardless of other local economic conditions likely to constrain industrial investment. Union interest in industrial urban renewal appears not to be contingent upon local economic conditions.

But in some sense, the unions themselves were a local economic condition. The labor unions themselves posed an obstacle to further industrial investment. In cities where they were powerful and the level of unionization higher, firms were making less new industrial investment. Because of the local nature of the labor market, the unions were interested in stimulating new industrial investment within the city. To the extent that their very presence, their very power, dampened industrial investment, the unions had strong interests in using public stimulants to overcome these effects.

The difference between the impact of corporate power upon office-serving urban renewal and union power upon industrial urban renewal is striking. Land-use constraints on the growth of the office economy have a greater impact on office-serving urban renewal where corporations are powerful. Land-use constraints on the growth of the industrial economy do not have a greater impact on industrial urban renewal where unions are powerful. In fact they have no effect on industrial urban renewal under any conditions. Corporate power has a greater impact upon the process of office-serving urban renewal policy-making than does union power upon that of industrial urban renewal. This reflects the differences in the sources of corporate and union power. Because they controlled private investment, the corporations controlled the economic conditions necessary to the success of urban renewal. The unions' economic powers were largely negative; they were themselves – their ability to make wage and working conditions demands – constraints upon local economic growth, and thus upon the potential success of public policies designed to stimulate growth. Thus while corporations and unions shared interests in local economic growth, they were unequally able to shape policies designed to achieve it.

Urban renewal used the central city's public purse and eminent domain powers for the benefit of private interests. But the politics of economic growth are always so. The redevelopment of the central city posed a thornier problem. If a city's politics are to be in equilibrium, then public policies must support the local economic growth that provides local jobs for those who maintain support for the public officials who legislate the policies of economic growth. The growth of the central city economy increasingly provided benefits for people who did not live there and costs for many of those who did. Office employment drew on the technical and social skills of suburban workers. Housing was constructed that local residents could not afford, while their own housing was destroyed. The problems of urban redevelopment were not that it provided public monies for private corporations, but that these corporations could not provide benefits for those who lived in the cities from whose treasuries the monies had come.

Appendix: decomposition of mean differences into slope and composition effects

The total difference in urban renewal activity between high and low corporate power cities can be decomposed in the following way. The mean level of urban renewal in high corporate power cities is given by

$$\overline{U}_c = a_c + \sum_{i=1}^{5}(b_{ic}\overline{X}_{ic})$$

and in low corporate power cities by

$$\overline{U}_{\bar{c}} = a_{\bar{c}} + \sum_{i=1}^{5}(b_{ic}\overline{X}_{i\bar{c}})$$

where $\overline{U}_c$ and $\overline{U}_{\bar{c}}$ are the mean levels of urban renewal in high and low corporate power cities; a_c and $a_{\bar{c}}$ are the intercept values for high and low corporate power cities; b_{ic} and $b_{i\bar{c}}$ are the metric parameter values for the effects of local economic conditions in high and low corporate power cities; and $\overline{X}_{ic}$ and $\overline{X}_{i\bar{c}}$ are the mean values of the local economic conditions in high and low corporate power cities.

The total difference in urban renewal activity between high and low corporate power cities is $\overline{U}_c - \overline{U}_{\bar{c}}$, or the difference in mean urban renewal activity in the two types of cities. The difference in mean levels of urban renewal activity is also equal to

$$\sum_{i=1}^{5}(b_{ic}\overline{X}_{ic}) - \sum_{i=1}^{5}(b_{ic} - \overline{X}_{i\bar{c}}) + (a_c - a_{\bar{c}})$$

The part of that difference due to differences in composition – differences in the nature of local economic conditions in high corporate power as opposed to low corporate power cities – is

$$\sum_{i=1}^{5} b_{ic}(\overline{X}_{ic} - \overline{X}_{i\bar{c}})$$

This is the additional amount of urban renewal that low corporate power cities would have if they had the same economic conditions as high corporate power cities but maintained their same level of responsiveness to local economic conditions.

The part of that difference due to differences in slope – in the impact of local economic conditions on local urban renewal – is

$$\sum_{i=1}^{5}(b_{ic} - b_{i\bar{c}})\overline{X}_{i\bar{c}}$$

This is the additional amount of urban renewal that low corporate power cities would have if local economic conditions had the same effect on urban renewal activity as in high corporate power cities but their local economic conditions did not change.

Notes

1. It might be objected that this analysis captures only the interests/power of the corporate offices and that central city newspapers, retailers, developers, land owners and bankers were also critical participants and beneficiaries of the urban renewal process. That is true. My assumption in this analysis is that they are non-dominant economic functions, whose economic well-being depends upon the 'export' – both office and industrial – economy controlled by these corporations. The importance of urban renewal was not that it saved the value of certain real estate parcels, but that it promoted the development of particular economic functions within the city. Therefore I focus on the dominant economic functions whose activity is furthered in the central city, rather than those who own or build the structures in which these functions are housed. This is not to deny that there are often serious tensions between them. Thus I take the position that urban renewal was not defensive, but offensive.

2. For those unversed in regression analysis, the parameters estimated in Table 5.1 are unstandardized regression coefficients. Within each group of cities – corporate and non-corporate – they assume a linear relationship between local economic conditions and local urban renewal. The unstandardized regression coefficient measures the number of its units that the dependent variable changes for each unit change in the independent variable, controlling for all other independent variables. For example, parameter estimate 3.58 indicates that for each percentage change in the level of CBD retail growth, the average high corporate power city had 3.58 more urban renewal acres between 1961 and 1966.

3. Another analysis including city size, associated with corporate headquarter location and potentially the size of the city's urban renewal program, was done. Inclusion of size had no effect on the results.

4. The assessment of the mean difference between two subpopulations with differing slopes is somewhat arbitrary. Comparison of the dependent variables at the intercept is less meaningful than comparison at the grand mean. None the less, the decomposition into slope versus main effect difference depends on the point at which the comparison is made.

Chapter 6

The Politics of Social Control: The Case of the War on Poverty

The public costs of economic transformation of the central city were high. The private costs – the costs borne personally by some of the city's residents – were even higher. The growth of the office economy was felt on dinner tables, in tax bills, in razed urban neighborhoods, in job and welfare lines. The people who bore these costs comprised a large bloc of city votes. And those who bore the costs most heavily were non-white. Because the economic transformation of the central city hurt them disproportionately and because they were then organizing successfully for civil rights in particular, and political power in general, the non-white communities were particularly disruptive.

The victims of central city economic change increasingly pushed against those policies which affected them most directly, most visibly. Corporate location and employment policies were bureaucratically opaque, legally private and politically inaccessible. Its victims were dispersed, ethnically diverse and unorganized. Urban renewal was a public policy, politically vulnerable to the votes and tax dollars of the city's citizens. Its victims were geographically concentrated, ethnically homogenous, and naturally organized on neighborhood lines. Public ire could not get a political handle on the private decisions which were transforming the city's landscape. It could, however, be mobilized toward derailing complementary public decisions. The victims of economic growth had to be socially controlled.

The threat to corporate and labor union power

After the Second World War, major corporations and labor unions forged new political coalitions in many central cities. Organized around policies to maintain the city's economic growth, the coalitions pushed forward with urban renewal projects, intra-metropolitan transportation, industrial parks, development corporations, zoning variances, under-assessments, subsidized water and power, etc. For the corporations, such policies promised subsidized profits; for the labor unions, unionized employment (Bok and Dunlop, 1970). The political coalitions were often centered around strong Democratic mayors who had the partisan identification, if not the political machine, necessary to deliver the central city vote (Mollenkopf, 1976; see also Chapter 4).

Political challenge by the poor, and especially the non-white poor, threatened the corporations and labor unions and the growth policies they pursued. It was the poorest communities who were displaced by urban renewal and highway construction, whose housing stock was depleted by clearance, whose employment opportunities were reduced by both central business district office growth and restrictive unionization on large construction projects and municipal jobs, and whose social services were constrained by the fiscal costs of the growth programs. Yet without the support of the central city non-white and poor communities, many of the Democratic mayors – the political focal point of these pro-growth coalitions – could not long remain in office. Thus the policies of the coalition conflicted with its electoral base. While the electoral base of coalitions included the central city poor and non-white populations, their political mobilization was inevitably directed against the growth policies on which corporate and labor union support was contingent (Mollenkopf, 1976; Morlock, 1974).[1]

Labor unions in particular had an ambivalent relationship to the central city poor and non-white communities. Labor's political power is dependent on its position within the Democratic Party. Given the absence of a cohesive, centralized national party system in the US, this means that urban political organizations are the elemental building blocks of national Democratic victories, victories that labor unions consider essential to pass pro-labor legislation. Since 1936, northern blacks have been central to the Democratic coalition. Labor unions have traditionally played an important role in organizing the Democratic vote of non-unionized workers and dependent populations. At a local level, while the unions experienced growing difficulties in building a political coalition with central city non-whites in the 1960s, they none the less, continued to play an aggregative role. Unions in cities like Chicago, Detroit and Los Angeles helped the new non-white immigrant to vote, select candidates and formulate programs (Greenstone, 1970). In northern cities at least, non-whites were politically influential only where labor unions were also strong (Morlock, 1974).

At a national level, labor unions have been more effective in securing broad redistributive legislation benefiting the entire working class, than in passage of regulatory changes beneficial to their particular unions (Lowi, 1967). National labor union leaders are as ideologically supportive of national programs for welfare expansion and income equalization as national corporate élites are opposed (Barton, 1975). Support for welfare and social service expansion flows both from their desire to maintain the electoral base of the Democratic Party and from their objective interests in increasing the 'floor' under union wages (Greenstone, 1970).

If labor union political interests pushed them into coalition with the urban poor, their economic interests undercut the coalition. Labor unions have been concentrated in more productive, less competitive, and hence more profitable industrial sectors. The high wages and secure jobs of disproportionately white union workers contrasts sharply with the low-wage, cyclical employment available to the central city non-white poor. That central city industrial jobs have been increasingly taken by suburban union workers has exacerbated the political visibility of the problem. Further, labor unions have been willing supporters of growth policies from which black communities found few benefits and many costs. It was precisely the unionized, 'affluent' workers who resented the rapid collective gains that blacks were making in the 1960s (Vanneman and Pettigrew, 1972). And this resentment fuelled their feelings that the government was doing too much for the blacks. The labor unions were caught in a double bind: eager to build up the base of the Democratic Party but anxious about the growing potential for mass union defections from the Democratic ticket.

Unorganized in production, excluded from well-paying unionized industries, the non-white poor's rising political mobilization was directed at targets most readily at hand. Doubly denied high-wage jobs due to declining industrial employment and the market privileges of the unions, the non-white communities turned to public agencies for services and employment. Because many of the bread-and-butter services they required were either financed or delivered locally, their politicization was directed at city hall. Labor union support for expansion of the local welfare state was an alternative to desegregating their privileged labor market on the one hand, and to taking stronger steps to expand national employment on the other.

But non-white efforts to gain greater control over public services and access to public jobs also ran into union resistance. Judicious dispersal of patronage positions had historically been a means of assuring immigrant loyalties to a political machine well oiled with business monies. Gradually, civil service reforms and municipal employee unions had consolidated white-ethnic controls over city jobs:

> when blacks entered the cities, they were confronted by a relatively new development in city politics: large associations of public employees, whether teachers, policemen, sanitation men, and the like. These groups had become numerous, organized and independent enough to wield substantial control over most matters affecting their jobs and their agencies: entrance requirements, tenure guarantees, working conditions, job prerogatives, promotion criteria, retirement benefits. When blacks arrived in the cities, local political leaders did not control the jobs – and in cases where job prerogatives had been precisely specified by regulation, did not even control the services – which might have been given as concessions to the newcomers [Piven, 1975; see Hill, 1976].

As a result of these economic strains between the non-white communities and the labor unions, non-whites began to bite the political hands which fed them. At a local level, their growing numerical strength and militancy undercut their political alignment with labor (Greenberg, 1974). Melvin King, of the Boston Urban League, declared, 'those in power in the labor movement are the enemy' (Bok and Dunlop, 1970: 452). Equally important, black politicization threatened the capacity of the Democratic Party to secure non-white votes, votes which had become of extreme strategic importance to national Democratic power. National Democratic victories were also important to the labor unions, struggling to reverse their steady decline as a percentage of the workforce.

Between 1940 and 1960, of the three million blacks who left the south, the vast majority moved into the industrial cities of the most populous northern states (Piven and Cloward, 1977: 216). Their allegiance to the Democratic Party was thus of extraordinary strategic significance to Democratic Presidential victories. The failure of the Democratic Party after the war to push for civil rights legislation, in hopes of containing southern defections from the party, undercut traditional black Democratic allegiance. By the late 1950s black support for the Democrats was slipping dangerously (Piven and Cloward, 1977: 226). In the 1960 Kennedy–Nixon context, it was the resurgence of the black northern Democratic vote that helped Kennedy carry key states (Piven and Cloward, 1977: 226). The emergence of mass civil rights protest across the country combined with the strategic significance of the black vote precipitated a series of concessions – from the Civil Rights Act of 1964 to the War on Poverty – which brought American blacks firmly and overwhelmingly into the Democratic Party (Piven and Cloward, 1977).[2]

These federal concessions to growing black protest affected the central cities deeply. To finance a significant material response to the demands of the non-whites and poor without cutting into growth programs or raising taxes, and thus further reducing the competitive advantage of the central city as a location for plant or office investment, the city looked to new federal monies which became available as civil disobedience became increasingly widespread and violent.

The War on Poverty: a contradictory strategy of social control

As protest intensified in the early 1960s, the federal War on Poverty forged new mechanisms of social control. The War on Poverty attempted to absorb the political participation of non-white and poor communities within new bureaucratic structures without increasing their political power. If by coopting them, it prevented a more comprehensive repudiation of the structure of urban power, it also brought them within the political system and thus exposed dominant institutions to more direct attack.

The War on Poverty – established in 1964 under the Office of Economic Opportunity – consisted of a range of federally sponsored bureaucratic agencies potentially independent of local government and long-established private community organizations. Pre-school education through Head Start, job training through Job Corps, litigation on behalf of welfare clients through Legal Aid, organizing residents to make demands on traditional public survice bureaucracies through Community Action Programs – all this grew chaotically under the aegis of the War on Poverty. The poverty agencies' intended purpose was to provide direct social services for the poor, new forms of public employment, referrals to other health, welfare and employment agencies, and a forum for the articulation and organization of community demands (Moynihan, 1969; Piven and Cloward, 1971). The War on Poverty was used to mobilize poor communities both for political participation in the poverty agencies themselves (Cole, 1974; Greenstone and Peterson, 1973) and as pressure groups in the city's electoral and bureaucratic politics (Piven and Cloward, 1971).

Within the city, poverty funds were allocated to those communities which had been hardest hit by the city's growth policies. The design of the War on Poverty's precursor, the Gray Areas project, clearly targeted those 'inner' areas which were the special victims of the renewal and highway bulldozers (Ford Foundation, 1963). The War on Poverty, however, was neither designed nor empowered to alter the urban growth programs or their deleterious effects on the housing and employment opportunities of the central city poor.

Incorporation into the new bureaucratic structures was not conducive to challenging the city's power structure (Kramer, 1969). Community groups were embroiled in bureaucratic politics – quarrels over agency patronage, struggles for agency survival and conflicts over agency mission – rather than mobilized to challenge the dominant interests and policies that actually created poverty (Kramer, 1969; Bachrach and Baratz, 1970).

The poverty agencies represented new bureaucratic targets for local political action. Community groups were absorbed with strategies for controlling the new bureaucracies rather than transforming existing ones. The creation of new, unorthodox agencies protected the existing municipal agencies and thus the powerful interest groups which controlled their services or employment. The mainline public services – police, fire, schools, transit, welfare, sanitation, roads – often remained in the hands of white workers who were protected by unions and civil service rules. The inequities in the distribution of their services between neighborhoods remained untouched. The inadequacies of their services for non-white communities were not challenged. Equally important, the agencies with some control over the location and nature of private investment within the city, as well as its fiscal contribution to the public weal – notably urban renewal, water boards, planning agencies, infrastructural bureaucracies of all types, the finance board – remained unaffected. Non-whites were given new kinds of jobs and services rather than better access to existing ones, new forms of participation rather than more power over those agencies with some leverage over private investment and thus the demand for their labor.

Locally situated corporations and labor unions integrated the cities into national networks of urban policy formation and diffusion which became increasingly important with growing federal intervention in the city. The War on Poverty evolved out of a series of urban programs sponsored by the Ford Foundation, dating back to the Great Cities program of 1960, the Gray Areas projects of 1961, and the federally supported Mobilization for Youth launched in 1962 (Urquhart, 1974;

Moynihan, 1969). Moynihan's interpretation of the poverty program evolution can be used to show how the structure and content of the Economic Opportunity Act of 1964 were essentially the same as those in the 1961 Ford Foundation Mobilization for Youth proposal (Urquhart, 1974). Both corporations and labor unions were represented in the cities receiving Gray Area Ford monies.

Further, the AFL–CIO actively lobbied for the initial War on Poverty legislation in Congress and subsequently devoted considerable resources to assure that local labor leaders were informed about how their cities could implement the program, and would actively participate in local poverty boards (Bok and Dunlop, 1970: 439–49). By 1967, over 500 local union officials were represented on poverty program-related boards.

Just as the central city was increasingly composed of poor, especially black poor, having electoral clout, the new federal project grants located the origins, and thus limits, of reform outside the city. While such a structure was critical to a Democratic President anxious to force local Democratic organizations to be more responsive to their rapidly growing black population, it simultaneously limited the growth of local black power.

If the War on Poverty located the origins of reform outside the cities, it also encouraged 'minority' citizen participation within the city. It is ironic that blacks were directed to city hall, just at that time when local authority was eroding. The economic function and physical structure of the city was increasingly determined by public agencies and private firms whose logic of operation lay beyond city limits. City revenues came increasingly from state and federal governments, and they came with strings attached. The public infrastructure necessary for the city's economic growth was increasingly determined by transit, water, port and highway authorities beyond local control. The level, content and location of private investment within the city was modulated by national tax laws, contract patterns, lending rates, and environmental regulations. The capacity of the central city to capture private investment within its boundaries depended on its relationship to firms whose network of plants spanned the nation, if not the globe. By encouraging participation at the city level in response to problems whose causes lay in government policies and economic processes outside the city, the War on Poverty insulated important centers of power from political challenge. By fostering an ideology and apparatus for local democracy as a response to an urban poverty whose causes were beyond the control of the localities, it severed the politics of poverty from the administration of wealth.

The War on Poverty was an incorporative strategy of social control, aimed at absorbing the blacks into new, but limited, centers of public authority. Rather than diffuse urban conflict, it could also be used by poor people to intensify their struggles for power, social services and employment. A new departure in federal urban intervention, the War on Poverty created direct relationships between poor communities and the federal bureaucracy, potentially undercutting the control of traditional city bureaucracies and party organizations (Piven and Cloward, 1971: 261–2). Further, under the banner of 'maximum feasible participation', the War on Poverty organized poor communities to demand procedural rights and improved benefits from traditional city bureaucracies (Piven and Cloward, 1971; Moynihan, 1969).

If the War on Poverty was a cooptive social control strategy, it was not without danger. Politically mobilized communities might break the back of bureaucratic politics, contesting not only poverty agency policy but the distribution of municipal employment and political power. The agencies created by the War on Poverty were often able to achieve considerable bureaucratic autonomy.[3]

Poverty agency leaders frequently went on to secure elective city office and to establish independent electoral organization at the city level (Piven and Cloward, 1971: 275; Urquhart, 1974: 36). This exacerbated the growing tensions between the social groups which formed the social base of the Democratic Party. As Piven and Cloward (1971: 254) note:

> In one city after another, racial strife led to polarization and division within the Democratic ranks. Local Democratic leaders in some cities became so threatened by cleavages in their constituencies that, to avoid further trouble, they simply ignored controversial national candidates and

worked mainly to win local contests. [See also Greenberg, 1974.]

While such tension hampered the national Democratic Party's efforts to win the Presidency, it also threatened the local Democratic pro-growth coalitions in Congressional and municipal politics. Many of the political activists who were organizing communities to oppose growth policies were employed in poverty agencies (Mollenkopf, 1973: 6, 11). Such community resistance was often effective enough to halt, delay and change urban renewal and highway developments, thereby raising their fiscal and political costs. With the assistance of attorneys provided by the War on Poverty, communities filed countless law suits which delayed re-development projects, forced them to include replacement low-income housing or stopped them altogether (Law Center, 1972, cited in Mollenkopf, 1973: 13).

The War on Poverty – particularly the Community Action Program – was frequently able to galvanize direct attacks on the city's mainline bureaucracies (Piven and Cloward, 1971; Glazer, 1965; Greenstone and Peterson, 1973). As a result the War on Poverty was often arduously fought by big city mayors (Bachrach and Baratz, 1970). This politicization of the poor was sufficient to induce Mayors Shelley (San Francisco) and Yorty (Los Angeles) to introduce a resolution at the 1965 US Conference of Mayors accusing OEO of 'fostering class struggle' (Urquhart, 1974: 33). Local programs also pushed up welfare rolls through political organization, litigation and improved referral and case-finding (Piven and Cloward, 1971).

On the one hand, the new poverty agencies coopted community activists through new forms of patronage, embroiled community organizations in inter-bureaucratic rivalries and increased competition for poverty program spoils among lower-income ethnic groups. This politically insulated those agencies upon which economic growth was dependent. On the other hand, the War on Poverty provided channels of access for poor, non-white leaders, legitimated their emerging political organizations and provided a new bureaucratic base for continued political mobilization. This exposed the central city's public service agencies and its growth programs to attack from within the city's political system. If the War on Poverty offered political benefits as a potent mechanism of social control, it also had political benefits as a potent mechanism of social control, it also had political costs as a potential bureaucratic base for further political challenge.

The inter-city distribution of War on Poverty funds: a hypothesis

It is again the argument here that cities responded to the War on Poverty not because of the local level of poverty *per se*, but because that poverty – its extent and color – threatened local corporate and union power. The War on Poverty was a soft stratagem for political control over poor and non-white communities who were growing in strength and challenging corporate and labor union political power and the growth policies they pursued.

In those cities where national corporations or labor unions are more powerful, high levels of War on Poverty funding will be a likely response to potential political challenge. In cities where national corporations or labor unions are less powerful, poverty funding levels will not be responsive to such potential political challenge. The combination of locally powerful corporations or labor unions, and social conditions which threaten their political dominance produces a cooptive policy of social control. Policy designed to maintain social control is the result of the coincidence of corporate or labor union *power* and *interest* in the containment of potential conflict. Where either is missing, cooptive public policy is less likely.

Piven and Cloward (1971, 1975, 1977) have cogently argued that the War on Poverty and the welfare explosion that accompanied it originated *nationally* as a Democratic Presidential response to non-white disruption and the changing strategic value of the non-white vote. My argument, however, does not concern the origins of the War on Poverty, but rather the inter-city adoption of this policy. In cities where corporations or labor unions are more powerful, the potential challenge will be a more important determinant of poverty funding levels than in cities where they are not.

Measurement

The local interest of corporations and labor unions in social control derives from the potential challenge posed by those groups who were the victims of the city's economic growth, and those policies designed to sustain that growth. Their potential political challenge is rooted in their growing numerical, and thus electoral, significance and in the extent to which public growth policies adversely affected their lives. The first is indicated by the extent of poverty in the city, the numerical strength of the non-white population, and the extent of non-white population increase. The number of urban renewal projects executed indicates the extent of the city's growth programs. These factors were quantified as follows.

Poverty is measured by the percentage of the city's families with annual incomes under $3000 in 1959 (1960 *Census of Population*). Urban poverty has a twofold status here. On the one hand, it is a measure of need, both in the sense of a legitimation for policy action and as an indicator of the city's fiscal incapacity to act on its own. On the other hand, it suggests the potential political power of the poor. Aiken and Alford (1970a) found that local poverty was related to federal War on Poverty funding in cities over 25 000 in population.

The numerical strength of the non-white population is measured by their percentage of the central city population in 1960 (1960 *Census of Population*). A study of fifteen major central cities shows that industrial executive, banker and Chamber of Commerce influence in city politics is *negatively* related to the influence of black groups (Rossi, Berk and Eidson, 1974: 38). Further, Morlock found that business influence, measured by reputational scores for downtown merchants, local industrialists and bankers was negatively correlated with both the percentage and absolute number of non-whites (Morlock, 1974).

The extent of non-white population increase is measured as the absolute percentage increase (or decrease) in the size of the city's non-white population between 1940 and 1960 (1940 and 1960 *Census of Population*). This taps the growth of the black electoral base, and the strain on the capacities of political organizations and city bureaucracies to absorb them.

The number of urban renewal projects executed between 1949 and 1966 indicates both policies to be protected and potential sources of protest (*Urban Renewal Directory*, 1966). On the one hand, it indicates the extent to which growth policies were at stake, on the other the number of affected neighborhoods in which political protest might emerge to challenge central city growth policies. Consequently, depending on its meaning, it may have either a negative or positive impact on War on Poverty activity.

The national political significance of the central city to the Democratic Party is measured by the percentage of Democratic votes in the Presidential election of 1960 in the county in which the city is located. (*County and City Data Book*, 1962).[4] The 1960 Presidential contest between Kennedy and Nixon was a 'normal' election in which the Democratic and Republican candidates took ideologically divergent stands on domestic social programs. The percentage voting for Kennedy indicates both urban bases of Democratic power, as well as local electoral support for a liberal, expanded federal role in urban affairs (Hamilton, 1972).

The level of War on Poverty activity is measured as the number of dollars received as of June 1966, standardized by the city's 1960 population (*Poverty Program Information*, 1966). This taps both the city's ability to secure funds from the Federal Government and the extent of its material response to federal program opportunities. Many cities were wary of involving themselves with the new federal programs as evidenced by late or minimal involvement in the program. A few large cities did not even have a poverty program as of 1966 and are coded zero.

Data analysis

Does corporate or union power affect the ways in which central cities responded to local political challenge? Does corporate or union power affect the city's willingness to use cooptive strategies of social control? The determinants of War on Poverty funding levels are presented in Tables 6.1 and 6.2.

TABLE 6.1   *Causes of War on Poverty activity in high and low corporate power cities: dependent variable – War on Poverty dollars per capita as of 30 June 1966, in cents*

Independent variables	High corporate power			Low corporate power			Difference of b_1-b_2
	$b_1(B_1)$	st. error	t	$b_2(B_2)$	st. error	t	
% poor	796 (0.04)	3564	0.22	17.3 (0.00)	1704	0.01	
% non-white	2999 (0.40)	1359	2.2**	377 (0.06)	918	0.41	2.32**
% non-white pop. change	−0.0008 (−0.00)	0.09	0.01	0.0238 (0.07)	0.042	0.55	
Renewal projects	−11.2 (0.10)	17.9	0.62	44.4 (0.17)	31.5	1.4*	2.12†
% Democratic	4250 (0.37)	1740	2.4**	2825 (0.28)	1236	2.3**	
Constant	−1744			−1001			
	$n = 58$	$r^2 = 0.230$		$n = 71$	$r^2 = 0.124$		

* significant at 0.10 level (one-tail).
** significant at 0.05 level (one-tail).
† significant at 0.09 level (two-tail).
b = estimated net effect of independent variable on dependent variable.
B = standardized net effect, controlling for the fact that independent variables have different variances.
t ratio = a statistic used to assess significance of estimated effect, or difference in effects.
r^2 = percentage of dependent variable variation explained.

Corporate power

Looking first at the determinants of poverty funding in high and low corporate power cities (Table 6.1), the impact of local social conditions is different in the two kinds of cities. Two variables have different effects in high as opposed to low corporate power cities: percentage non-white and number of urban renewal projects executed. Non-white percentage has a stronger positive effect on poverty funding levels in high rather than in low corporate power cities. Urban renewal activity has an insignificant negative effect on poverty funding in high corporate power cities, but a significant positive effect in low corporate power cities. These differences were statistically significant. Three variables have similar effects in high and low corporate power cities: poverty, non-white population growth and Democratic percentage. Poverty and non-white population growth has an insignificant effect in both high and low corporate power cities, while Democratic percentage has a strong positive effect in both high and low corporate power cities.

These results suggest that high corporate power cities were more responsive to the numerical strength of their non-white populations, but not to the poor as such. It was the black communities whose potential electoral strength and political protest could be directed against corporate élites and the growth program they pursued. The War on Poverty appeared to be a means to contain and deflect that challenge. That the magnitude of the urban renewal program only has a positive effect on poverty funding in low corporate power cities suggests that urban renewal was a vulnerable policy requiring protection from political challenge. The War on Poverty, particularly where it was directed towards political mobilization, often intensified community resistance against urban renewal and highway-related clearance.[5] Rather than mollify protest against the growth program, the War on Poverty could intensify it. Cities in which corporations were powerful were less likely to use such a cooptive policy where a large public growth program was at stake.[6] Finally the impact of partisan national electoral pressures on local poverty funding appears to be impervious to the local level of corporate power. Democratic administrations were eager to bolster local bases of national political support, and the local constituencies provided the local support for innovative forms of welfare state activity.

Union power

Turning to the impact of union power on poverty funding, two variables have significantly different effects in high as opposed to low union power cities. Non-white strength has a strong positive effect on poverty funding in high union power cities and an insignificant negative effect in low union power cities. The number of urban renewal projects has an insignificant negative effect in high union power cities, compared to a significant positive effect in low union power cities. These differences are both statistically significant. The three other variables – percentage of poor, non-white population change, and percentage of Democratics – have similar effects in both groups of cities: percentage of poor and non-white population growth have insignificant effects, and Democratic electoral strength has a strong positive effect, in both high and low union power cities.

TABLE 6.2   *The causes of War on Poverty activity in high and low union power cities: dependent variables – War on Poverty dollars per capita as of 30 June 1966, in cents*

Independent variables	High union power $b_1(B)$	st. error	t	Low union power $b_2(B)$	st. error	t	Difference of b_1-b_2
% poor	−494.9 (−0.03)	2750	0.18	−354 (−0.03)	1765	0.2	
% non-white	2981 (0.40)	1147	2.6**	−35.3 (−0.01)	967	0.0	2.83**
% non-white pop. change	0.013 (0.02)	0.095	0.14	0.03 (0.09)	0.04	0.7	
Renewal projects	−1.52 (−0.01)	17.1	0.09	89.6 (0.34)	34.8	2.6**	3.4†
% Democratic	3361 (0.28)	1632	2.1**	3349 (0.35)	1208	2.8**	
Constant	−1253			−1217			
	$n = 69$	$r^2 = 0.199$		$n = 60$	$r^2 = 0.23$		

* significant at 0.10 level (one-tail).
** significant at 0.05 level (one-tail).
† significant at 0.05 level (two-tail).
b = estimated net effect of independent variable on dependent variable.
B = standardized net effect, controlling for the fact that independent variables have different variances.
t ratio = a statistic used to assess significance of estimated effect, or difference in effects.
r^2 = percentage of dependent variable variation explained.

Partisan electoral determination of poverty funding was independent of local labor union power. The uniformly positive, significant effect of Democratic strength on poverty funding indicates that the city's position in the national political system was an important determinant of its War on Poverty funding. The policy impact of urban partisan pressures is independent of the city's position in the national corporate or union structure.[7] Finally, union power depresses the positive effect of urban renewal projects on the level of poverty funding, again suggesting a union interest in protecting growth policies from political attacks potentially launched by poverty activists.[8]

Because labor unions can't control the city's economic growth, they are particularly sensitive to social forces that might endanger their electoral influence. While the white poor remained ethnically fragmented and relatively unorganized, black politicization rose markedly in the postwar period. The central city black population was particularly threatening to the political position of the labor unions. In mayoral electoral politics, labor unions were likely to be key coalitional partners with the non-whites (Greenstone, 1970). But securing the support of the non-white political community for liberal, Democratic candidates, while maintaining racially restrictive unions and supporting disruptive growth programs was a difficult balancing act. The coalitional alliance between unions and blacks was contingent upon the survival of a relatively moderate, if independent, black leadership. Cooptation and patronage through incorporation in the new poverty bureaucracies was a means to contain the militancy of emerging non-white political organizations.

Interest, power and public policy

Corporate and union power affected the extent to which black communities translated their numbers into the new patronage. Corporate and union interests in cooptive social control were dependent on the extent to which blacks could contend for power. But does corporate and union power have an effect on social control policy independent of local conditions? Do corporations and unions have interests in social control which are independent of local social conditions? Is non-repressive social control policy a corporate or union response to local political challenge, or to national political or ideological factors which don't vary between cities?

Both high corporate and union power cities had higher

average War on Poverty funding than did low corporate or union power cities. Are these differences due to the fact that corporate and union cities responded differently to similar social conditions? Or did corporations and unions generate higher levels of cooptation regardless of local conditions? To

TABLE 6.3   *War on Poverty expenditure per capita, 1966, for the average central city*

	Corporate power	Union power
	($ per capita)	
High power	10.51	9.70
Low power	6.63	6.86

answer this question, the intercepts can be compared in high and low corporate power (and high and low union power cities), where the intercepts are adjusted for group differences in local social conditions. In this 'what if' exercise, the regression equations presented above in Tables 6.1 and 6.2 are used to generate the expected level of War on Poverty funding each city would have if each experienced the same local social conditions. Table 6.4 summarizes the projected results.

TABLE 6.4   *Expected War on Poverty expenditure per capita assuming similar local social conditions*

	Corporate	Union
	($ per capita)	
High power	27.32	21.22
Low power	17.83	21.62
Difference between high and low power	9.49	−0.40

Based on the projections in Table 6.4, if high corporate power cities faced the same local social conditions as low corporate power cities, they would have *higher* levels of War on Poverty activity. If high union power cities faced the same local social conditions as low union power cities, they would have almost exactly *the same* levels of War on Poverty activity.

The results suggest that corporate interest in cooptive social control policy was not entirely contingent upon the local political challenge. For the locally headquartered national corporations, cooptive social control was not a serious threat to their political power. Union interest in cooptive social control was dependent upon local political conditions. For the unions, such policies and political incorporation of challenging groups threatened the mainsprings of the union political power – their ability to organize participation.

Summary and conclusions

The War on Poverty was not a local policy response to poverty, but to the power of those who were poor. In part, that power grew out of their numerical strength and their blackness. Numbers meant votes, while color was the basis of cohesion and political visibility. In part, that power also grew out of the organizational complexion of local political élites who faced the political challenge of the black poor. Where corporations and labor unions were weak, blacks faced more conservative political groupings, dominated by smaller, more localized firms. Because such firms were more vulnerable to local decisions and thus more dependent on the outcomes of city political conflict, they were likely to be active in city politics. Given their dependency on low-wage, non-unionized labor, the depressing effect of racism on both wages and unionization (Reich, 1973; Hill, 1973), and their low profit margins and thus vulnerability to tax increases, such local firms were more resistant to political concessions to non-dominant interests. Without a strong union presence as a base for the Democratic Party or coalition partner, or a politically sophisticated corporate leadership, non-white communities lacked the political leverage necessary to secure even cooptive benefits. In such cities, police guns may have been a substitute for this new form of welfare.

Thus patronage and cooptation were not an automatic response either to poverty or to the potential power of the poor. The leverage of non-dominant groups depends on the power and interest of the dominant groups from whom they must wring concessions. The local War on Poverty was not just a response to mass electoral pressures, although these clearly mattered to a Democratic administration anxious to shore up urban support. Nor was it a governmental response to demands lying latent in impoverished silence or to the obvious failures of public services and private economy. The evidence suggests the policy impact of corporations and labor unions who were anxious to manage mass politicization, which was moving with increasing force at the ballot box and with increasing violence in the streets.

Notes

1. In her study of ninety-one northern cities, Morlock found that reputational influence based on successful *rejection* of major city programs was highest for non-white social groups. The most frequently rejected program was Urban Renewal (Morlock, 1974).

2. The percentage of black vote for the Democratic Presidential candidate was 79 per cent in 1952, 61 per cent in 1956, 68 per cent in 1960, 90 per cent in 1964, 87 per cent in 1968, 86 per cent in 1972, and 94 per cent in 1976.

3. This was especially so under conditions of a reformed city structure, where the dominant political coalitions were less able to determine agency recruitment patterns or policy implementation (Greenstone and Peterson, 1973: 203–25).

4. When a city was in more than one county, the county in which the majority of the city's population resides is used. Because the city and county are not coterminous, this measure probably underestimates the central city's Democratic vote because of the concentration of non-white, low-income individuals likely to vote Democratic in the central city and the concentration of white, higher-income individuals likely to vote Republican in the suburbs.

5. This interpretation is bolstered by the fact that when analysis was done specifically for the level of Community Action Program activity, the program most likely to politicize poor communities, the differential impact of renewal activity was even more marked ($b = 8.6$, $F = 4.92$ v. $b = 19.7$, $F = 2.48$) and the difference in regression coefficients between equations was significant at the 0.01 level.

6. An alternative interpretation of this indicator, which is consistent with the empirical findings, is that the number of renewal projects indicates the city's political and administrative experience in acquiring project grant funds from the Federal Government. Although Urban Renewal was under the jurisdiction of different Congressional committees and lodged in different federal agencies than the War on Poverty, Urban Renewal probably provided the city with critical experience in the preparation of grant applications and the development of administrative and political linkages with Washington, DC. In cities where corporations were powerful, these administrative and political linkages may have been less important because the corporations themselves provided a lot of the informational and influential linkages to national centers of power and decision-making. This interpretation is not consistent, however, with the strong negative effect of renewal activity on Community Action Program activity which obtains in both corporate and union power cities.

7. This is consistent with other studies which have found that electoral politics

matters most for welfare policies (Fry and Winters, 1970; Booms and Halldorson, 1973; Hicks, Friedland, Johnson, 1975).

8. Controls were made for population size in all equations. Population size did not have any effect on the dependent variable in any of the equations, nor did its inclusion change the results.

Chapter 7

Public Policy and Black Political Violence

Corporate and union power shaped the central city's adoption of policies intended to stimulate economic growth – Urban Renewal – and maintain social control – the War on Poverty. If their power influenced the causes of public policies designed to serve their interests, it could not control the consequences of those policies. By the late 1960s, the black riots had razed cities across the country. What role did public policies – policies of growth and social control – have in this apparently national breakdown in urban social control?

The black struggle for civil rights, in the south and north, was waged in the face of popular and state terror. Mob attacks, bombings, intimidation, police violence – these were ordinary responses to the civil rights movement. From its original concern for equality before the law, the movement increasingly came to demand equality within the law: better housing, more jobs, better pay. Thousands of protest demonstrations – as many inside as outside the south – politicized the cities' ghettoes.

For urban blacks, poverty, inadequate services and restricted housing opportunities had less to do with blackness than with the changing economic structure of the city. Low-skilled industrial jobs were decreasingly available. Office jobs drew on the skills of suburban workers. Those firms requiring non-skilled labor had to pay extremely low wages in order to survive. The city's growing office economy was making extraordinary demands on the public purse while the property tax base of the city was eroding. Funds for more services or for public employment to absorb some of the non-white labor were difficult to find. Housing markets were restricted by the low rents non-whites could afford, and by the destruction of low-income housing supply through urban renewal and highway construction oriented to the downtown economy. Blacks could confront these powerful but faceless forces only indirectly. Voters could be mobilized; services could be obtained; jobs could be had – but the urban system, its genetic codes, could not be touched. The protests won what could be won – patronage, public office, public services. But they could not win enough, even as their victories told them that they were right to struggle in the first place.

And so the cities burned. Starting in 1961, the frequency of black collective violence steadily increased, climaxing in the horrible summers of 1967 and 1968. Of the 234 riots experienced by these large central cities between 1961 and 1968, over three-fourths occurred in 1967–8. In the midst of madness – of blood, death, fire – the forces governing the shooting, the shouting, the burning hardly appeared rational. Executives peered fearfully out of downtown office windows as smoke rose over the city. Suburban families watched with anger and morbid fascination as blacks seemed to destroy their own communities. That these violent conflagrations might be rational could hardly be fathomed. That, indeed, their number and severity might have local political origins strained the sociological imagination.

Social theory and collective violence

At some times, in some places, in some form, groups convert their pain into protest rather than individually endure. In so doing, they engage in extraordinary behavior. Not only do they act in concert, but their cooperation violates the legal and social canons that regulate daily life.

These events of collective defiance seem to be as difficult for social theory to explain as they are for political élites to manage. The explanations either emphasize a breakdown of *social control*, or breakdown in *state control*.

Explanations of collective protest – from riots to civil wars – which stress the erosion of social control locate the sources of conformity in the routines and experiences of daily life. It is a disruption of those routines which provides a basis for collective protest.

A first social-psychological explanation argues that people turn to political violence when a yawning gap between expectations and real opportunities suddenly emerges. It is not those who need the most who rebel, but those who can't get what they have been led to expect they should have. This theory of 'relative deprivation', whether from rising expectations or sudden emmiseration, argues that periods of rapid economic change generate widespread frustration and consequent aggression against the powers that be (Gurr, 1971, 1968; Davies, 1962).

A second social control explanation points to the ways in which social change disrupts the regulation embedded in daily life. Disruption of families, of work routines, of communities often follow from rapid economic changes. For large numbers of people, social life is suddenly deregulated. The rewards for conformity are absent. The routines of compliance are unpracticed. And the time to think other thoughts and act other deeds is all too abundant. Piven and Cloward (1977: 11) write:

> Ordinary life for most people is regulated by the rules of work and the rewards of work which pattern each day and week and season. Once cast out of that routine, people are cast out of the regulatory framework that it imposes. Work and the rewards of work underpin the stability of other social institutions as well. When men cannot earn enough to support families, they may desert their wives and children, or fail to marry the women with whom they mate. And if unemployment is longlasting entire communities may disintegrate as the able-bodied migrate elsewhere in search of work. In effect daily life becomes progressively deregulated.

According to this explanation, political violence is but one expression of social deregulation which also surfaces in higher divorce, crime, drug addiction and suicide.

If the social control approach locates stresses in the

relationship between individuals and society, a second approach locates them in the power relationship between social groups and the state. It is not the level of discontent or deregulation that explains the pattern of collective defiance of the state, but political opportunities available to oppressed groups. Again there are two basic orientations.

A first, state control approach locates the causes of political violence in the problems of political modernization. Modernization continuously catapults new social groups into the political arena, anxious to use political power to redress their economic grievances. Often political participation rises more quickly than the state's capacity to absorb it within legitimate channels, to socialize each new group's leaders to the rules of the game, to build autonomous agencies to handle new demands, to widen parties to incorporate new constituencies.[1] At such junctures, political deviance is highly likely (Huntington, 1968; Rokkan, 1970). Where the system is not able to absorb new groups through corruption or patronage, political violence erupts. This approach stresses the non-instrumental nature of political violence, 'a symbolic gesture of protest which . . . is not designed to be requited' (Huntington, 1968: 64). In modern society, social cohesion is forged within political institutions. Political violence results not from politicization, but from the insufficient power of the state to absorb it.

Political violence may not be symbolic, but strategic – a way to force open the doors of the state house when other routes have failed or when the frailties of the state structure suggest that it will work. This alternative approach, denies the neutrality of the state. Depending on their interests, their demands, the political empowerment of some groups may be costly to dominant groups. Consequently, dominant groups will purposefully organize the state to minimize the probabilities that non-dominant groups obtain political access, or to reduce the efficacy of what access they do achieve. From this alternative perspective, political violence is one of the many strategic options available to oppressed groups. Political violence frequently emerges out of peaceful patterns of political expression, particularly as a consequence of state violence. Political violence emerges when its efficacy appears probable –

notably when the balance of power between the social group and the state has appreciably shifted. From this perspective, the emergence of political violence is one indicator that a realignment in the power structure is taking place (Tilly, 1978). Political violence, whether by oppressed groups or by the state, is an effective option. Groups that are able to mount an 'unruly' opposition are more effective in securing gains from the state than groups who obey the rules of normal politics (Gamson, 1975). Conversely, where the state violently represses protest, social groups are demobilized, their political expression individualized and redirected into institutionalized channels (Tilly, Tilly and Tilly, 1975).

According to Piven and Cloward (1977), periods of rapid economic change destabilize the relations between political parties and their constituencies. At such times, political élites – anxious to stabilize a new electoral base – make concessions to clear the streets, concessions that legitimate the mobilization of disaffected groups. The concessions suggest not only that disruption is just, but that it works. Because initial concessions tend to be insufficient, political violence is likely when the state lacks the capacity to repress disorder – whether because recalcitrant groups posses many resources or because the state does not (Tilly, 1978).

The black riots: towards a sociological explanation

Relative deprivation, the deregulation of social life, the failure of the political system to incorporate new groups, rising political power and symbolic concessions – each explanation seems to offer an explanation for the black riots of the 1960s. Each has in fact been offered.

Blacks migrated to the cities with expectations of work. Yet the central city economy imposed depression levels of structural unemployment on the black communities in the 1960s. After the Second World War, the relative unemployment rates of non-whites continued to worsen, even while black families, as a whole, were closing the income gap with their white counterparts (Farley, 1977). While many blacks were moving up, many others were not. Black anger at the insufficiency of individual or group gains has been argued to dispose urban blacks to political violence (Gurr, 1968).

The massive migration of blacks to the cities tore at the texture of social life. The structure of black communities was strained by a tremendous inflow of people suddenly cut away from traditional institutions, unable to find jobs to maintain families, unable therefore to regulate their children (Piven and Cloward, 1971: 222–40). It appeared that it was in cities which had the highest influx of non-whites – where social controls were presumably weakest – that the black riots were most severe (*ibid:* 239).

So too it can be argued that many urban governments were not capable of incorporating rising black politicization. In the cities still run by political parties, white ethnics controlled the Democratic Party and the Democratic Party controlled the cities. There were few local incentives for incorporation of new black citizens (Piven and Cloward, 1977: 216). Cities whose electoral logic ran along ward and partisan lines tended to be more responsive to the interests of their citizenry (Lineberry and Fowler, 1967; Alford and Scoble, 1968). Even so, the black community had little impact on urban policy in such cities (Lineberry and Fowler, 1967). Black communities were also unsuccessful in 'machine cities' in securing any political influence. In response to the mobilization of black communities, the partisan city distributed favors, not power (Greenstone and Peterson, 1973: 168).

Finally, the political power of urban blacks was on the rise in the 1960s and the city's white power structure seemed permeable to assault. Black communities were sufficiently large and concentrated to support independent institutions – churches, stores, organizations – and thus independent black leadership (Piven and Cloward, 1977: 203–4). Black numbers meant potential votes, but in the 1960s they also meant black protests, thousands of them. The concessions these protests were then winning indicated the vulnerability of the political system.

Both the riot participants and the black communities in which they rioted viewed their violence politically (Feagin and Hahn, 1973; Fogelson, 1971). The rioters tended to be well informed about the political system, but with little trust in its capacity to respond to black needs (Paige, 1971). Rioters were not alienated, they were angry.[2]

The local sources of black political violence

Most of these explanations of the urban riots have failed to account for the local incidence and severity of black riots. In the most extensive comparative studies of black riots, Spilerman analyzed variations in riots in 673 cities of 25 000 or more population (see also Morgan and Clark, 1973; Lieberson and Silverman, 1965). Not only did he analyze city variation in the number of riots a city experienced, but he analyzed the local determinants of severity for 322 riots in 1967 and 1968 (Spilerman, 1971 and 1974). Spilerman found that when controls were made for the number of blacks resident in the city and whether the city was located in the south, indicators of absolute deprivation (e.g. non-white unemployment), relative deprivation (e.g. ratio of black to white median family income), social disorganization (e.g. growth in non-white population), or political structure (e.g. mayor-council government) had no significant effect on either riot frequency or severity (Spilerman, 1971, 1974). Spilerman interprets the positive effect of black population size as a control for the availability of participants. Spilerman argues that the ghetto riots were *nationally* determined by the limitations of federal court and legislative action, by the national diffusion of a militant riot ideology and by the transmittal of uniform political stimuli to all cities by the mass media.[3]

The findings that local social conditions had little impact on local riot activity were also used to argue that the black riots lacked any political logic at all. Eisinger (1973: 13), for example, wrote: 'protest against local government targets is likely to be related to the nature of local politics, while ghetto violence is not'. Protesters make strategic calculations as to how to maximize their policy gains, while minimizing their losses. Rioters, because they expose themselves to injury, imprisonment and death, are irrational, having 'thrown cost considerations to the winds' (ibid: 13). While protesters implicitly manipulate the fear of violence and thereby maintain legitimacy, the rioters do not. While protests are instrumentally motivated by specific local grievances, the riots reflect expressive impulses diffused by the national media. The urban riots thus are nationally rational and/or locally irrational political behavior. In either case, they do not appear to be determined by local conditions.

Public policy and black violence

Economic conditions have different political qualities than urban policies. While high rents, deteriorated housing, unemployment and poverty were highly visible, the economic processes which reproduced them were not. The logic of housing or labor markets was opaque, and many of its dominant agents exerted their silent influence through mazeways of mortgage flows, tax write-offs on plant investments and networks of absentee ownership. The effects of these economic processes were individualized through market exchanges between customers and merchants, tenants and landlords, and wage laborers and employers. Lacking a unified political or union movement, politics aimed at the exploitation of the black consumer, tenant or worker tended to fragment the black community. For the demands which were consistent with the logic of the market were demands against racial discrimination, for equality before the market. Because blacks were not equal in the market, such political movements tended to be supported by and benefit those upwardly mobile blacks who were moving into higher-income occupational roles and the residential areas such income could afford. Finally, these economic processes seemed to have no beginning, nor end. While economic conditions could not effectively mobilize the black community, urban policies could.

Blacks viewed the riots politically – as protests against injustice, as strategies for change. Yet studies have not analyzed the impact of urban policies on their frequency or severity. Two major urban policies – the War on Poverty and Urban Renewal – directly impinged on the political expectations and material conditions of the black community.

These urban policies were highly visible at a local level. They simultaneously affected large numbers of people. They provided public targets for which collective political action was both legitimate and feasible. Their implementation was localized in time, the War on Poverty beginning in 1964 and the bulk of residential urban renewal being executed after 1960.

Urban renewal programs had particularly deleterious effects on the black community. First, urban renewal, particularly residential renewal, physically destroyed large amounts of black housing and housing potentially available to blacks. Between 1949 and 1966, the average central city destroyed 1511 housing units. Of these housing units, an average of 79 per cent were substandard and thus likely to be occupied by low-income renters. The amount of black displacement involved was considerably greater than would be expected by their proportion in the population. Between 1949 and 1966, the average central city displaced 1220 persons, according to official HUD statistics. These statistics are very conservative estimates, as many people moved out of renewal areas after clearance announcements were made but before official ennumerations were taken. While non-whites constituted on average 16 per cent of the 1960 central city population, they were about 61 per cent of those displaced by urban renewal.

Urban renewal inflicted large uncompensated costs on those it displaced, as well as destroying valued social networks which were dependent upon their location in the renewal areas (Downs, 1971). By destroying a large segment of the low-rent housing stock without replacement, urban renewal put upward pressures on rental levels in the remaining low-income housing. Those relocated by urban renewal experienced large rental increases, continued occupation of substandard housing, overcrowding and intensive deterioration of the housing stock (Hartman, 1967; Abrams, 1965).

Urban renewal – 'Negro removal', as it was angrily called – became a target for rising black militancy. In Newark, for example, black opposition to the renewal displacement caused by School of Medicine construction was a political stimulus for the 1967 riots (Castells, 1970). Across the country, black communities organized to resist urban renewal displacement, secure adequate relocation housing and demand construction of low-income housing to replace that destroyed by renewal.

If Urban Renewal was a policy loss for the black community and thus a target for black opposition, the War on Poverty appeared to be a policy gain. The War on Poverty assiduously wooed black support. It funneled services into black communities, while absorbing their newfound political participation. The programs were especially targeted to those areas which had been the special victims of urban renewal. The War on Poverty was a strategy of state control which coopted community activists through new patronage structures (Greenberg, 1974; Katznelson and Kesselman, 1975). And yet it embroiled them in inter-bureaucratic struggles to protect the domain, funding and very survival of the poverty agencies (Kramer, 1969; Bachrach and Baratz, 1970). Blacks captured a piece of the local state. But it was a new piece, without power to change the policies of dominant agencies.

In the process, the streets were deprived of their best black political leadership. The new structures of black participation were irrelevant to a large segment of the black community, particularly young black men. The poverty agencies could only provide a limited number of new municipal jobs. Without power, they could not change the material conditions of the black poor.

Public policy, political violence and social theory

These two local policies might impact local riot activity in various ways. Each policy affects the central processes that the social theories reviewed above claim are central to explaining political violence. From the point of view of the psychological social control theory, Urban Renewal imposed serious costs on the black community and was thus a political defeat. Just when black access to housing was expanding, urban renewal was destroying the housing they had or might have taken. It was a political source of *deprivation*. The War on Poverty, on the other hand, by its rhetoric of a total war on poverty, by its delivery of new services and its apparent empowerment of the black community, certainly raised expectations. Given the limits on the power of the poverty program, it probably raised expectations relative to gains. In this perspective, it was a political source of *relative deprivation*.

From the point of view of social-structural social control theory, both Urban Renewal and the War on Poverty might be seen as a political source of *social disorganization*. The renewal process literally destroyed black communities, as well as areas in which they might expand. In the same vein, the War on Poverty left the streets without political leadership, often undermining the independence and coherence of those political organizations which did exist within the community. From the point of view of the theory of political modernization, the basic causes of political violence lay in the insufficient 'institutionalization' of the government. Where government agencies are differentiated, able to maintain autonomy from the citizenry yet able to absorb new constituencies, political violence will be averted. Thus, a strong renewal program indicates an *institutionalized government program*; while the War on Poverty indicates the ability of the local political system to *incorporate new groups*.

From the point of view of a theory of political violence as a strategy of political empowerment, the explanation of political violence lay in the growing power of oppressed groups and the variable vulnerability of the local state to them. Urban Renewal was a *vulnerable target*. Electoral politics seemed to have no effect. Yet, community resistance had slowed, altered,

TABLE 7.1   *Social theory, public policy and the determinants of black collective violence*

	Public policy	
Social control	*Urban Renewal*	*War on Poverty*
Social psychological	deprivation (+)	relative deprivation (+)
Social disorganization	social disorganization (+)	social disorganization (+)
State control		
Political modernization	state autonomy (—)	incorporation of new groups (—)
Political conflict	vulnerable target (+)	symbolic concession (+)

or stopped renewal programs altogether. Urban renewal and residential renewal in particular was decidedly opposed to the interests of the black community. The War on Poverty was a *symbolic concession*, legitimating the rising political mobilization of the black community. The War on Poverty indicated that the walls of city hall might be breached, that at least, it was worth a try.

The conceptualization that each social theory might make of these policies, and their expected impact on black political violence is presented in Table 7.1.

Measurement

To measure the extent to which riot frequency and aggregate severity are affected by local policies, two measures of local riot activity will be used: the number of riots occurring in 1967 and 1968, and an aggregate severity score for riots occurring in 1967 and 1968.

The data used to construct these indicators were generously provided by Seymour Spilerman and the reader is referred to his empirical studies for more complete information on index construction (1970, 1971, 1974). To count as a disorder the incident had to involve thirty or more individuals, be a result of Negro aggression, and not grow out of a civil rights demonstration. I have used the more delimited period between 1967 and 1968 because riot frequency increased markedly in 1967 and 1968. Spilerman suggests that this increase was not a function of local reinforcement processes, but due to some 'uniform national stimulus' (1970: 636). This short time-frame in which the bulk of the riots took place would be the least likely to provide empirical support for a theory of local determination of riot frequency and aggregate severity.

The riot severity index for 1967 and 1968 was constructed using Spilerman's riot severity scale. The scale was a unidimensional, intervally scored index which excluded what kind of police assistance was called (e.g. national guard). The severity scale is reproduced in Table 7.2 (Spilerman, 1974).

To create an aggregate riot severity score, I added the riot severity scale, for the *most* intense riots in 1967 and 1968. If a

TABLE 7.2   *Riot severity scale*

---

1. Low intensity – rock and bottle throwing, some fighting, little property damage. Crowd size < 125; arrests < 15; injuries 8.
2. Rock and bottle throwing, fighting, looting, serious property damage, some arson. Crowd size 75–250; arrests 10–30; injuries 5–15.
3. Substantial violence, looting, arson and property destruction. Crowd size 200–500; arrests 25–75; injuries 10–40.
4. High intensity – major violence, bloodshed and destruction. Crowd size > 400; arrests > 65; injuries > 35.

---

city had more than one riot in either year, its most intense riot was coded. Riot severity is analyzed as an attribute of the city's political system, not as an independent instance of collective behavior. Thus the aggregate riot severity score expresses the level of aggregate political violence created by a city's black population.

When blacks rioted in American cities in the 1960s, they collectively violated property rights and defied police authority. Given the institutional centrality of the targets of opposition, state violence was quite likely. And thus the intensity of the riot was in part a measure of the level of state violence the rioters were prepared to endure and resist.

The *city's* severity score is not the same as in Spilerman's analysis of riot severity. In Spilerman's analysis of riot severity, the individual riot was the unit of analysis, and the city was an attribute of the riot event. Here the aggregate level of riot activity is an attribute of the city. There are a number of differences with Spilerman's study of riot severity. First, Spilerman excludes all cities without riots in the study of riot severity. This results from considering the riot as an independent political event and then analyzing its severity, rather than as a component of the total level of black political violence in the city. Second, by considering all riots as independent units of analysis, the impact of local social conditions, which are invariant for each political event within that city, are weighted towards those cities which have the most riots and those which have the highest average riot severity.

The level of residential urban renewal is operationalized by the number of urban renewal acres slated for residential re-use in projects executed between 1961 and 1966 (*Urban Renewal Directory*, 1972; *Urban Renewal Project Characteristics*, 1966). The execution stage begins with federal approval of a local plan and authorization of a federal funding contract. It is at this stage that local clearance begins.

The level of War on Poverty funding is operationalized by the number of War on Poverty dollars per capita which had been allocated to the city between its inception in 1964 and 30 June 1966 (*Poverty Program Information*, 1966).

Six other variables will also be used: non-reform government structure, size of non-white population, the rate of non-white population growth, the level of low-rent housing supply, the level of local police activity and a regional control for southern location.

To indicate non-reform government structure, the presence of mayor-council government is used. This is highly correlated with other structural aspects of the non-reformed structure: partisan elections, large city councils and ward-based election. Non-reformed cities tended to use patronage to incorporate non-white communities and resisted attempts to increase their power.

The absolute size of the non-white population is measured by the logarithm of the number of non-white residents as of 1960. Spilerman (1974: 23) has argued that size of the local Negro population indicates the size of the pool of potential participants. In addition, a large black community was necessary to provide a milieu in which concealment was possible and which provided large enough crowds to deter immediate and total repression. Spilerman (1970, 1971, 1974) has consistently found this indicator to be the single most powerful predictor of riot frequency and severity.

The rate of black population increase is measured as the percentage growth in the non-white population between 1940 and 1960. This has been used to indicate social dis-organization, and the existence of a large number of people who are not subject to informal social controls and are unfamiliar with formal procedures for redress of grievances (Spilerman, 1974: 20). However, the data indicate that riot participants were not more recent migrants to the cities

(Feagin and Hahn, 1973). An alternative interpretation of this indicator is that a large increase in the non-white population strained the systems of social control by overburdening the constricted structure of city patronage, overflowing social service agencies with new black clients and exacerbating racial tensions in the housing and labour markets.

I constructed an indicator of low-rent housing demand relative to supply. Other studies have used indicators of housing quality such as the percentage of dilapidated housing (see Spilerman, 1970; Downes, 1970). One of the most salient problems to the black community was the limited availability of rental housing at a price they could afford. Congress has argued that families should not have to pay more than 25 per cent of their income on housing, yet according to census reports, more than 2.8 million renter households payed 35 per cent or more of their income on rent (Abrams, 1965: 147). An adequate indicator of low-rent housing supply must take low-rent housing demand into account. To construct an indicator of supply, I used the number of rental housing units which had rents of $80 or less per month which would be 24 per cent of an annual family income of $4000 (*US Census of Population and Housing*, 1960). As an indicator of demand, I used the number of all central city families who had annual income of $4000 or below. The index of low-rent housing demand relative to supply was the ratio of these two values. A high value would indicate a high level of demand for low-income housing relative to low-rent supply.

Local police activity was measured by the per capita local expenditures for police in 1965 (*City Government Finances*, 1965–6). The probable impact of local police activity is ambiguous. On the other hand, high levels of police activity suggest a larger repressive capacity of local government. Such a capacity would deter potential black violence. On the other hand, high levels of police activity also suggests a repressive orientation of the local government to local problems, as well as a larger police presence in the black community. Given the higher visibility of police, the greater number of contacts that blacks were likely to have with policemen and the important role that such contacts had in catalyzing the riots, a city's police activity could also increase local riot activity.

Finally a regional control variable was used to control for the distinctive pattern of black experience in the south. All cities located in the deep south – Louisiana, Alabama, Mississippi, Florida, Georgia, North Carolina and South Carolina – were included in this dichotomous regional variable. Spilerman (1974) has found that riots were less severe in southern cities.

Data analysis

The local determinants of black riot levels are presented in Table 7.3. Looking at the causes of the number of central city riots in 1967–8, non-white population size, the level of police

TABLE 7.3   *The local origins of the black urban riots, 1967–8*

Independent variables	Riot frequency 1967–8			Aggregate riot severity 1967–8		
	b	beta	*t*	*b*	beta	*t*
Socioeconomic conditions						
Non-white population growth, 1940–60	—0.00002	—0.03	0.33	0.00004	0.04	0.54
Non-white population size, 1960	0.42	0.45	5.3‡	0.59	0.44	5.6‡
Low-rent housing demand, 1960	0.10	0.05	0.69	0.62	0.21	3.2‡
Political conditions						
War on Poverty funding, 1966	0.00016	0.10	1.18	0.00035	0.15	1.95‡
Urban Renewal activity, 1961–6	—0.0024	—0.11	0.18	0.0045	0.13	1.88†
Police activity, 1965	0.07	0.27	2.85‡	0.085	0.24	2.8‡
Non-reformed government	0.62	0.22	2.95‡	0.74	0.18	2.7‡
Region (1 = south)	—0.39	—0.09	1.2	—0.81	—0.13	1.9†
n = 118		r^2 = 0.47			r^2 = 0.57	

* significant at 0.10 level (one-tail).
† significant at 0.05 level (one-tail).
‡ significant at 0.01 level (one-tail).

activity and the existence of a non-reformed government all have significant positive effects. Neither War on Poverty funding, nor Urban Renewal funding have significant positive effects. Turning to the aggregate riot severity, both non-white population size and the level of low-rent housing demand have positive effects. Further, every single political variable has a significant positive effect on the city's aggregate level of black political violence: poverty funding, urban renewal activity, police activity and non-reformed government. Finally, the aggregate level of riot activity tended to be lower in cities in the deep south.

Local public policies played an important role in conditioning the city's level of black political violence. Underneath the national simultaneity of the riots of those 'hot summers' of 1967 and 1968 lay a local logic, a political logic. Riot activity was stronger in machine cities, cities which converted potential political conflicts into distributive favors (see also Downes, 1970). So too the level of police activity increased the level of riot activity. The black community viewed the police as a source of harassment, a white, repressive presence. The riots tended both to begin and end with police violence (Skolnick, 1969).

The level of social disorganization – indicated by a precipitous rise in non-white population – had little to do with the level of riot activity. Social disorganization did not produce local political violence. Rioters tended to be long-term residents, residents who knew the local political scene most intimately, not newcomers. Indeed, given the strong informal community support necessary to sustain a riot, a transient black community may have been socially ill equipped to engage the police and national guard for days at a time.

Cities with a large urban renewal program have more intense political violence. Urban renewal was a visible indicator of the city's commitment to displace the black community, to woo a whiter, wealthier clientele. But such a visible target was also a vulnerable target, one subject to legal and political opposition. By this time, federal officials had written in procedural guarantees which legitimated black opposition to urban renewal projects which did little for those who actually lived there. If Urban Renewal was vulnerable to political opposition, the War on Poverty emboldened the black community.

The poverty program contributed to the intensity of a city's black political violence. By providing new sources of black public employment and new avenues of legitimate black participation, it brought blacks closer to urban power than they had ever been before. But because it conceded limited employment and formal participation, it could not contain the rising political mobilization of the black community. Indeed it legitimized black politicization. This was also the view of OED officials. What the rioters said on the streets, the poverty leaders now said to city hall. The program absorbed much of the more skilled, and more moderate black political leadership from the streets. In so doing, it left the mass of unemployed, young black men without the basis for creating their own political organizations. Outflanked by the new poverty politics, bombarded by the rhetoric of 'participation' and given low-paid summer jobs, the young black men were left on the street corners with nothing but their righteous anger. A routine arrest, an explosion.

The riots appeared to be a strategy of political empowerment. There was a local rationality to the riot, rationality linking it to injustices on the one hand, and to its potential efficacy on the other. The riot was a political resource, to be used strategically like any other. The data indicate that poverty funding and renewal activity only affect total riot severity and not riot frequency. How to explain this difference? If the riot were a strategy of political empowerment, the community's unconscious calculation would weigh the costs and benefits of repeated rioting, costs that would certainly escalate with each incident, while benefits would probably not. In order to be effective, the community would have to capitalize on its political violence – convert it to jobs, services, power. Part of that conversion would be contingent on its ability to prevent another riot. From this perspective, that public policies have less effect on the local number of riots than they do on the aggregate severity of the riot activity would not be unexpected.

Local social controls had counter-productive effects on black political violence. The War on Poverty coopted black leaders.

Urban Renewal physically displaced the black community. Cities with large police budgets were able to monitor the black community more closely, maintain a believable deterrent to political violence. Yet both cooptation and repression increased the severity of black violence, when it occurred.[4]

In the streets, perhaps as much as in the voting booth, politics mattered. The data cannot reveal whether the causes were political privation, political disorganization or the potentialities of political empowerment. They suggest, at least, the need to locate the public sources of private anger and the conditions under which that anger propels people against the state.

In part, the riots counterposed popular violence to state violence. In part, the riots were a violent veto to the policies of local government – policies of growth and social control. The city's residents had privately borne many of the costs of this new pattern of urban growth – in constricted housing supply, unemployment, inadequate services. The riots forcibly presented the pains of the private household to city hall. It would be the public household that would now try to absorb them.

Notes

1. Huntington (1968: 1) writes, 'The most important political distinction among countries concerns not their form of government, but their degree of government.'

2. The rioters often chose their targets carefully. The looting of stores was not random, but followed community norms as to the sources of exploitation. Stores that had treated their black clientele favorably were often spared (Feagin and Hahn, 1973; see also Berk and Aldrich, 1972; and Rossi, Berk and Eidson, 1974 for evidence of target selectivity during the 1967–8 period in general).

3. Spilerman (1974: 27) writes:

Taken together, these studies suggest that despite considerable differences in Negro circumstances from one city to the next, this consideration did not find expression in the two aspects of the disturbance process that we have examined. Although we would not claim that local conditions never influenced disorder proneness or disorder severity, we do assert the absence of a systematic tendency for either of these facets of the racial turmoil to be associated with the extent of Negro deprivation in a community. This assessment is neither unreasonable nor counter-intuitive when viewed against other characteristics of the disturbances, and against trends which were operative during the period. In particular, the incidents tended to cluster in time following a few dramatic events such as the massive Newark disorder in July 1967 and the assassination of Martin Luther King in April 1968. Also the entire time interval during which disorder occurred in larger numbers itself concentrated within a few years in the mid-1960s. It is difficult to conceive of the kinds of developments in individual communities which could account for this sudden and practically simultaneous occurrence of hundreds of outbursts.

4. That black political violence did not carry over into the 1970s was a result of the massive deployment of repressive strategies of social control involving new weapons, new riot tactics, new anti-riot legislation and new federal programs. Law enforcement federal military training schools trained national guard, army and local police units; revenue-sharing funds were spent disproportionately on local law enforcement; and new anti-guerilla SWAT teams were established. The political trade-off switched towards guns and away from butter. Equally important, the riots of the 1960s had incurred enormous costs, given the paucity of long-term benefits. Thousands of people had been arrested and injured; hundreds had been killed. The black community had destroyed many of its homes and its shops. In the absence of a unified political movement, the utility of further collective violence appeared marginal indeed.

Chapter 8

The Costs of Urban Power

The black urban riots of the 1960s suspended the calculus of social control.[1] During the height of the rioting in 1967 and 1968, some 10 000 persons were injured, 100 000 arrested and 300 killed (Feagin and Hahn, 1973). In some cities, the police fired indiscriminately at blacks. In others, a massive deployment of federal troops brought the violence to an uneasy end. As the armoured cars rumbling down the boulevard made clear, the central cities were occupied.

The riots expressed both the success and failure of the civil rights movement, which had legitimated black political mobilization. Elimination of racial restrictions in labor markets could not increase the demand for low-skilled labor in the central city, nor could it appreciably improve the wages at which such work could be had. The origins of urban poverty lay not in market imperfections, but in the logic and location of profitable production (see Chapter 3). When the rioting was over, the large division separating civil rights leaders and the ghetto community was painfully apparent (Skolnick, 1969).

Black violence politicized the black community even more than did the civil rights movement. Countless voices rose to speak on behalf of blacks. Black violence empowered those voices, to which the city now listened intently. The riots enhanced the efficacy of more normal forms of black participation. The black's role within the Democratic Party became more volatile. If labor accommodated black demands for more jobs, ethnically balkanized public services and racially restrictive craft unions were threatened. The Italians ran this, the Poles ran that and the Irish ran something else. Yet more rioting would mean less investments and fewer jobs. Further, the riots undermined support on both sides of the color line for the electoral coalitions that had engineered central city redevelopment (Mollenkopf, 1976). As black communities intensified their resistance to urban development and their demands for public jobs, the Department of Housing and Urban Development rapidly increased the construction of low-income housing units (Button, 1978). Whites then intensified their opposition to black encroachment on their neighborhoods and share of the public's goods. They voted for law-and-order mayors. They also voted with moving vans that took them to the suburbs.

Central city blacks – whether riot participants or not – viewed the riots as political rebellions, tactics that many thought would have significant political and economic effects (Aberbach and Walker, 1973; Campbell and Schuman, 1968). Whites, on the other hand, viewed the riots as criminal aberrations to be forcibly contained. The riots were a violent coda to a decade of individual resistance to structural unemployment, police harassment, inadequate housing and poor public services. By shattering a fragile coalition, black violence quickly led to parallel politicization of white ethnic neighborhoods. The politics of bureaucratic turf, of inter-neighborhood distribution generated expensive interactive demands for patronage and protection.

City governments could do little about the structural sources of urban poverty. They could do nothing to change the fact that many of the small firms remaining in the central city had to pay low wages if they were to survive. They could not reverse the deterioration of low-rent slum housing except by transformations that ended with new, wealthier tenants.

In short, city governments could not solve the blacks' problems, but they could manage them. They could convert demands for private jobs into a supply of public ones. They could divert protests against public programs into competitions for public spoils. They could convert participants in movements for power into clientele for new services.

The riots terrified both corporation and union executives who established urban affairs programs, stepped up non-white hiring and financed black businessmen (Perrow, 1972; Powledge, 1970). Organizations like the Urban Coalition were formed, bringing corporation executives, union officials, civil rights leaders and local government administrators. The Coalition sought to galvanize local support for expanded government services for minorities, greater local participation in federal programs and more private hiring and job training for minorities. Similarly, in concert with the Federal Government, the National Alliance of Businessmen provided hundreds of thousands of jobs for blacks. So too the US Chamber of Commerce rapidly expanded its urban affairs programs, aimed at everything from crime protection to manpower training.

The War on Poverty was intensified and the Model Cities program was launched, supplanting the more political role of Community Action Programs. If the former worked through symbolic participation, the latter stressed coordination of existent programs and symbolic administration. Yet Model Cities agencies lacked statutory authority to modify the programs they were to coordinate. They could only infuse them with more money.

The riots also ushered blacks into local politics. Shortly after the rioting, blacks captured the mayor's offices of Cleveland, Gary and lesser cities. Blacks were elected to city councils and appointed to committees and commissions. As blacks came to power, they expanded social welfare spending and slowed bureaucratic growth (Welch and Karnig, 1978).

But as city government scrambled to deliver more services and more jobs to blacks, calls for 'law and order' became deafening. Cities stock-piled riot technology, spending thousands in local funds for tear-gas training, armored cars, steel helmets and helicopters. Congress treated the riots as a problem of crime, transforming collective violence into individual felonies and misdemeanors. The 1968 Omnibus Crime Control and Safe Streets Act created the Law Enforcement Assistance Administration, which financed research on riot technology and reimbursed cities for their helicopters and other weapons. The US Army and federal police agencies expanded their intelligence systems, enabling them to anticipate riots (Button, 1978). Still, local governments remained the primary agents for repressive control. Even in 1974, local governments employed almost 70 per cent of all criminal justice employees (Quinney, 1977: 115).

Guns and butter: the economics of power

When a minority group openly and consistently violates the rules of political empowerment, governments must calculate the costs of containment with some precision. Concessions aimed at restoring social peace can be interpreted as weakness, thus stimulating further mobilization and, what is worse, counter-mobilization among groups – perceiving infringements on their traditional prerogatives. Because concessions often cannot solve the problems which provoke revolt, repression is often necessary to enforce the limits of reform. But repression too has its social costs. Repression which is too complete can harden resistance, by reducing the 'consent of the governed' so essential to social peace (Rosett and Cressey, 1976). The solution is to concede and repress simultaneously, hoping for an effective balance. Concessions legitimate repression, while repression requires strategic concessions to prevent full-scale rebellion. In short, gun barrels must always be buttered.

Political violence has been a common complement to most struggles for power. Cities facilitate mass organization because they are the place of primary popular contact with the government. As a result, their histories are filled with the blood of citizen and state. And yet there is little research to inform us of the conditions under which a government will either grant concessions to those who rebel or repress them with counter-violence. We know little about why men and women rebel, but we know even less about what they get when they do.[2]

A recent work by Tilly (1978) suggests an initial framework to explain the extent to which collective political mobilizations are repressed or tolerated. Tilly argues that the larger the scale of action (number of participants, duration, degree of force), the more likely the state is to try to repress the group. On the other hand, the more powerful the group, the more likely the state is to tolerate it (Tilly, 1978: 111–12).[3] The argument that large-scale rioting leads to repression, while at the same time more powerful black communities secure patronage, fits with the notion that state control involves a delicate balance between repression and concession. But I would also argue that concessions won by violence, whether or not they were an announced goal of the rioters, are also contingent on the dominant political powers which constitute the status quo. For example, in cities experiencing riots, corporation and urban power should affect both the patronage and the repression stemming from votes and violence.

A group's political power is in part a function of the resources they can bring to bear in the local polity. Specifically the ability of the blacks to secure greater patronage and more services should come both from their potential electoral strength and the intensity of their political violence. But this power to command patronage and services also depends on the resources controlled by groups with which the blacks must deal.

I contend that the efficacy of black numbers and black violence depends on the class structure of local political power. Black power and black violence affect the interests of these powerful organizations. Accordingly, the city's response to black power and black violence should be determined not simply by the nature of the challenge, but also by the nature of those whose power and interests are challenged.

The policy impact of the riots

Several studies have measured the impact of the urban riots on public policy. For example, in an analysis of forty cities, Button (1978) found that federal grant increases to the cities were an outcome of riot activity. The cities experiencing riots between 1963 and 1968 received more Office of Economic Opportunity (OEO) funds in 1967-9, relative to funds they received in 1965-7. On the other hand, riot activity between 1963-70 had a distinctly negative effect on OEO expenditure increases between 1970-2, relative to 1968-70. From these data Button argues, logically enough, that while the riots were originally effective in securing federal largesse, they later lost their punch. Perhaps political orientation makes a difference. The Nixon administration (1968-74) seemed to be trying to punish black violence. Local riot activity increased the level of federal funds for low-income housing flowing into the cities, but there was no linear relationship between local riot activity and the inflow of federal funds for riot control.

Button concludes that political violence is likely to produce material benefits when governments have ample resources (as the Federal Government did until the 1968 escalation of the Vietnam war), when it is not too frequent so as to lose its bargaining power; where it is accompanied by limited, concrete objectives paralleled by specific stratagems of political empowerment.

Button's study is the most comprehensive analysis to date of the federal response to the urban riots, being concerned particularly with the riots' impact on the distribution of federal funds to ghetto areas. Yet the study is limited by the measure of federal funding it used. This is in part a technical issue, in part a theoretical one. Measures of expenditure growth are frequently correlated with the initial level from which they deviate. Thus, cities which have initially low levels of expenditure often exhibit precipitous increases, but cities with initial high levels of expenditure show more moderate patterns of subsequent growth. Accordingly, findings of a negative or low effect of riot activity expenditure growth may indicate only that cities which had large numbers of riots also had high pre-riot expenditure levels.

More theoretically, I have argued that local public policies were an important determinant of local riot activity (see Chapter 7). From this point of view, the models used by Button are misspecified, with potentially misleading results. For example, Button estimates the impact of 1963–8 riot activity on the growth of OEO funding in 1967–9, relative to that of 1965–7. This scheme uses as the denominator of the dependent variable what could be considered an independent variable, a determinant of riot activity. Whether the impact of pre-riot poverty funding on riot activity is stronger or weaker than the impact of riot activity on post-riot poverty funding remains an empirical question.

Other studies also have found that urban riots have had significant policy effects. For example, Welch (1975) studied all cities over 50 000 (n = 310) and found that riot cities had larger increases in inter-governmental police funding than cities which had experienced no riot. Given the fact that most of the cities Welch studied had experienced a riot, this dichotomous characterization of a city's riot activity does not sufficiently differentiate between the 310 cities. Various analyses have also looked at the impact of major riot activity on welfare expansions, primarily a state and county function rather than a city function. Jennings (1978), for example, found that state welfare rolls expanded in response to rioting and in response to changes in the unemployment rate (see also Albritton, 1979; Piven and Cloward, 1979). All told, the evidence suggests that the urban riots affected expenditure patterns at all levels of government.

Method

The impact of black numerical strength and black violence on repression and patronage was assessed by regression analysis. The level of police funding in 1970 and the level of personal spending in 1970 was regressed on the numerical strength of the non-white population and the aggregate severity of black violence in 1967–8. Controls were made for the level of police and personnel spending at a point in time before major black rioting took place. This lagged control for the endogenous variable is an alternative to potentially artificial change scores. Using this technique, the net effect of pre-riot patronage on post-riot patronage, for example, summarizes unmeasured causal relationships which are operating at *both* points in time but are not estimated in the model. Estimating the impact of the initial level of this variable on its later level is an alternative to using a direct measure of change as a dependent variable, which assumes a particular relationship between spending levels over time, net of other variables.

To assess the impact of corporation and union power on the city's patronage and repressive response to black political challenge – whether by numbers or by violence – the cities were split into high and low corporation and union power. The cities' post-riot level of police and personnel spending was regressed on black numerical strength and aggregate riot severity in each group of cities (high and low corporation power, high and low union power). The differential efficacy of numerical strength and riot activity in different groups of cities was then used to infer the impact of corporation and union power on repressive and patronage responses to black disruption.

Measurement

Black power was measured by the numerical strength of the non-white population as a percentage of total city population in 1960. Greater relative numbers give blacks more influence in the local polity (Morlock, 1974).

The scale of black political violence was measured by the aggregate severity of the most intense riot experienced by the city in 1967 and 1968 (Spilerman, 1974; also see Chapter 7).

Repression was measured by the per capita spending for police in 1970 and 1960 (*City Government Finances*, 1970–1; *County and City Data Book*, 1962).

Patronage was measured by the level of personnel spending in 1970 and 1965.[4] This consists of all monies paid by the city for compensation of its employees, before deductions for taxes or retirement contributions. This measure taps the level of increased spending for employment, improved quality or level of labor-intensive services and increased benefits to existing workers.

Finally a measure of city poverty, the percentage of a city's families with incomes below $3000 in 1960, was used to tap both the potential demand for public services and the city's capacity to pay for them. Its bivariate relation to median income, a traditional measure of local fiscal capacity, is very strong.

Data analysis

How do black power and political violence affect a city's use of repression and patronage? How does corporation and union power affect city governments' response to such power and violence? The results are presented in Tables 8.1–4.

Tables 8.1 and 8.2 indicate that corporate power in the

TABLE 8.1 *Corporate power and the sources of urban patronage expansion, 1965–70: dependent variable, per capita personnel expenditure, 1970*

Independent variables	High corporate power			Low corporate power			Statistical significance of $b_1 - b_2$
	b^H	(B)	t	b	(B)	t	t
Personnel costs, 1965 per capita	172.5	(0.92)	19.1**	128.5	(0.83)	11.8**	—
Percentage poor, 1960	−0.23	(−0.11)	2.1	−0.09	(−0.09)	1.1	—
Percentage non-white, 1960	0.02	(0.03)	0.6	0.08	(0.14)	1.6*	1.36
Black violence aggregate severity, 1967–8	0.004	(0.08)	1.8**	−0.002	(−0.06)	0.9	2.31‡
	$n = 58$	$r^2 = 0.89$		$n = 69$	$r^2 = 0.69$		

* significant at 0.10 level (one-tail).
** significant at 0.05 level (one-tail).
‡ significant at 0.05 level (two-tail).

TABLE 8.2 *Corporate power and the sources of urban repression, 1960–70: dependent variable, per capita police expenditures, 1970*

Independent variables	High corporate power			Low corporate power			Statistical significance of $b_1 - b_2$
	b	(B)	t	b	(B)	t	t
Police costs, 1960 per capita	0.002	(0.76)	9.2**	0.0014	(0.62)	7.5**	—
Percentage poor, 1960	−0.03	(−0.11)	1.3	−0.04	(−0.33)	3.3‡	—
Percentage non-white, 1960	−0.004	(−0.04)	0.5	0.015	(0.22)	2.2**	2.47‡
Black violence aggregate severity, 1967–8	0.0015	(0.23)	3.0**	0.0007	(0.13)	1.6*	2.53‡
	$n = 58$	$r^2 = 0.78$		$n = 69$	$r^2 = 0.63$		

* significant at 0.10 level (one-tail).
** significant at 0.05 level (one-tail).
‡ significant at 0.05 level (two-tail).

determination of local policy makes a difference. Black power has no effect on public employment expansion in high corporate power cities, while in low corporate power cities, blacks were able to translate their numbers into employment expansion after the riots. Nor did high corporate power cities respond to black power with increased repressive capacity. The cities with low corporate power, on the other hand, increased their police spending in response to the numerical strength of the non-white population.

Although the impact of black numbers was unimportant in cities with high corporation power, the political productivity of black violence was much greater. In high and low corporate power cities, black violence led to large increases in police expenditures.

Repression was an omnipresent response to intense black violence, but high corporate power cities took a significantly more repressive response to that violence than did low corporate power cities. Violence begat violence in both types of cities. It was only in high corporate power cities that black violence also led to expansions of the public payroll. In low corporate power cities, black violence was singularly ineffective in prying loose more public patronage.

Union power also makes a difference, but of a different kind. In cities with high union power, unlike cities with high corporate power, black power increases the level of municipal patronage. In cities where unions are powerful, the patronage effect of black power is greater than where they are not. The impact of black power on repression is also positive in strong union cities. In weak union cities, black power has no effect on the expansion of repression.

Union power also makes a difference to the impact of black violence. In high union power cities, black violence increases the level of municipal patronage. In low union power cities, it has no effect. The impact of black violence on repression is not affected by union power. High union power cities are as likely to meet black violence with increased repressive capacities as low union power cities.

TABLE 8.3 *Union power and the sources of urban patronage expansion, 1965–70: dependent variable, per capita personnel expenditure, 1970*

Independent variables	High union power			Low union power			Statistical significance of $b_1 - b_2$
	b	(B)	t	b	(B)	t	t
Personnel costs, 1965 per capita	143.6	(0.81)	12.9**	174.8	(0.95)	22.1**	—
Percentage poor, 1960	−0.25	(−0.15)	1.8‡	0.01	(0.01)	0.22	—
Percentage non-white, 1960	0.10	(0.13)	1.5*	0.025	(0.05)	1.0	1.46*
Black violence aggregate severity, 1967–8	0.006	(0.13)	2.0**	0.0005	(0.01)	0.23	2.2**
	$n = 66$	$r^2 = 0.80$		$n = 61$	$r^2 = 0.90$		

* significant at 0.10 level (one-tail).
** significant at 0.05 level (one-tail).
‡ significant at 0.05 level (two-tail).

TABLE 8.4 *Union power and the sources of urban repression, 1960–70: dependent variable, per capita police expenditure, 1970*

Independent variables	High union power			Low union power			Statistical significance of $b_1 - b_2$
	b	(B)	t	b	(B)	t	t
Police costs, 1960 per capita	0.0019	(0.70)	10.5**	0.0015	(0.66)	6.1**	—
Percentage poor, 1960	−0.076	(−0.32)	4.3‡	−0.008	(−0.06)	0.5	—
Percentage non-white, 1960	0.03	(0.23)	3.0**	−0.003	(−0.05)	0.5	4.26‡
Black violence aggregate severity, 1967–8	0.001	(0.16)	2.4**	0.0009	(0.19)	2.0**	—
	$n = 66$	$r^2 = 0.84$		$n = 61$	$r^2 = 0.52$		

* significant at 0.10 level (one-tail).
** significant at 0.05 level (one-tail).
‡ significant at 0.05 level (two-tail).

Local power, local interests

Although corporate and union interests in both soft and hard strategies of social control were shaped by the extent and manner in which blacks were contending for power, the question remains as to whether corporation and union power have an effect on public expenditures which is independent of local social conditions. To answer this question, the regression analyses presented above were maneuvered so as to generate intercepts, which compare the two groups of cities (high *v.* low corporation power cities; high *v.* low union power cities) while assuming that the two have the same local social characteristics. The adjusted intercepts, and their statistical significance, are presented in Table 8.5.

TABLE 8.5 *Corporate and union impacts on police and personnel expenditures, 1970: adjusted intercepts*

Intercept	Difference		Statistical significance of difference
	High–low corporation power	*High–low intercept ratio*	
Personnel	+ 0.018	117%	1.05
Police	+ 0.008	158%	2.13*
	High–low union power	*High–low intercept ratio*	
Personnel	− 0.05	68%	2.64*
Police	+ 0.0014	92%	0.36

* significant at 0.05 level (two-tail).

High and low corporation power cities spent equally on personnel. However, high corporate power cities spent significantly more on police than did low corporate power cities, when controls for local conditions are made. High union power cities spent considerably *less* on personnel than did low union power cities when local conditions were controlled. They spent equally for police, unlike high and low corporate cities.

These results suggest that the impact of corporation and union power was not entirely contingent upon local political challenge. High corporation power cities tended to be heavily armed, while high union power cities tended to have lower levels of personnel expenditure. However, when local conditions threatened their power, union cities were highly responsive to black political challenge.

Discussion

The results are summarized in Table 8.6, which indicates the conditions under which black power and black violence have significant positive effects. As expected, large-scale black political violence uniformly provokes an expansion in the repressive efforts of local governments. This occurs regardless of whether corporations or unions are locally powerful. Black

TABLE 8.6   *Class power, black power and the determinants of patronage and repression*

| | Corporate power | | |
| High | | Low | |
Patronage	Repression	Patronage	Repression
—	—	Black power	Black power
Black violence	Black violence	—	Black violence
	Union power		
High		Low	
Patronage	Repression	Patronage	Repression
Black power	Black power	—	Black power
Black violence	Black violence	—	Black violence

violence also produces a cooptive response – an expansion of public services and employment – but it does so only where the power and interests of large corporations and labor unions are at stake. Where corporate and union power are absent, popular violence only begets state violence. In such cities, blacks probably faced more conservative political authorities whose power base lay in smaller, less profitable firms and unorganized workers. Thus, whether political violence sparks an expansion of the public pork barrel depends on the class composition of local political power.

On the other hand, black power does not uniformly lead to

an expansion in municipal patronage. Cities where blacks were numerically powerful did not always increase their employment and service levels after the riots. The patronage impact of black power is conditional upon the level of union and corporate power. High union power cities responded to black power with both patronage and repression. In low union power cities, powerful black communities faced only expanded local repressive capacities. In high corporation power cities the reverse took place. Corporate cities did not respond at all to the numerical strength of the black population. Only in low corporate power cities did black power lead to expanded local public employment.

Thus the powerful union cities responded to both black power and black violence with patronage and repression. In weak union cities, blacks faced only increased repression. Powerful corporate cities, on the other hand, responded only to black violence. That corporations were responsive to violence and not to votes, while unions were responsive to both, suggests the different bases of corporation power and union power. For the corporations, the containment of black politicization was a strategic problem of pacification, of diffusing opposition to the city's growth program. Corporation élites are ideologically opposed to redistribution and welfare expansion, and union élites favor such expansion (Barton, 1975). Thus corporate power stood between the black electorate and city hall. It took black violence to wrest concessions from corporation élites. Numbers were not enough.

For the unions, black politicization was a more fundamental problem. The political power of the unions depends on electoral arithmetic. Corporations can invest and not invest, thereby encouraging the city to do their bidding. Labor unions must rely on their leverage at the polls and within the Democratic Party. Black numbers, especially volatile black numbers, threatened these bases of union power. Then, like an ambivalent lover, the unions came down on the blacks with both concessions and fists.

Notes

1. I am indebted to Don Cressey for his critical and editorial comments on this chapter.

2. In a historical survey of groups which mobilized an unorganized constituency in the US between 1800 and 1945, Gamson (1975) found that those who were willing to violate the political rules – including prohibitions against use of violence – were most successful in winning concessions from the government and in building their membership. However, the low comparability between these different movements – from the Christian Front Against Communism to the Tobacco Night Riders – makes it difficult to assess the effects of protest *per se*.

3. The causes of repression are also said to be functionally determined by the problems of controlling a surplus labor supply. Economic downturns throw large numbers of people out of work and thus weaken the social controls implicit in work. Because the state cannot control the sources of crime – poverty and unemployment – it must control the criminal. Thus admissions to US prisons rise and fall with the unemployment rate (Jankovic, 1977a, 1977b). Sutherland and Cressey (1978) discuss several other theories pertaining to relationships between social structure and repression.

4. This patronage measure would include some percentage of police personnel. This would decrease the probability of obtaining different findings for patronage and repression. The obvious question is why not use black or non-white local public employment figures. I tried to obtain these figures from the Equal Employment and Opportunity Commission but was not successful.

Chapter 9

Central City Fiscal Strains: The Public Costs of Private Growth[1]

Corporate and union power shaped city responses to the violent breakdown in social control. Public employment expanded rapidly in the wake of the riots, as cities attempted to pacify those who found little place in the city's emerging economy. This imposed new costs on the public budget. Corporate and union power also shaped the city response to the constraints on economic growth. Public capital spending, such as urban renewal, also grew in response to the emerging office economy. This too imposed new costs on the public budget. Did the public policies of social control and economic growth have a role in generating fiscal strain, the symptoms of which first became visible in the 1970s? How effective was the new economic growth in counteracting the fiscal strains normally attributed to industrial and residential decline?

Urban fiscal strain

By the mid-1970s, fiscal strains began to afflict many American central cities. Tax burdens increased. Cities turned to the state and federal governments for revenues. City debt charges consumed an ever larger percentage of current expenditures. Unable to make ends meet, cities resorted to short-term borrowing at high interest rates. The technical default experienced by New York City was only the most dramatic and visible symptom of a syndrome variously experienced across the country.

Conventional wisdom locates the origin of urban fiscal strains in the economic decline of the cities, their inability to stimulate private growth – in jobs, in housing construction, in population. Such economic decline erodes the tax base and intensifies the demands of the resultant low-income residents for public jobs and public services. A declining revenue base, when combined with expanding popular demands for public spending, leads to increasing tax burdens. Thus the remaining businesses and residents endure an ever growing tax burden and mounting incentives to move out of the city.

The public costs of economic decline were expanding public budgets to provide sustenance to a dependent, increasingly non-white population. The growing political strength of this dependent population undercut the political power of city leaders, and thereby provided an opportunity for the rising militance of municipal workers (Piven, 1975). Slowdowns, sick-outs and strikes disrupted municipal services in cities across the country. At the same time that the revenue base was eroding and demands for services increasing, wage costs were also escalating.

The remedies which flow out of such an analysis are straightforward and painful. The public household must be put in order. Not only must the municipal unions be stopped, but unproductive social services and public employment must be cut back. The city's residents, particularly its poor residents, must sacrifice today in order to provide incentives in lower taxes and more infrastructure spending that will lure private investment to the city tomorrow. Thus the Municipal Assistance Corporation of New York has called for a reduction in

the disproportionate tax burden on those persons and businesses whose continued presence in New York City is peculiarly significant to its survival as a great metropolitan community [cited in Marcuse, 1980: 37].

Those whose tax burdens should be reduced, the banker-dominated agency argues, include corporate headquarters, manufacturers, high-income families and the financial community. Because the city is vulnerable to the geographical mobility of its tax-payers, it cannot provide redistributive services to those who do not pay taxes without pushing out those who do (Peterson, 1979; Piven, 1974; Bahl *et al.*, 1978). Cities simply cannot afford to support the idle, the poor, the unproductive segment of the city's population. Especially at the city level, there are no free lunches.

The problem with the received wisdom is that it doesn't ask who's paying for dinner. The analysis makes assumptions which have not received empirical scrutiny. It assumes, most importantly, that the public benefits of economic growth are larger than the public costs. Local private investments are assumed to increase the tax base and thus reduce local tax burdens. Further, local private investment should increase local incomes and thus decrease the demand for public services and public employment which can now be obtained in private markets. Private incomes will substitute for public incomes. Finally, it assumes that the public investments required by local private investment are self-financing. The pouring of public concrete should generate enough taxable private investment to pay for itself. The more sanguine view suggests that they will reduce tax burdens by stimulating private investments that would otherwise not take place.

In this chapter, I want to provide a preliminary empirical examination of these assumptions by analyzing the sources of central city fiscal strain in the 1970s.

Explaining urban fiscal strains

The analysis of urban fiscal strain, and the location of its sources in various aspects of economic decline, has become a growth industry. I shall review some of the already vast literature.

In an analysis of fiscal differences in twenty-seven cities with 500 000 or more population, Muller (1975a) showed that those cities which lost population between 1960–73 experienced most fiscal strains. Population decline is associated with a declining tax base, due to the fact that emigrants have higher income levels. Those cities who lost most population also lost employment and were unable to adapt through annexation of adjacent territory with higher-income residents. The resultant low-income population has more demand for public services, but has less ability to pay for them (see Logan and Schneider, 1979). At the same time as the city is losing low-skill, blue-collar jobs and gaining higher-skill, white-collar jobs, it is gaining unskilled residents and losing skilled residents (Kasarda, 1979). The growing mismatch of jobs and residents, exacerbated by the lack of transport access to suburban unskilled jobs and the comparative advantages of suburban secondary workers, only reinforces central city poverty. While declining cities have declining fiscal capacity, they must also continue to provide supportive services for businesses which occupy a relatively large percentage of the city's total property, and pay relatively high wages to municipal workers due to high costs of living and strong unionization.

Clark and Ferguson (forthcoming) have made one of the only comprehensive comparative political analyses of spending and tax habits of large US cities during the 1960s and 1970s. They argue that the fiscal impact of citizen preferences depends upon the stability and homogeneity of a city's social composition. Where cities experience rapid shifts in residential composition and increases in social heterogeneity, there are high levels of uncertainty about citizen preferences. During such periods, organized political activity and leadership preferences come to dominate spending decisions. Their findings suggest that fiscal strains emerged during the late 1960s and early 1970s when black political mobilization pushed up expenditures and municipal unionization increased the level of compensation. The resultant taxation burdens were opposed to the preferences of the urban middle class; and in those cities where they were numerically strong, spending increases were smaller and retrenchment in the mid-1970s was greater. Thus fiscal strains result from the lack of political power by the increasingly fiscally-conservative urban middle class, whose preferences became more important as social and political conditions stabilized.

That economic declines have been concentrated in the central cities of the older northeast has struck many fiscal observers. Between 1970 and 1975, northeastern cities lost employment at an annual average rate of 2 per cent, while southern city employment grew at 3.2 per cent (Bahl *et al.*, 1978: 9). Older cities lose more employment during periods of national economic decline, and grow more slowly during periods of growth (ibid: 29).

Gordon has argued that a city's physical form reflects the stage of capitalist development at which it reached maturity. Delineating three stages – commercial, industrial and corporate – of capitalist growth, Gordon (1977: 108) argues:

> A city grows rapidly until it reaches the size appropriate to its economic functions and its place within the urban system. When cities reach their own 'level', their growth begins to slow.

Fiscal strains reflect the difficulty that old cities have in adapting to structural changes in the economy. Thus old cities have declining employment and high levels of fiscal stress (see also Howell and Stamm, 1979, below).

In part the economic declines of older, northeastern cities reflect the comparative advantages of the 'new' southern and western regions of the US. Such old cities are at a comparative disadvantage due to their high wages, high unionization and more expensive energy costs (Sternlieb and Hughes, 1977; Marcuse, 1980). But labor cost differentials may not be so important given that major industries must often import labor, as well as the unions, to their new locations (Mollenkopf, 1979). Mollenkopf (1979: 29) argues that it is the low fiscal costs of adapting the new locations to new forms of private investment that is their main attraction:

> The Southwestern cities, being largely built on a clean slate, did not require the massive redistribution of land and employment under way in the Northeast during the 1950s and 1960s. Indeed, Southwestern society remained so racially segmented and politically underdeveloped that little need be spent on resident population to assure political stability.

Some analysts have focused on the problematic nature of urban capital spending as a source of fiscal strain. Older cities also have an aging public capital stock and must upgrade it to remain competitive with younger cities for private investment. Yet at the same time, older cities face mounting current expenditure demands and declining fiscal capacity. Rising public employment demands on limited revenues may undercut their ability to finance the infrastructure necessary to stimulate private investment (Phillips, 1979; Howell and Stamm, 1979). High current expenditures associated with large dependent populations, high tax burdens and low private investment levels all inflate borrowing costs by lowering city bond ratings.

The borrowing problems of declining cities were exacerbated by the downturns in the economy in the late 1960s and mid-1970s. The financial intermediaries who purchase the bulk of tax-free municipal bonds increase their bond purchases during periods of expansion in order to reduce tax liabilities (Boast, 1977). As a result of these economic downturns, which hit the older and less productive industrial plant of the older cities hardest, these cities had to pay more to raise capital to provide the infrastructure necessary to attract new private investment. The disadvantage of northeastern cities was compounded by their greater reliance on general city governments, as opposed to special districts, to finance capital spending (Boast, 1977). When compared to special districts which have accounted for a growing share of all borrowing, such cities are seriously disadvantaged in the capital market.

In a study of sixty-six cities between 50 000 and 1 000 000 in population, Howell and Stamm (1979) found that a city's industrial age was an important determinant of fiscal stress.

Cities in their early growth stages generally have rapid and extensive private sector investment as well as substantial population growth. As cities pass into the stage of industrial maturity, there is a fall-off in investment and, in turn, a sustained loss of manufacturing employment [ibid: 8].

Industrial age was operationalized by changes in industrial employment and population between 1950 and 1970. The study analyzed mean fiscal performance characteristics within differentially aged cities. In aging industrial cities, public capital expenditures increase rapidly, but they have a much smaller effect in 'leveraging' private investment. Further, the erosion of the tax base is accompanied by higher demands for public services and public employment. An economically sound and growing economy provides revenue growth while simultaneously taking pressure off the expense side of the budget by providing job opportunities to population groups that would otherwise become heavily dependent on municipal social services (Howell and Stamm, 1979: 54).

Because federal grants to the cities are targeted to geographical concentrations of adversity – like unemployment, poor housing and poverty – rather than low levels of private investment, declines in the local tax base are not accompanied by increases in federal revenues. As a result, cities have higher tax burdens, as measured by taxes per capita and taxes as a percentage of personal income. Howell and Stamm (1979: 24–5) suggest:

> Maintaining the economic base through private investment is critical to maintaining revenue from local sources. In younger cities, this investment occurs relatively spontaneously. However, maturing and older cities must allocate both capital and services toward maintaining this process. In some cases this may require difficult trade-offs between immediate social services versus long-term job opportunities and tax base growth. But the private–public investment partnership is essential in dealing with potential fiscal stress.

The uneven distribution of private investment among cities appears to explain the geography of fiscal strain. Yet some have argued that while the differential location of private investment may create large private benefits, the governmental structure assures that it also creates larger net public sector costs (Marcuse, 1980; Bluestone and Harrison, 1979). Inter-city competition for private investment leads to public investment *de novo* in areas where private investments are expanding, and underutilization of existent capacities which could have been upgraded at less cost (Marcuse, 1980: 21). The absence of any locational controls on private investment lead to suboptimal production of public infrastructure. The social costs of private investment loss, as well as the resultant inefficiencies of public service delivery, must be borne by the municipalities no longer favored by private investors. Finally, government policies are biased towards new investment, thereby shortening the useful life of existent private and public investments and accelerating mobility (Marcuse, 1980; Peterson, G., 1978).

But even in those cities which are the recipients of new investment and population growth, the public costs of growth may outweigh the public benefits. In a study of Santa Barbara, Appelbaum *et al.* found that all growth trajectories, 1974–2000, which varied by zoning and density characteristics, would result in more rapid increases in expenditures than revenues (1976; Appelbaum, 1978). The result would be an increase in property tax rates. The anticipated net revenue losses were particularly striking for water, waste-water and general fund categories (Appelbaum *et al.*, 1976: 142–222).

Central city fiscal strains: a description

The fiscal strains of central cities emerged between 1965 and 1975. It was during this period that municipal worker unionization, black riots and inflation increased the costs of political peace. Population declined and industrial loss intensified. But it was also the period when central cities' downtown economies expanded skywards and public infrastructure was built as a foundation for this new growth.

In this decade the central city's revenue structures changed dramatically. Tax burdens on the central city's population continued to increase. This increase in tax burdens per capita was above the level of increase in current wages, indicating a real cut in disposable incomes. Faced with growing tax-payer resistance, an eroding tax base and mounting costs and expenditures, central cities tapped other sources of revenues. Sales taxes, fees and user charges increased much more rapidly than traditional property taxes. More profound in its implications for local control, was the meteoric rise in the central city's dependence on revenues from state and federal governments. In ten short years, the average central city increased the revenues it received from higher levels of government some nine times! (These figures do not adjust for inflation.) In 1965, inter-governmental revenues were less than half as large as local tax revenues. By 1975 the average city received as much inter-governmental revenues as local taxes. For many cities, such strategies to obtain more revenues were still insufficient to cover the revenue–expenditure gap. As a result they entered short-term capital markets to cover expenses, borrowing at high interest rates to make ends meet. While many cities did not resort to such borrowing, those that did, did not do so as a temporary expedient. For municipal budgets to approach the red became a common phenomenon. Short-term borrowing accelerated over the decade.

What was driving this rapid expansion in taxation, short-term borrowing and dependence on state and federal revenues? To be sure expenditures for city employees were increasing rapidly, faster than tax revenues. Municipal union strategies of bargaining for increased municipal contributions to their pension programs is evidenced by the ever more rapid increase in municipal contributions to retirement programs. The costs of fringe benefits for pensions, social security and health insurance grew faster than wage costs in private industry, and by the mid-1970s accounted for up to one-half of the pay for time actually worked (Bahl *et al.*, 1978: 23–5).

But municipal capital expenditures were increasing just as rapidly as current expenditures. Municipalities borrow in different forms, forms which correspond to the function performed by the capital expenditures which they finance. Debts backed by the 'full faith and credit' of the municipal treasury are generally used to pay for projects which improve the general welfare but do not have direct and discernible impact on taxable private investment. They consequently require the approval of the city's electorate. Parks, schools and hospitals are examples. Non-guaranteed debt, however, lacks such a general obligation on the part of the municipal treasury. Rather it is used to finance projects which increase local profitable investment which can be taxed or otherwise charged. The local electorate does not have strong political controls over such municipal debt. Such non-guaranteed debt was used increasingly for industrial aid bonds where cities subsidize land building and equipment acquisition for private firms. The findings indicate that while the first general obligation form of borrowing was increasing slowly, at a rate roughly comparable to increases in tax revenues, non-guaranteed forms of debt were increasing considerably more rapidly. The percentage of total state and local bond value approved by the electorate dropped consistently since 1968. In 1968, referendum-approved bond value accounted for more than half of all bond value. By 1975 the percentage was down to something like 10–15 per cent (Peterson, G., 1978: 58–9).

The sources of fiscal discomfort lay not simply in the demands of the urban poor and public workers who were then unraveling long-standing political alignments. They lay also in the public capital programs which accompanied new forms of central city economic growth.

The sources of urban fiscal strain

Cities clearly vary. Did those cities in fiscal distress conform to the conventional image: old cities with declining population, militant unions and decaying downtowns? What role did different factors play in exacerbating a central city's fiscal difficulties in the mid-1970s? In this last section I will model the sources of urban fiscal strain.[2]

Municipal budgets have two sides: current and capital. Analyses of the local finances have focused their attention and criticism on the software of public finance – expenditures for public employment, social services and transfer payments. Such public expenditures are used to provide public employment for those who cannot find private jobs and public services for many who cannot buy them in the market place. Such expenditures constitute a significant component of the social wage and as such are consumed by the resident population.

But there is the other side of the local budget which, like the other side of the moon, has not received careful scrutiny. Such hardware expenditures, whether financed by borrowing, user charges or current expenditures, are used for physical construction. A large portion of all local capital spending was for infrastructure necessary to local private investment – in offices, industrial plants and new houses. Such public capital spending was for physical inputs into the investment process, benefits capitalized in the profitability of local business. Such expenditures constitute a component of social capital and as such are consumed by the local private investors.[3]

It is generally assumed by analysts of current expenditure that it does not stimulate subsequent taxable private investment and thus increases tax burdens. Such social wage payments are generally redistributive, and whatever increased effective demand results is likely to leak out of the local economy. Capital expenditures, on the other hand, are assumed to produce collective benefits *in excess* of their costs and thus are self-financing (Steiss, 1975; Peterson, 1979). Consequently, capital spending should be less likely to increase subsequent fiscal burdens. What was the relative impact of these two forms of municipal expenditure in generating central city fiscal strains?

That local public revenues are dependent upon taxes is one of the facts of fiscal life. Local taxes, in turn, are ultimately dependent upon private incomes. Private incomes are ultimately dependent upon private investments in the locality. The virtuous circle of investment, employment and income thereby increases the level of local taxable resources. Local economic growth is consequently argued to be self-financing, a boon to the local treasury (Bahl, Jump Jr and Schroeder, 1978). Surveying the economic decline of many central cities, public finance analysts came to gloomy predictions about the consequences for the fiscal future. What were the actual fiscal consequences of growth?

By the mid-1970s local frictions between citizen and state had taken form in political conflict between home-owners and municipal workers. Central cities relied heavily upon property taxes, which by 1976 still accounted for over two-thirds of all local taxes. For the home-owner such taxes were highly visible, held down property values and could not easily be passed on. Home-owner agitation for lower property taxes gradually became a groundswell of national significance. Municipal workers were also organizing during this period for higher wages, better working conditions and more fringe benefits. If home-owners wanted to limit revenues, the city's workers wanted to increase compensation and employment. How significant were these two groups in the shaping of local fiscal strains?

Measurement

To measure *local fiscal strains*, three different measures will be used. Local taxes per capita, 1975; local property taxes per capita, 1975; and short-term debt per capita, 1975 (*City Government Finances*, 1975–6; 1965–6). Local tax burdens reflect the total tax liability per person. This measure has been found to be highly correlated with tax effort, the ratio of taxation to local income (Howell and Stamm, 1979). It is used because cities vary in their reliance on property taxation. Local property tax burdens reflect the tax liability experienced by property owners, both residential and commercial. Finally, short-term borrowing (debt repayable within one year of issue) reflects a relatively expensive means to cover short-falls in revenues, whether to pay for interest obligations or operating expenses. Increasingly, central cities used the short-term borrowing market, indicating serious fiscal strains.

To measure *local economic growth* various dimensions of growth will be used: increase in number of office-serving business establishments, 1963–72;[4] the number of national corporate headquarters per capita, 1966; the total number of new residential units constructed in 1961 and 1966 per capita, 1960; the level of new industrial investment per establishment, 1963; and the percentage decline in population, 1960–75 (*Census of Business*, 1972; *Fortune*, 1967; *Construction Reports*, 1961 and 1966; *Census of Manufacturing*, 1963; *City Government Finances*, 1975–6). Office activity, residential construction, industrial investment, population growth[5] – in various combinations these were the components of urban growth.

To measure *municipal union militancy*, the frequency of municipal strike activity was used as of 1967 (*Municipal Year Book*, 1967). An ordinal scale was constructed ranging from 0 to 5.

To measure *home-owner strength*, the percentage of all household units which are owner-occupied as of 1960 was used (*Census of Population and Housing*, 1969).

To measure *growth-related capital spending* I used three categories: highway capital spending per capita, 1970–5; sewage capital spending per capita, 1970–5; and urban renewal capital spending per capita, 1970–5 (*City Government Finances*, 1970–1; 1975–6). The capital expenditures were totaled over the two time points both because of their lumpiness and thus potential unevenness in capital spending, as well as the cyclical nature of capital spending. These forms of capital spending were regressed on the various indicators of local economic growth to assess the assumption that they were growth related. Each was significantly related to different growth components, even when the previous level of capital spending and other relevant variables, like median income, were controlled.[6]

To measure local spending for *public employment*, local personnel services expenditure per capita 1975 was used (*City Government Finances*, 1975–6). This measure captures all expenditure for any form of compensation to municipal employees and is thus an aggregate measure of expenditure for labor-intensive public services. It includes all monies paid to city employees before deduction for taxes or retirement contributions. This variable includes the impact of black power and black violence (see Chapter 8).

To measure central city internal revenue dependence, the percentage of all general revenues which are raised from the city's own sources as of 1970 is used (*City Government Finances*, 1970–1). Cities which raised the bulk of their own revenues might be more sensitive to the local tax consequences of local expenditure decisions. This variable will also control the functional responsibility for revenue raising.

To measure central city characteristics likely to affect fiscal capacity, costs of service delivery or needs for public expenditures, a number of variables are used: age of city, median income and population density. City age which indicates the public costs of land-use change is measured by the year the city first reached 25 000. Median income, measured in 1960, is both a measure of local fiscal capacity and a

potential source of demand, depending on the income elasticity
of demand for public expenditures (Borcherding and Deacon,
1972; *Census of Population*, 1960). This control allows us to
interpret the net tax effects as indicating determinants of
strain. Finally, population density indicates both the costs of

TABLE 9.1   *The central city's changing revenue structure, 1965–75**

	Revenue per capita	
	1965–70 % change	1970–75 % change
Taxes, all	48%	47%
Property taxes	35%	35%
General sales taxes	59% (35)	92% (54)
Current charges	73%	107%
Inter-governmental revenue	193% (129)	266% (129)
Short-term debt	310% (88)	526% (87)

* Number of cases is 130 central cities with population of 100 000 or more in
1960 unless otherwise stated in parentheses. Inflation is not controlled.
SOURCE: *City Government Finances*, 1965–6, 1970–1 and 1975–6; US
Department of Commerce, Bureau of the Census, 1967, 1972 and 1977.

TABLE 9.2   *The central city's changing expenditure structure, 1965–75**

	Expenditure per capita	
	1965–70 % change	1970–75 % change
Personnel	56%	78%
Retirement	83% (105)	103% (106)
Current, total	70%	86%
Total capital spending	101%	81%
Gross debt outstanding	47%	42%
Long-term debt	43%	49%
Full-faith and credit debt	31% (128)	49% (127)
Non-guaranteed debt	343% (101)	143% (98)
Long-term debt issued	239% (92)	300% (85)

* Number of cases is 130 central cities with population of 100 000 or more in
1960 unless otherwise stated in parentheses. Inflation is not controlled.
SOURCE: *City Government Finances*, 1965–6, 1970–1, 1975–6; US Department of Commerce, Bureau of the Census, 1967, 1972 and 1977.

service delivery, older pre-automobile pattern of urban settlement, as well as the areal size of the incorporated city. Density is measured as the number of thousand persons per square mile in 1960 (*County and City Data Book*, 1960). These three variables have been found to be important determinants of municipal expenditures (Appelbaum, 1978; Mushkin and Cotton, 1969).

As an alternative to change measures, the level of taxation and borrowing ten years earlier (in 1965) is included as a control. If the model is improperly specified and variables have been left out of the model which affect the dependent variable (taxation or borrowing) across the decade, then the effect of this variable will be inflated. This estimation of the relationship between taxation or borrowing across the decade cannot be taken as a measure of trend, given that it would include residual correlation across time.

Empirical findings

The relative impacts of these different factors: infrastructure spending, local economic growth, constituency characteristics and other local ecological conditions are presented in Table 9.3. Those variables which are statistically significant determinants are summarized, along with their standardized effects in Table 9.4.

Looking first at the determinants of a city's *total tax burden*, different forms of infrastructural spending have different effects. Highway spending has no effect, while sewage spending reduces tax burdens and urban renewal increases them. Most forms of local economic growth do not reduce the local tax burden. Indeed growth in the office economy increases the local tax burden. Only a city's resident population growth is associated with a lower level of tax burden, probably due to the ability to annex higher-income adjacent population. As expected, cities with more militant municipal labor unions have significantly higher tax burdens. Conversely, cities whose populations are largely composed of home-owners have lower tax burdens. Cities with high median incomes do not have significantly lower levels of tax burden.

TABLE 9.3 *The sources of central city fiscal strain, 1975*

Independent variables	Tax per capita, 1975			Property tax per capita, 1975			Short-term debt per capita, 1975		
	b	B	t	b	B	t	b	B	t
Highway 1970–5	0.13	0.03	0.8	−0.03	−0.01	0.2	0.19	0.04	0.5
Sewage 1970–5	−0.20	−0.07	1.48*	−0.01	−0.01	0.1	−0.18	−0.05	0.6
Urban renewal 1970–5	0.35	0.08	1.78†	0.44	0.10	2.6††	0.94	0.19	2.1††
Corporate headquarter dominance 1966	162	0.01	0.4	379	0.03	0.97	1789	0.14	1.8†
Office growth 1963–72	0.005	0.09	2.3††	0.001	0.02	0.5	0.002	0.05	0.6
Industrial investment 1963	0.00	0.01	0.2	0.00	−0.01	0.4	0.9^{-5}	0.22	2.4††
Housing construction 1961–6	−0.002	−0.01	0.3	0.006	0.03	0.9	0.002	0.01	0.1
Population growth 1960–75	−2.17	−0.07	1.6*	−0.43	−0.01	0.4	0.51	0.01	0.2
Municipal union militance 1967	0.006	0.08	2.5**	0.002	0.02	0.8	−0.001	−0.01	0.1
Home-owner strength 1960	−0.14	−0.15	2.4**	−0.16	−0.17	3.1**	−0.05	−0.05	0.4
Median income 1960	0.00	0.00	0.2	0.00	0.01	0.5	0.8^{-5}	−0.04	0.5
Personnel exp. 1975	0.24	0.27	3.6**	−0.01	−0.01	0.2	−0.02	−0.02	0.2
City age	0.002	0.06	1.17	0.001	0.03	0.6	0.002	0.04	0.4
Population density	0.00	0.00	0.00	−0.004	−0.14	2.7††	0.001	0.026	0.2
Internal revenue independence	0.06	0.06	1.27	−0.02	−0.02	0.5	0.00	0.00	0.007
Tax per capita, 1965	138.7	0.62	7.9**	—	—	—	—	—	—
Property tax per capita 1965	—	—	—	192	0.88	17.4**	—	—	—
Short-term debt per capita 1965	—	—	—	—	—	—	0.91	0.62	6.7**
	$r^2 = 0.94$		n = 84	$r^2 = 0.95$		n = 84	$r^2 = 0.74$		n = 84

* significant at 0.10 level (one-tail).
** significant at 0.05 level (one-tail).
† significant at 0.10 level (two-tail).
†† significant at 0.05 level (two-tail).

TABLE 9.4 *Determinants of central city fiscal strain, 1975: significant variables, beta coefficients*

	Tax per capita, 1975	Property tax per capita, 1975	Short-term debt per capita, 1975
Sewage	—0.07	—	—
Urban renewal	0.08	0.10	0.19
Corporate headquarter dominance	—	—	0.14
Office growth	0.09	—	—
Industrial investment	—	—	0.22
Population growth	—0.07	—	—
Municipal union militance	0.08	—	—
Home-owner strength	—0.15	—0.17	—
Personnel expenditures	0.27	—	—
Population density	—	—0.14	—

High levels of personnel expenditures also significantly increase the total tax burden. Finally older cities, dense cities and cities with a strong revenue independence do not have higher total tax burdens. The effect of internal revenue dependence is positive, but not significant. This effect is partially artifactual given that cities which raise revenues locally obtain them through taxation.

Looking second at the determinants of a city's *property tax burden*, no infrastructural spending is associated with lower property tax burdens. Urban renewal spending is again associated with high levels of property taxation. No form of local economic growth significantly reduces local property tax burdens. While cities with a strong home-owner population again have lower levels of property tax burden, municipal union militance has absolutely no effect. Personnel expenditures also have no effect on property tax burdens. Cities with high median incomes again have no higher or lower property tax burden. And older and fiscally self-reliant cities again have no higher levels of property tax burden. Dense cities have lower levels of property tax burden.

Finally, the determinants of *short-term indebtedness* exhibit an interesting pattern. Highway and sewage spending do not lead to lower levels of short-term debt. Cities with high levels of urban renewal spending again have higher levels of short-term debt. This relationship is partially explicable by federally backed, short-term bond issues in support of urban renewal. Cities with strong local economies again do not have lower levels of fiscal strain. On the contrary cities with a strong corporate office economy and those whose industrial plants are making new capital investment have high levels of short-term debt. Unlike the determinants of taxation, neither municipal union nor home-owner strength have any effect on short-term debt, nor do personnel expenditures. High-income cities, old cities, dense cities and fiscally autonomous cities also do not have higher levels of short-term debt.

Discussion

Contrary to conventional wisdom and widespread policy prescription, local economic growth does not reduce local fiscal stress. Those localities with strong patterns of investment in industry, office and housing do not have lower tax burdens. On the contrary, strong downtown office economies have high levels of tax and short-term debt burdens. Only population growth appears to be associated with lower levels of tax burden.

The public infrastructure spending to accommodate local private investment is alleged to have salutary, or at least neutral effects on the local fisc. This appears to be the case for local sewage expenditures which reduce subsequent local tax burdens, and for highway expenditures which have no discernible effect on fiscal stress. Such is not the case for urban renewal. Local redevelopment expenditures appear to exacerbate local fiscal strains.[7] Contrary to the advertisements of local redevelopment supporters who argued that renewal would stimulate private investment that would not otherwise have taken place and thereby increase the tax base manifold, the data suggest otherwise. While redevelopment may have increased private investments on the site, it may also have involved serious fiscal losses elsewhere in the city. Not only does the redeveloped land remain fallow for a period, but the new sites compete with business activities elsewhere in the city; urban renewal takes other taxable lands off the rolls for parking and transit, and the city must absorb the social costs of population displacement leading to unemployment and public dependency. While the present research cannot specify the source of this relationship, it suggests that urban renewal was not a fiscal boon to the local treasury.

Home-owners were a significant force in holding down local tax burdens. Sensitive to highly visible taxes once or twice a year, absorbing these taxes out of their disposable income and watching these taxes affect the sale value of their only capital, their homes, home-owners were increasingly mobilized against property tax expansion.

The municipal unions were an important force in pushing up local tax burdens. Union demands for higher wages, better working conditions and more fringe benefits forced cities to increase their tax burden. But public employment expenditures were increasing for other reasons as well. In response to structural unemployment, to the role of the local government in stimulating a city economy which provided them little place, which destroyed their housing while policing their streets, the city's black community had rebelled. Black political violence had left its mark on the trajectory of public employment, as local governments scrambled to provide jobs and services to a community which had long been marginal to city politics. High levels of public employment, rooted in the militance of municipal workers and the black community, now made their contribution to fiscal strains.

In sickness, as in health, there are two worlds of public finance. When revenues don't cover expenditures, the local government can turn to its resident tax-payers or to the banks. The politics of these two forms of bandaging are different. To obtain the latter, the city turns to financial institutions with strong links to the interests of local investors, who calculate the wisdom of the loan in terms of its effects on their behavior. To obtain the former, the city turns to its residents who calculate the bite of the burden in terms of the services they receive.

The data suggest an asymmetry in the determination of the symptoms of fiscal strain. Local economic growth has fiscal costs, costs borne equally in higher taxation and short-term debt. The expansion of public services and public employment is also costly, but these costs are not absorbed through local borrowing, only taxation. It is striking that neither local economic growth, nor expansion in the costs of public employment, make an impact on property tax burdens. The costs of local economic growth and public employment expansion were probably absorbed by other forms of local revenues – sales taxes and user charges. Home-owners and enterprises shared one thing – property. It was this common liability to an undifferentiated form of property taxation that was the basis of a deepening political bond.

Conclusion

By the mid-1970s, fiscal strains afflicted many US central cities. The technical default of New York in 1975 was a dramatic example of underlying national trends. Rising expenditures and limited tax revenues forced cities into higher tax rates, greater short-term debt and accelerating dependence on state and federal finance. Yet urban residents resisted public service cutbacks, as well as the increasing cost they bore to finance them. Those who owned homes resisted the growing tax burden most intensively and with greatest effect. Public workers, who were increasingly well organized, used their ability to mount paralyzing strikes and to provide the infrastructure of electoral support to resist cuts in public employment and public wages. In part, the fiscal strains of the 1970s were a reflection of these divergent political forces which pulled at the public's purse strings with growing ferocity.

In the face of economic downturn in 1974–5, dominant investors in the cities demanded more subsidies, better infrastructure, fewer restrictions on location and effluence, and yet lower taxation. This economic decline and the power it gave to urban business certainly exacerbated the tendency for fiscal strain. It did not create it however. The fiscal strains of the 1970s were not the result of economic decline, but of the nature of urban economic growth.

Private growth was publicly expensive because it increasingly failed to provide employment and income for the city's residents, and because it made demands on the public purse for infrastructure expenditures which were not self-financing.

On the one hand, new economic growth in the central cities did not provide sufficient employment and income benefits to the central city's residents. Industrial jobs were taken by suburbanized union workers. Construction work was dominated by restrictive craft unions. And the new office economy was drawing on the better educated, better heeled, suburban workforce. Industrial investments were now part of vast multilocational networks of plants, thus weakening the local multipliers from local plant investments. This export of the income benefits of local economic growth meant a continuous reservoir of poor, structurally unemployed people who turned to city governments for jobs and services.

On the other, the rising office economy of the central city required a restructuring of urban space to move people and information most efficiently. This required a massive investment in public capital for mass transit, parking, urban renewal and the more traditional forms of infrastructure. The urban electorate was decreasingly willing to approve bond issues at the polls. To protect these infrastructural investments from popular pressures, their design and financing were put beyond the reach of electoral controls. Through new forms of revenue and tax increment bonding, through autonomous special districts which rose rapidly in number over the period, the public infrastructure of private economic growth was structurally insulated. (Even within the city, capital planning was frequently not integrated into the city financial management system.) Such structural insulation – appointed agencies, banker committees and private investor clientele – assured that the projects would be evaluated in a businesslike manner. The local business clients argued that such public investments would pay for themselves, or that perhaps the city, and its other bond obligations, would be jeopardized if it didn't back new capital spending. Out of this structural insulation and the absence of a social accounting that electoral influences would make necessary, private investors were able to obtain public largesse that was not self-financing. The intense competition between cities (and states) for private investment allowed them to further sweeten the deal (Molotch, 1976; Apilado, 1971).[8]

There were two worlds of local expenditure: one oriented to providing services and public employment for the city's residents, the other to constructing the infrastructure necessary to profitable private investment. These two worlds – of social wage and social capital – were structurally segregated. The former was governed by electoral politics and the excesses of patronage. The latter was housed in bureaucratic agencies, dominated by men of business who survived by their efficiency. The politics of consumption appeared irrational and inefficient, a hog trough of benefits for those who couldn't begin to pay for them and probably didn't deserve them. The local politics of production appeared rational and efficient, a politically neutered self-financing building program.

The resultant rise in local tax burdens fell most visibly on those most able to resist them – the home-owners. It was the home-owners who pushed most vigorously against expansion in taxation and spending. Their populist success eventually became a movement of national import. When the central city home-owners began to resist, they turned against those groups which were most politically vulnerable – the urban poor and municipal workers. In some places, the property tax revolt was married to an anti-statist ideology, proclaiming the ills of excessive public intervention. The populist wildcard was again played in American politics, but against the losing hand.

The local organization of private investment remained unquestioned, untouched and unruffled. Movements for exclusionary zoning and growth controls were only intimations that there were social costs to growth, costs which higher-income communities were best able to refuse to pay (Logan, 1976). That a locality's residents should capture a share of the private benefits of local investment and should not be forced to bear its public costs was not yet part of the central city's political agenda. A rough and uneasy political coalition began to emerge linking corporations whose interests lay in profits and corporate growth, labor unions anxious to protect employment and home-owners eager to protect their declining incomes from rising tax burdens. However, it is a coalition that can become unglued by local political limitations on the public spending necessary to private investment (McWatters, 1979) by mounting unemployment and by the inadequacies of public services.

Since the recession of 1974–5, city governments have reversed the previous decade's continuous growth in local public employment. Given the difficulty of increasing productivity, let alone measuring it, this suggests serious declines in municipal services. The ability of central city residents to substitute private services for public has been remarkable. Private security systems now patrol commercial buildings and higher-income residential neighborhoods. Private schools increasingly substitute for public. The privatization of public life is limited by income. Whether the private adaptation to public poverty will be extensive enough to provide a new political majority for public austerity remains to be seen.

But fiscal constraint has also been achieved at the cost of serious local reductions in economic infrastructure. In 1965, gross capital investment was 20 per cent of all municipal general spending in the forty-eight largest city governments. By 1977, it was down to 13 per cent (Peterson, G., 1978: 52). According to Peterson, urban fiscal stress has been associated with drastic reductions in capital spending. New York, for example, cut capital spending by half and local contributions to the capital budget by 80 per cent, after the fiscal crisis (*ibid*: 57). Tax limitation initiatives have undercut the ability of local governments to borrow against general revenues and limited the increase in revenues associated with new private investments. This has seriously undercut the ability of cities to make public capital investments.

Reductions in urban capital spending, particularly for economic infrastructure, may ultimately reduce the profitability of local private investment. The deterioration of the central city's capital stock due to the deferred maintenance, has attained crisis levels. Events such as the collapse of NYC's West Side Highway and estimates that some 50 per cent of its water now leaks out of the antiquated distribution system are serious indicators (Peterson, G., 1978). The actual replacement cycle for NYC roads is 150 years, for Los Angeles 130 years. Technical studies indicate that repaying should be done on a twenty-five-year cycle.

The ability of the city to provide economic infrastructure now depends increasingly on its ability to use new capital expenditures to stimulate private investments whose taxability can be tied to finance the public investment. The rise of revenue bonds and user charges reflects this option. It also depends on the growing role of the Federal Government, whose share of local economic infrastructure spending has increased. The federal share for highways, waste-water, mass transit and airport project grants have all increased since 1972 (Peterson, G., 1978: 60).[9] Finally it depends on the ability of cities to force local businesses to absorb directly the public infrastructure costs of local private investment. George Peterson (1978: 56–7) notes

the increasingly severe capital construction requirements imposed on developers by local communities. These typically require that developers install roads, sewer and water systems, and recreational areas at their own expense . . . In rapidly growing southern and western communities as much as one-half of the total value of assets added to public ownership come from 'private' investment of this type. Nationwide, in the range of $4 billion to $5 billion per year probably is spent by private builders on public capital construction.

Because tax reductions are tied both to declines in municipal services and economic infrastructure, the survival of a local coalition around public austerity is uncertain. It depends on the ability of central city residents to obtain sufficient income from local private investment to obtain the services they require from the private market, and upon the ability of central city investors to obtain the public infrastructure at sufficiently low cost to maintain profitability. The current solution appears to take spending decisions for economic infrastructure ever more completely out of the hands of the central city electorate and to reduce the dependency of the middle-income electorate upon public services. The result will be to further bureaucratize social capital, while returning social wage policies to the market.

Notes

1. I am grateful to Harvey Molotch, Merrie Klapp and Jimy Sanders for criticism of an earlier draft of this chapter.

2. As will become clear it is a tentative and incomplete model. The structure of causes and consequences of local public budgeting are not well understood; none the less it is a first approximation.

3. This is what Hansen (1965) calls 'economic overhead capital'.

4. To check the possibility that the effects of headquarter or office employment were associated with high levels of communication and potential 'suburban exploitation', the percentage of central city employment by place of work that was resident in 1970 was controlled. This did not have a significant effect on any of the three measures of fiscal strain. It was not included in the analysis because of the serious loss in cases that would result from missing data.

5. Cities were differentially able to expand through annexation. The impact of population growth and residential construction will reflect this, as well as employment declines.

6. Industrial investment and headquarter location were significant determinants of urban renewal; population growth of highways; and office growth, industrial investment and population growth for sewerage. The effects of the various measures of local economic growth upon fiscal strain are effects net of their indirect effects through public spending on infrastructure.

7. An alternative and benign interpretation of the positive net effect on tax revenues per capita of urban renewal spending is that this reflects an increase in aggregate tax revenues due to increased aggregate economic activity. To date, I have seen no aggregate local economy studies that suggest a net effect on total levels of economic activity. Indeed, my own initial studies suggest that urban renewal did not have a net effect on industrial or residential construction levels, although it might have affected their location (Friedland, 1977).

8. Two-tailed tests were used where the relationships were not in the direction hypothesized in the literature, or where no relationship was hypothesized.

9. President Reagan's search for budget cuts may reverse that trend.

Conclusion: The Structure of Power

The fiscal strains which emerged in the 1970s were not simply the result of economic downturn and militant public sector unionism. They had their roots in past policies of economic growth and social control, and in the powers of corporations and unions which shaped those local policies – policies which catalyzed intense breakdowns in local social control.

The black riots of the 1960s had a local political logic. Public clearance for private property, for example, not only helped provoke severe black riots, but probably did not make a net

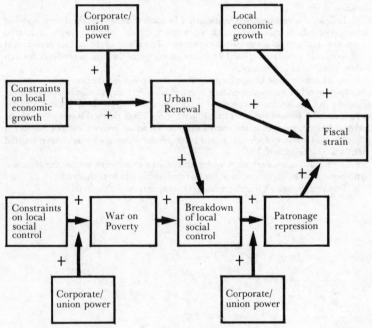

FIGURE C.1   *Power, policy and contradiction*

contribution to the public treasury. Indeed, even the new pattern of local economic growth seemed to eat up more in public expenditure than it contributed in public revenues.

Figure C.1 shows the causal logic of the book. Corporate and union powers shaped local policy responses to local constraints on local economic growth and social control. These policies had consequences – breakdowns in social control and fiscal strains – which were not anticipated or subject to control. These were the contradictions of power because they produced new constraints on economic growth and social control.

The impact of corporate and union power

Corporate and union powers shaped the central cities' policy responses to local economic and social conditions. Public policies intended to stimulate economic growth or maintain social control were not automatic responses to local constraints upon economic growth and social control. Neither did corporate or union power affect local policies similarly wherever they were locally powerful. The local powers of national corporations and labor unions influenced which local conditions affected public policies and which did not. More important than the effects of corporate or union power on policy, were their effects on the determinants of policy. The results point beyond technocratic or instrumental models of local policy-making.

Corporate and union powers were not the same. The differences between them are reflected in the policies on which those powers had greatest impact and the local conditions whose policy impact they shaped. Urban renewal was intended to stimulate local economic growth, particularly office growth. In cities where corporations were powerful, constraints on office growth – built-up land-use, inner-city slums and tax constraints on the provision of a new economic infrastructure – motivated those cities to adopt urban renewal. In cities where corporations were not powerful, such constraints did not motivate the adoption of urban renewal. Where corporations were powerful, a high level of office-serving urban renewal was adopted, regardless of local conditions; where they were not, the level of such urban renewal was considerably lower.

Labor unions were less powerful in determining policies intended to stimulate economic growth. In cities where unions were powerful, comparable constraints on industrial investment did not lead cities to adopt industrial urban renewal, nor did union power, by itself, motivate those cities to adopt a larger industrial renewal program.

Corporate power shapes the process of policy-making for economic growth in a way that union power does not. National corporations controlled the dynamics of the urban economy which urban renewal was designed to affect: labor unions did not. For the corporations, urban renewal was a way to manage growth; for the unions, to combat decline.

The War on Poverty, the expansion in public employment and the growth in local police capacity were all designed to sustain local social control, the first two through cooptive incorporation and the last through repression. Again corporate and union power had different effects on the determination of social control policy. The fundamental source of revolt was the cities' blacks, whose numbers and ultimate violence threatened the policies of economic growth, the powers of the corporations and unions, and ultimately the economic functioning of the city. The power of the urban blacks to participate – whether inside or outside the confines of electoral channels – had to be controlled.

In those cities where corporations were powerful, blacks were better able to convert their numbers into federal War on Poverty funds, but *less* able to secure higher levels of local public employment and public expenditure. In cities where corporations were powerful, only black violence engendered a local response – both cooptive and repressive. Further, cities where corporations were powerful adopted a more repressive policy, independent of the local political threat that blacks posed.

In those cities where unions were powerful, blacks were also better able to convert their electoral strength into federal poverty funding, *and* were also better able to obtain higher levels of local public largesse. Further, cities where unions were powerful had higher levels of public employment independent of local black political power. As in the case of corporate power, union power increased the policy impact of black violence upon both cooptive and repressive forms of social control policy.

Union power shaped the process of policy-making for social control in a way that corporate power did not. The national labor unions were highly dependent upon their ability to organize mass political participation, which these policies were designed to affect. For the unions, public sector expansion to sustain the electoral allegiances of the blacks was essential to their power base, while to the corporations it was not. The unions remained as ideologically supportive of such public sector redistribution as the corporations were opposed. None the less, black power threatened the unions – their exclusion of non-whites, their support of growth policies which hurt the black communities and their power-broker role in many local Democratic parties to which the blacks were allied. Thus while powerful black communities were more likely to receive higher levels of public employment and public services, they were *also* likely to face a more repressive local state response where the unions were powerful. For the corporations, black electoral strength did not threaten the bases of their local powers, which were economic. While black violence was threatening to corporate power, black numbers were not. As a result black communities were likely to face more repression only when they took to the streets.

Thus corporate powers are rooted in their control over the local economy and those powers seem to have greater impact on the economic determination of public policies designed to affect the economy. Union powers are rooted in their mobilization of the masses, and those powers seem to have greater impact on the political determination of policies designed to affect that mobilization.

State intervention to stimulate the local economy is not a technocratic response to the limits of local growth. State intervention in response to the demands of the populace is not an automatic political market response to their electoral power, nor simply a strategic response to the requirements of pacification of a rebellious citizenry. The response of the state to the economy and to its citizens depends upon the organizational structure of political power.

The local organizational structure of national corporations

and unions is a critical element of the local power structure. Their powers did not derive from the voices of their organizational élites who spoke out for and against public policies. Their powers derived from the different resources they controlled: their control over the economy, their privileged position in the structure of the local state and their ability to organize the participation of others. Thus corporate and union powers did not necessarily depend upon the voices of their élites, but could shape public policies without speaking.

Just as voices may be powerless, powers need not have voices to be heard. The silent powers of national corporations and unions shaped the cities' policies of economic growth and social control.

The sources of political power: participation, structure, system

The concept of 'political power' is a powerful one. Conflicts over its meaning and empirical measurement are endemic to social research. Part of the divisiveness over its meaning reflects a diversity of *sources* of power to which different groups have access.[1]

Political power is commonly thought of as the ability of individuals or groups to influence government actions. Such an approach locates the source of power in the political *participation* of individuals, groups or organizational élites. Similarly, the political power of corporations or labor unions is measured by observing their participation in the resolution of political issues that generate controversy and contention. Power is conceptualized as *influence* over government action or inaction. Those who study political participation as a source and an indicator of political power ask: who governs, who rules? This view of political power typically assumes that the government is either a neutral instrument – a pliable bureaucratic tool which can be used equally by all potential participants – or an unbiased political market in which all can participate.

A second approach to political power rejects the assumed

political neutrality of the state. On the contrary, it views the *structure* of the state within which public decisions are made as a source of political power. The structure of the state is considered a cause of political organization and consciousness, a determinant of the kinds of issues and participants that can penetrate the political arena.

Analyses of participation as the primary source of political power tend to map the participants, their stratagems and the outcomes in single units of analysis: program, decision, policy area. This assumes that the points of government policy-making and the groupings of participants who swarm about them can be analytically isolated. It also assumes that the government aggregates across different interests as indicated by the aggregation of participation rates across the issues (see Clark, 1968). The participational approach does not analyze the political relationship between the components of government, between the policy arenas they manage and thus between the groups which they differentially absorb.

To be sure, the political relationship between social groups is fought out in particular policy arenas. But the structural approach illuminates the fact that one of the most important political relationships between social groups is their distribution within the government apparatus. Some groups have access to local governments, while others are concentrated at the national level; some gain the ear of elected representatives, while others are beholden to bureaucratic agencies; some depend on highly politicized programs, while others benefit from routine government allocation year after year.

Thus the organization of the state mediates the political relationship among social groups. The structure of the state is a source of power because the organization of political authority differentially affects the level and effectiveness of different social groups' participation. In this viewpoint, the state is not a competitive marketplace where interests are brokered by the government, but a structured battleground where some groups are strategically placed while others are located far from the real centers of power. The structure of the state selects which demands can be handled by the government, and thus which kinds of participants will most easily gain access. It also channels participants into government locations with differential capacities to respond to their demands.

Finally, by implication, the state organizes the political relationship among social groups, such that some groups must regularly confront each other while others rarely do. Structural power is therefore observed in two ways: first, by examining the political effects of a group's location within government – for example, its ability to maintain a program from which it routinely benefits and which is insulated from potential opponents in other government locations; second, by examining those critical junctures when new structures of political authority are created. Such reorganizations in the structure of authority involve more than a victory over the selection of government personnel and the policies they pursue. They involve the organizational bedrock of political power, conceptualized as domination.

During the Progressive period, for example, corporate-backed reformers successfully restructured the governments of many cities. These reforms – the shift from ward to city-wide elections, introduction of non-partisan elections, shrinkage of city council size and institution of an appointed city manager – shifted the pattern of political participation and the power of different participants. In particular they reduced the power of political parties.

Non-partisan elections made it more difficult to align the working-class vote systematically, and city-wide elections made it more difficult to elect working-class candidates to office. The city manager system, including the rise of a local civil service merit system together with the absence of partisan organization for electoral office, reduced the legislative accountability of city agencies, rendering them more vulnerable to the most intensely organized and economically important interests (Hays, 1969; Williams and Adrian, 1963; Alford and Lee, 1968; Morlock, 1974). During a period when city governments were rapidly taking on new functions as a result of urban industrialization, the reformed government structure allowed the economic interests who were most dependent on the city's efficient performance of these functions to insulate them from potential political challenge by the new urban working class, then organizing an urban-based socialist party. If those who search for the source of power in participation ask *who* governs, this approach asks *how* they govern.

A third approach locates the source of political power in neither the participation of actors, nor their ability to maintain politically biased governmental structures. Rather, it argues that the nature of the social system in which a government operates limits the policies that can be adopted and implemented. The social system's limit on public policy is *systemic* power.[2] All social systems can be described in terms of the social relationships which produce and allocate the most important values. Continuity in their production and allocation is of importance to all members of society, and also to the government whose effectiveness and legitimacy depend upon the groups which can provide it.

As long as the government is imbedded in a particular social system, it must confront the power of those who control the processes of production and allocation of key values. The power does not derive from their superior political organization, but from their control over the material conditions which generate both the problems which the government must solve and the solutions from which it must choose. In the USA, private ownership organizes the production and allocation of material goods. Such ownership allows private control of local investment, production and employment decisions, decisions which largely determine not only a city's problems but also its policy solutions. Local government structure in the USA – because of its revenue dependency on local taxes and its competitive position in a decentralized market for public goods – reinforces this systemic power of private investors (see Chapter 2).

From this perspective, the political power of local owners derives from their control of local investment and land-use decisions, rather than from their political participation.

Systemic power is observed in the policy impact of those investment and allocation processes which are most important to the local economy, processes upon which local land values, employment, income and taxes are most dependent. It is observed in the large impact of economic growth upon public expenditure and taxation when compared with measures of electoral representation of all kinds (Dye, 1972; Hofferbert, 1972; Schumaker, 1974). And it is observed in the ways in which public policies are more likely to sustain important economic processes than they are to serve those resident citizens who do not benefit from the processes and may even be its victims.

The social system limits public intervention to forms which reinforce capitalist social relationships. Capitalist social relationships – based upon private ownership – shape the ways in which social problems are experienced and the kinds of political solutions which appear viable. Thus, unemployment is often perceived as a defect in the individual's productive capacities, rather than as an inability of the system to make the most productive use of society's resources. Or bad housing is perceived as an absence of sufficient market incentive for the production or sale of good low-priced housing, rather than an inability of a profit-based system to provide adequate housing for all. In the first case, the unemployed demand job training or unemployment compensation. In the second, the ill-housed organize around rent subsidies or rent control. Such political efforts by the victims of economic growth may be successful, even in the face of political opposition. Yet they indicate the systemic power of the owners.

There are three sources of political power: participation which expresses the preference and the electoral powers of those who wish to decide public issues; governmental structures which condition the accessibility of participants to points of greatest public authority; and those social relationships which generate the participants, the problems and interests which motivate their participation, and the solutions among which they are likely to choose.[3]

Corporate and union powers

Corporations and unions drew differentially on these sources of political power. Corporate and union élites participated in the public policy-making of economic growth and social control. National corporate élites dominated the origins of the city's growth programs, while the unions were incorporated as secondary supporters of the pro-growth alliance. The unions, because of their infrastructure for political mobilization, drew their power from their ability to organize the participation of others, to provide the channels for popular influence. Their local power shaped the policy impact those participants could have.

Corporate, and secondarily union, interests were served by urban growth policies, while the central cities' poor and non-white populations were hurt by the same policies. The policies designed to stimulate economic growth, and those intended to provide benefits for the victims of that growth, were housed in government locations that were both different and distant from each other. Policies designed to stimulate economic growth were *structurally segregated* from those designed to sustain social control. Urban renewal agencies which reshaped land-use patterns and thus had some power over the demand for labor and the availability of low-income housing, were structurally distant from agencies charged with housing those displaced by changes in land-use and finding employment for those who could not find work in the city's changing economy. This structure of local authority assured that the beneficiaries of economic growth did not confront its victims.

When the ill-housed and unemployed protested, their protests were often directed against a public housing agency which had no authority to insure low-income housing construction for those persons whom urban renewal displaced. Or they were channeled into poverty and manpower agencies which could not shape the private demand for labor; or they were channeled into demands for the provision of more public services and public employment, rather than into demands that cities use their public expenditure to sustain economic growth so as to ensure greater benefits to local residents from that growth – more public revenues and private employment.

The structural differences between city agencies oriented to sustain social control and private investment are striking.[4] Agencies whose aim is to absorb mass participation, particularly through the provision of public services and public employment, are structured to be relatively accessible to popular influence. Agencies whose aim is to sustain private investment are structured to make popular access difficult and to leave control by private investors unhampered.

Agencies that make land-use and infrastructural decisions which are critical to profitable investment tend to be controlled by officials who are not elected and financed by revenues which do not depend upon electoral approval. There has been a steady proliferation of special districts and public authorities to finance critical infrastructure – ports, highways, water, sewerage, industrial parks. These agencies have independent sources of financing, particularly revenue bonds and federal supports. Such special districts have accounted for a growing share of all borrowing (Boast, 1977). Because they are oriented to capital-intensive services, and because municipal borrowing occurs in a highly concentrated market for private capital, the private investment community is able to assure that such investments are oriented to stimulating profitable local economic activity. Because the resultant profitable investments provide the long-term flow of public revenues – whether in charges or tax increments – necessary to finance such borrowing, these agencies have the greatest potential to generate current surpluses (Boast, 1977). Such surpluses provide these agencies with advantages in the capital market through better credit ratings, minimize their revenue dependency on other jurisdictions, and assure that a large share of the private profits derived from public expenditures are used to refinance other public expenditures which will provide still more profits.

Because such agencies are freed from partisan political constraints, they develop strong clientele relationships with those private investors that have the most intense interests in their policies. Their success depends upon their ability to serve those interests, a dependency intensified by the agency's insulation from electoral control. Because of the greater predictability of private investment behavior, the translucent rationality of profit and the tight bonds which tie the agency to the market, a technical ideology pervades the operation of the agency. The agency clientele understand the complex criteria of public decision-making, given that such agencies themselves approximate the logic of a business. This technocratic lexicon legitimates insulation of the agency and dissuades popular groups who would try to intervene, for it argues that what is being done is not political.

By contrast, agencies which provide public consumption goods and absorb mass political participation are far more visible and politicized. The provision of local public consumption goods – schools, fire, police, parks, transit, health care, housing, welfare – tend to be controlled by municipalities or districts whose officials are elected, and their budgets derive from general revenues which must face electoral approval. Capital spending for such public services is more likely to be raised through general obligation bonds and thus face electoral scrutiny at the polls. Because such services tend to be more labor intensive and supported by current expenditures, their financing is subject to greater political review. Also, since they are provided city-wide and are not targeted to areas of high economic growth potential, their aggregate impact on local private investment is likely to be minimal. Because such services are not self-financing, the jurisdictions tend toward deficit financing which undercuts their relative ability to borrow funds.

The structural segregation of agencies charged with maintaining the profitability of private investment, and those responsible for coping with the public service and public employment demands of the city's residents, insulates the state's role in economic growth from its role in social control, thereby improving its capacity to perform both roles simultaneously.

There are serious limits to this dual welfare state: economic growth and the public infrastructure it requires may not contribute to the government's ability to finance public services and employment; the public infrastructure may not be self-financing; public subsidies may be extracted for private investments that would have occurred without them; public investments will be made to stimulate private investments without regard to their local income and employment consequences; and residents who cannot obtain what they need from the local private economy are likely to make demands for public expenditures which contribute nothing to local profitability and may indeed cut into the public revenues available to stimulate private investment.

Under such conditions, the structural segregation of the government's role in sustaining profitable investment and popular quiescence is likely to be reinforced, leading to private investments with high social costs and social programs with high private costs. The fiscal strains which emerged in the 1970s reflected this perverse logic.

Thus the bureaucratization of the city's growth programs and the politicization of its social control program were a structural source of power for the beneficiaries of central city economic growth, and of powerlessness for the victims. For the corporations, such structural segregation rendered them more powerful without having to participate. For the non-white poor, such segregation increased their participation without increasing their power, thereby increasing the likelihood of local political protest and even violence.

Beyond participation and government structure, the national corporations also drew on a systemic source of power – their control over the dynamics of local economic growth. Thus their presence shaped both the determinants and level of local urban renewal programs designed to stimulate a local economy whose expansion depended on their continued presence. Their systemic power is reflected in the patterning of local conditions which stimulate office-serving urban renewal. Constraints on the growth of the local office economy, centered downtown, stimulated higher levels of office-serving urban renewal in cities where they were powerful. The general problem of slum housing, which was used to legitimate urban renewal, was singularly ineffective as an inducement to local renewal in all cities.

These powers – rooted in the participation of élites and their ability to organize the participation of others, in the structure of governmental authority, in the control of production and allocation – allowed national corporations and unions to shape local policy-making. Because such powers operate silently, they are difficult to observe. The empirical analyses presented above suggest their existence may be indicated by their effects upon local policy-making. To be sure there are other voices with other powers, other interests, which have been omitted from the analysis. Future research will require a more inclusive, more formal modeling of the alliance structure of these groups and how their different powers and interests shape local policy. It will also be necessary to relax the implicit assumption made here of a local state which derives its interests from those who privately appropriate its powers (see Piven and Friedland, 1981). This is but a crude beginning, a suggestion that groups can wield power without participation, that that power can be measured and that group interests can be inferred from those local conditions which affect local policies where groups are powerful.

The current crisis: beyond the welfare states

The central cities of the US remain torn between the politics of economic growth and social control. In part this is due to economic decline – of the industrial economy which undercut the local employment possibilities for the cities' growing poor and non-white resident population; in part to economic growth – of an office economy which draws on non-resident labor. These economic conditions created a large pool of structurally unemployed residents who made large demands on the public economy for jobs and services. But these conditions also made large demands on the city for public capital expenditures, the benefits of which were not captured by a large share of the local population and whose costs – taxation and displacement – they did absorb.

The new economic structure places large demands on the public budget, but does not provide commensurate revenues. The poor resident population makes large demands, but contributes little in revenues. The old forms of industrial investment require that infrastructure be maintained, even though total levels of industrial investment, and thus fiscal productivity, are lower. The new forms of office investment contribute less in revenues than they eat up in expenditures, both directly in new capital expenditures and indirectly in the resident employment displaced or forgone.

Thus the new office economy fails to provide either the local employment necessary to sustain mass political support or the public revenues necessary to deliver public jobs and services that are otherwise necessary to shore up political stability. The central city economies are neither self-legitimating nor self-financing.

Locally, corporations and labor unions have strong interests in sustaining central city economic growth. But the basis of that interest derives primarily from their role in production. For both corporation and union, interests as residents and producers are no longer politically defined in the same localities. The severance of corporate élite production and consumption interests had taken place long before. The capitalist residential community had less and less to do with the localities in which production took place. But the post-1945 period had also witnessed the segmented suburbanization of the American working class. Thus corporate and union organizations approach the problem of managing the local politics of growth in the central city in isolation from their own residential interests.

The policy requisites of political control and economic growth increasingly diverge. As the gap widens, the structural segregation of the two policy arenas also increases. This tends to minimize conflicts between the city's residents, particularly those most disadvantaged in the new economy, and the city's producers. But isolating the politics of public services and patronage from the politics of production and economic infrastructure also assures that the popular and economic shocks experienced by the central city lead to rapid, parallel expansion in current and capital expenditure.

When rebellion erupted in the 1960s, a violent index of the ways in which changing social composition was eroding the power of the local regime, vulnerable political élites responded with large expansions in public employment. When rapid structural changes reshaped the central city economy, local investors were able to dominate the bureaucracies which provided the infrastructure necessary to profitable local investment.

Structural segregation of local social wage and social capital assured that the city's resident population and its investors would not confront each other in the political arena. Conflict was expressed in inter-city confrontations over zoning, annexation and infrastructural siting. But political peace within the central city was purchased at a price. Because public spending to stimulate private investment was depoliticized, local growth policies were not governed by their local employment and income consequences. And because public spending to support directly local living standards was more politicized, the local investment consequences of such public expenditure were not part of the political calculus that governed their expansion.

The result was fiscal strain. The expenditure requirements for social control and economic growth became increasingly competitive. The policies necessary to growth have high social costs while the policies necessary to social control cut into the revenues necessary to support growth.

The Federal Government had, until the election of Reagan, stepped into the breach. The central government increasingly intervened in the 1970s in the local financing of patronage and capital financing. By 1976, federal funds accounted for 60 per cent of all social welfare outlays, which themselves constituted over 20 per cent of GNP (Erie and Brown, 1979). As a result the poor, and particularly the black poor, were increasingly dependent on transfer incomes which originated outside the local political arena. As the federal welfare state absorbed the public financing of the urban poor, the local black population were converted into depoliticized clients for national bureaucracies. So too the central government absorbed an ever larger share of the financial obligations for local economic infrastructure. At the same time, special districts proliferated to finance economic infrastructure. The result has been to reduce city governance to a problem of good housekeeping, and thereby lay the institutional groundwork for fiscal conservatism and anti-statist populism.

A long-term solution does not lie in more progressive and thus redistributive forms of financing public services, nor more regressive patterns of expenditure which more closely serve economic growth. Because of intense inter-city competition for new investment, the former strategy will lead to investment losses to other cities. Because of the structural nature of much urban unemployment and poverty, the latter will ultimately require vast amounts of misery and repression in anticipation of a full-employment recovery that may never come.

A long-term solution requires structural and political

integration of social wages and social capital. The externalization of the social costs of popular power and private growth cannot continue. To maintain popular incomes, whether through public or private spending, the public must be given more control over private investment and government's role in sustaining it. The growing role of the state in capitalization could be used to assure that the local wage and employment consequences of economic growth are part of the political agenda. To maintain profitable investment, the logic of private and public wage expansion must be structurally integrated into the policy framework of economic growth. The growing role of the state in wage formation must be calibrated to the public expenditure requirements of private economic growth.

At both local and national levels of government, the choice cannot be between a Keynesian welfare state and supply-side economics. The zero-sum trade-offs between social wage and social capital are a product of the increasingly segregated structure of politics and policy that house them. The distributional incidence of public revenue must be politically integrated into the distributional incidence of public expenditure. The trade-offs between social wage and social capital must be fought out in the context of the relationship between private wages and private profits. Not to do so will lead to further decomposition of the American state and rising privatism and irresponsibility on the part of both citizenry and state, and we will continue to cycle through fiscal crisis, political conflict and economic stagnation.

It is true that the central city may return to urban civility. Rising energy and housing costs, suburban building restriction, the need for maximum access to a metropolitan job market for the dual-wage family, the rise of the single person household – all these augur well for the return of the political and fiscal balance to the central city. But they will not solve the problem – only move it elsewhere.

Notes

1. The idea that there are multiple sources of political power – participation, structure and system – was originally proposed in Alford and Friedland (1975).

2. In an excellent article, Stone (1980) has also proposed the concept of systemic power as a type of power relationship. Stone argues that systemic power involves the ways in which the relationship between the government and the socioeconomic system predisposes public officials to favor the interests of one group as opposed to another. The 'top stratum' contribute revenues, rather than demand services; they command large-scale organizations with superior capacities for mobilization, as opposed to other groups which either have to rely on mass membership organizations or do not possess organizations at all and thus have inferior capacities for mobilization; and they have cultural advantages and high esteem as opposed to other groups which have cultural disadvantages and lower esteem. Public officials want to maintain revenues, work with private sector organizations which are most capable of visible accomplishments, and work with clients where contact is personally and professionally rewarding. Public officials will therefore favor the interests of the upper strata.

Stone argues that systemic power operates most strongly where popular or electoral constraints are weakest: in the initiation and implementation stages of policy-making, in the interpersonal, labor-intense processes of service-delivery, in those policies which bear upon revenue generation. In his study of urban renewal politics in Atlanta, Stone found that although pro-business proposals were politically advantaged at the preliminary stages of screening and later implementation, they had no advantages over pro-neighborhood proposals at the most visible stages of policy-making. He also found that pro-neighborhood policies required neighborhood pressures to be considered by the government, while pro-business proposals were more likely to be solicited by government officials (see Stone, 1976).

The implication of Stone's analysis is that depoliticization of public policies results in systemic bias. While the predisposition of public officials to large private investors is conditioned by their revenue dependence, it is not clear that the policy benefits businessmen receive are necessarily net producers of public revenue. The systemic bias may allow private investors to cannibalize the state and use its funds and authority to enlarge their private profits without commensurate public benefit.

3. Participation, government structure and social system – each is a source of political power in the city. The multiple sources of political power suggest that three kinds of questions should be asked to map the local power structure.

First, what social groups are the primary participants in local policy-making? Which are influential and which marginal? Which social groups, are dominant in the origin of a policy, its legislative initiation, adoption and implementation? Second, how is public authority organized to formulate and execute local policy? Does the structure of local public authority differentially affect the ability of different groups to influence the public levers appropriate to their interests? Third, what is the dominant logic of the local social system in which policies are adopted? What processes have most impact on the overall performance of the local economy and government? How do these processes affect, and how are they affected by, local policy?

Different social groups in the city have different access to these three sources of political power. Some may control critical economic processes, others may have access to the centers of public decision-making, still others may control votes. The uneven distribution of political resources – systemic, structural and participation – among different groups describes the *resource-specificity* of each social group. The relative efficacy of each of these resources in the determination of public policy describes the *power-specificity* of public policy. The two together – the distribution of political

resources among social groups and the impact of those resources on public policy –
describe the *power structure*.

The distribution of political resources among social groups does not indicate
whether those resources are used, nor their efficacy in determining local policy.
Knowing the distribution of resources may incorrectly predict the distribution of
policy outcomes. The use and policy impact of resources depends on the kinds of
interests at stake in the policies under consideration and the distribution of resources
and interests among other social groups. The consistent disagreement between those
who ask local notables to identify influential groups and those who ask which groups
win particular decisions, indicates the indeterminate relationship between
distributions of political resources and policy outcomes. The former find concentrated
power structures; the latter, dispersed power structures. To determine public policy
outcomes, the study of a power structure must link the distribution of political
resources among groups to the distribution of groups and policies. Thus a power
structure is a distribution of politically effective resources. The old debate between
élitists and pluralists reflects a false dichotomy. The élitists studied power as a capacity
to shape policy, focusing on the distribution of political resources among social groups.
The pluralists studied power as actual victories in decision-making conflicts, focusing
on the distribution of victorious groups among policy decisions.

4. These ideas were first developed in Friedland, Piven and Alford (1977). They are
extended and applied to the conflictual logic of vote and revenue generation in Piven
and Friedland (1981).

Bibliography

AARON, HENRY (1975) *Who Pays the Property Tax?* (Washington, DC: Brookings Institution).

ABERBACH, JOEL and WALKER, JACK (1973) *Race in the City* (Boston: Little, Brown).

ABRAMS, CHARLES (1965) *The City is the Frontier* (New York: Harper & Row).

ABRAHAMSON, MARK and DUBICK, MICHAEL, A. (1977) 'Patterns of Urban Dominance: the US in 1890', *American Sociological Review*, 42, October, 756–68.

ADDE, LEO (1969) *Nine Cities – the Anatomy of Downtown Renewal* (Washington, DC: Urban Land Institute).

AIKEN, MICHAEL (1970) 'The Distribution of Community Power: Structural Bases and Social Consequences', in M. Aiken and P. Mott (eds), *The Structure of Community Power* (New York: Random House).

AIKEN, MICHAEL and HAGE, JERALD (1968) 'Organizational Interdependence and Intra-organizational Structure', *American Sociological Review*, 33, 912–30.

AIKEN, MICHAEL and ALFORD, ROBERT (1970a) 'Comparative Urban Research and Community Decision-Making', *The New Atlantis*, 1, 85–110.

AIKEN, MICHAEL and ALFORD, ROBERT (1970b) 'Community Structure and Innovation: the Case of Urban Renewal', *American Sociological Review*, 35, 650–65.

AIKEN, MICHAEL and ALFORD, ROBERT (1974) 'Community Structure and Innovation: Public Housing, Urban Renewal and the War of Poverty', (New York: Halsted Press).

AKIN, JOHN S. (1974) 'Fiscal Capacity and the Estimation of the Advisory Commission on Intergovernmental Relation', *National Tax Journal*, XXVI, 2, 275–91.

ALBRITTON, ROBERT B. (1979) 'Social Amelioration through Mass Insurgency?: a Reexamination of the Piven and Cloward Thesis', *American Political Science Review*, 73, 1003–11.

ALFORD, ROBERT and FRIEDLAND, ROGER (1975) 'Political Participation and Public Policy', *Annual Review of Sociology*, 1, 429–79.

ALFORD, ROBERT and LEE, EUGENE (1968) 'Voting Turnout in American Cities', *American Political Science Review*, 67, 796–813.

ALFORD, R. R. and SCOBLE, H. M. (1968) 'Sources of Local Political Involvement', *American Political Science Review*, 62, 1192–1206.

ALLEN, MICHAEL (1974) 'The Structure of Interorganizational Élite Cooptation: Interlocking Corporate Directors', *American Sociological Review*, 39: 393–406.

ALONSO, WILLIAM (1964) *Location and Land Use* (Cambridge, Mass.: Harvard University Press).

ALONSO, WILLIAM (1971) 'A Theory of the Urban Land Market', in Larry S. Bourne (ed.), *Internal Structure of the City* (New York: Oxford University Press).

ALYEA, P. E. (1969) 'Property-tax Inducements to Attract Industry', in R. W. Lindholm (ed.), *Property Taxation–USA* (Madison: University of Wisconsin Press) 139–58.

ANDERSON, MARTIN (1964) *The Federal Bulldozer* (Cambridge, Mass.: MIT Press).

APILADO, V. (1971) 'Corporate Government Interplay: the Era of Industrial Aid Finance', *Urban Affair Quarterly*, 7, 2, 219–41.

APPELBAUM, RICHARD (1976) 'City Size and Urban Life', *Urban Affairs Quarterly*, 12 (2), December, 139-70.

APPELBAUM, RICHARD (1978) *Size, Growth and U.S. Cities* (New York: Praeger).

APPELBAUM, RICHARD, BIGELOW, JENNIFER, KRAMER, HENRY P., MOLOTCH, HARVEY L. and RELIS, PAUL M. (1976) *The Effects of Urban Growth: a Population Impact Analysis* (New York: Praeger).

ARMSTRONG, R. B (1972) *The Office Industry: Patterns of Growth and Location* (Cambridge, Mass.: MIT Press).

AVERITT, ROBERT (1968) *The Dual Economy* (New York: W. W. Norton).

BACHRACH, PETER and BARATZ, MORTON (1970) *Power and Poverty* (New York: Oxford University Press).

BAHL, ROY, JUMP, BERNARD JR. and SCHROEDER, LARRY (1978) 'The Outlook for City Fiscal Performance in Declining Regions', in Roy Bahl (ed.), *The Fiscal Outlook for Cities* (Syracuse: Syracuse University Press) 1-47.

BANFIELD, EDWARD C. and WILSON, JAMES Q. (1963) *City Politics* (Cambridge, Mass.: Harvard University Press).

BARLOW, R. (1974) 'The Incidence of Selected Taxes by Income Classes', in James Morgan, Katherine Dickinson, Jonathon Dickinson, Jacob Benus and Greg Duncan (eds), *Five Thousand American Families – Patterns of Economic Progress* (Ann Arbor: Institute for Social Research) 213-45.

BARSS, REITZEL AND ASSOCIATES (1969) *Community Action and Institutional Change* (Cambridge, Mass. July 1969).

BARSS, REITZEL AND ASSOCIATES (1970) *Community Action and Urban Institutional Change* (Cambridge, Mass. August 1970).

BARTON, ALLEN (1975) 'Consensus and Conflict Among American Leaders', *Public Opinion Quarterly*, 38, 507-30.

BELLUSH, JEWEL and HAUSKNECHT, MURRAY (1969) *Urban Renewal: People, Politics and Planning* (New York: Doubleday).

BERK, RICHARD and ALDRICH, HOWARD (1972) 'Patterns of Vandalism During Civil Disorders as an Indicator of Selection of Targets', *American Sociological Review*, 37, 533-47.

BERGSMAN, J. GREENSTON, P. and HEALY, R. (1972) 'The Agglomeration Process in Urban Growth', *Urban Studies*, 9, 263-88.

BERRY, BRIAN J. L. (1967) *Geography of Market Centers and Retail Distribution* (Englewood Cliffs, N.J.: Prentice-Hall).

BERRY, BRIAN J. L. (1968) *Theories of Urban Location* (Washington, DC: Association of American Geographers).

BETZ, MICHAEL (1974) 'Riots and Welfare: Are They Related?', *Social Policy*, 21.

BINGHAM, RICHARD D. (1974) 'The Impact of Federal Grant on City Revenue: The Case of Public Housing and Urban Renewal', 1974 Midwest Political Science Association (Chicago, Illinois).

BINGHAM, RICHARD D. (1975) *Public Housing and Urban Renewal: an Analysis of Federal–Local Relations* (New York: Praeger).

BIRCH, DAVID (1970) *The Economic Future of City and Suburb* (New York: Committee for Economic Development).

BLUESTONE, BARRY and HARRISON, BENNETT (1979) 'Capital Mobility and Economic Dislocation', mimeo, cited in Marcuse, 'Public Crisis for Private Profit'.

BLUESTONE, BARRY and HARRISON, BENNETT (1980) *Capital and Communities: the Causes and Consequences of Private Disinvestment* (Washington, DC: The Progressive Alliance).

BOAST, TOM (1977) 'Federal Programs, Urban Resources and the American Capital Market' (paper at the Conference on Urban Resources and State Power, Center for International Studies, Cornell University, New York) June.

BOGUE, DONALD J. (1949) *The Structure of the Metropolitan Community* (Ann Arbor, Mich.: Horace H. Rackman School of Graduate Studies, University of Michigan).

BOK, DEREK C. and DUNLOP, JOHN T. (1970) *Labor and the American Community* (New York: Simon & Schuster).

BOLLENS, J. C. and SCHMANDT, H. J. (1970) *The Metropolis: Its People, Politics, and Economic Life*, 2nd edn (New York: Harper & Row).

BONNEN, J.T. (1969) 'The Absence of Knowledge of Distributional Impacts: An Obstacle to Effective Public Program Analysis and Decision', from *The Analysis and Evaluation of Public Expenditures: The PPB System*, a compendium of papers prepared for Sub-Committee Economic Government Joint Economic Commission US Congress, 91st Congress, 1st Session (Washington, DC: US Government Printing Office).

BOOMS, B. H. and HALLDORSON, J. R. (1973) 'The Politics of Redistribution: a Reformulation', *American Political Science Review*, 67, 924–33.

BORCHERDING, THOMAS E. and DEACON, ROBERT T. (1972) 'The Demand for the Services of Non-Federal Governments', *American Economic Review*, 62; December 891–901.

BOURNE, LARRY S. (1967) 'Private Redevelopment of the Central City', Research Paper no. 112 (Department of Geography, University of Chicago).

BOURNE, LARRY S. (1971) *Internal Structure of the City* (New York: Oxford University Press).

BRADFORD, D. F. and KELEJIAN, H. H. (1973) 'An Econometric Model of the Flight to the Suburbs', *Journal of Political Economy*, 81, 566–89.

BRECKENFELD, GURNEY (1972) '"Downtown" Has Fled to the Suburbs', *Fortune*, 79, 80–7, 156, 158, 162.

BROWN, D. M. (1974) *Introduction to Urban Economics* (New York: Academic Press).

BROWN, JAMES and KAIN, JOHN (1970) 'The Moving Behavior of San Francisco Households', in John Kain (ed.), *The NBER Urban Simulation Model*, vol. II.

BROWNING, C. E. (1961) 'Recent Studies of Central Business Districts', *Journal of the American Institute of Planners*, 27, February, 82–7.

BURNS, LELAND (1977) 'The Location of the Headquarters of Industrial Companies: a Comment', *Urban Studies*, 14, 211–14.

BURNS, LELAND, and PANG, WING NING (1977) 'Big Business in the Big City: Corporate Headquarters in the CBD', *Urban Affairs Quarterly*, 12, 4, June, 533–44.

BURT, RONALD (1977) 'Power in a Social Typology', in Roland Liebert and Allen W. Imersheim (eds), *Power, Paradigms and Community Research* (Beverly Hills, Calif.: Sage).

BURT, RONALD and FISCHER, MICHAEL G. (1978) 'Comparative Community Power Structures in 51 Cities Representative of American Places of Residence Circa 1967', Survey Research Center Working Paper 22 (University of California, Berkeley).

BUSSE, DAVID (1978) 'The Application of Multiple Regression Analysis to the

Appraisal of Commercial Property', unpublished M.A. thesis (University of California: Department of Economics, May 1978).

BUTTON, JAMES W. (1978) *Black Violence: Political Impact of the 1960's Riots* (N.J.: Princeton University Press).

CAMPBELL, ALAN K. and SACKS, SEYMOUR (1967) *Metropolitan America: Fiscal Patterns and Governmental Systems* (New York: Free Press).

CAMPBELL, ANGUS and SCHUMAN, HOWARD (1968) *Racial Attitudes in Fifteen American Cities*, Supplemental Studies for the National Advisory Committee on Civil Disorders (Washington, DC: US Government Printing Office).

CASTELLS, MANUEL (1970) 'La Rénovation urbaine aux États-Unis: synthèse et interprétation des donnés actuelles', *Espaces et sociétés*, 1, 107–35.

CASTELLS, MANUEL (1972) 'Urban Renewal and Social Conflict in Paris', *Social Science Information*, 11, 93–124.

CENTRAL LABOR COUNCIL OF ALAMEDA COUNTY AND THE CENTER FOR LABOR RESEARCH AND EDUCATION, INSTITUTE OF INDUSTRIAL RELATIONS (1965) *Report on Union Member Attitude Survey* (Berkeley: Center for Labor Research and Education).

CHILD, J. (1973) 'Parkinson's Progress: Accounting for the Number of Specialists in Organizations', *Administrative Science Quarterly*, 18, 328–48.

CLARK, TERRY (1968) 'Community Structure, Decision-Making, Budget Expenditures, and Urban Renewal in 51 American Communities', *American Sociological Review*, 33, 576–93.

CLARK, TERRY (1974) 'Money and the Cities' (presented at the Eighth World Congress, International Sociological Association, Toronto).

CLARK, TERRY (ed.) (1974) *Comparative Community Politics* (New York: Halsted Press).

CLARK, TERRY and FERGUSON, L. C., (forthcoming) *Political Leadership and Urban Fiscal Strain* (University of Chicago Press).

CLOWARD, RICHARD A. and PIVEN, FRANCES F. (1974) *The Politics of Turmoil* (New York. Pantheon).

COHEN, B. (1971) 'A Look at Suburban Office Space', *Skyscraper Management*, 56, 6–10.

COHEN, BENJAMIN and NOLL, ROGER G. (1968) *Employment Trends in Central Cities* (Pasadena: California Institute of Technology).

COHEN, ROBERT B. (forthcoming) *The Corporation and the City* (New York: Columbia University, Conservation of Human Resources).

COLE, R.L. (1974) *Citizen Participation and the Urban Policy Process* (Lexington, Mass.: Lexington Books).

COLEMAN, JAMES S. (1977) 'Notes on the Study of Power', in Liebert and Imersheim, *Power, Paradigms and Community Research*, 183–98.

COPE (Committee on Political Education) (1967) *New Frontier: Politics in the Suburbs*, publication no. 177C (Washington, DC: AFL–CIO Committee on Political Education).

COWART, A. T. (1969) 'Anti-Poverty Expenditures in the American States: A Comparative Analysis', *Midwest Journal of Political Science*, 13, 219–36.

CRENSON, MATTHEW A. (1971) *The Un-Politics of Air Pollution* (Baltimore: Johns Hopkins Press).

CRNCICH, P. (1973) 'The Influence of Chamber of the Commerce in United States Cities', unpublished paper, University of Wisconsin.

DAHL, R. A. (1961) *Who Governs: Democracy and Power in an American City?* (New Haven: Yale University Press).

DANIELS, P. W. (1975) *Office Location* (London, G. Bell & Sons).

DAVIES, JAMES C. (1962) 'Toward a Theory of Revolution', *American Sociological Review*, 27, 5–19.

DAVIS, OTTO A. and WHINSTON, ANDREW B. (1966) 'The Economics of Urban Renewal', in Wilson (1966: 50–67).

DEACON, R. T. (1977) 'Review of the Literature on the Demand for Public Services', *Papers of the National Conference on Nonmetropolitan Community Services Research* (US, GPO) prepared for the Committee on Agriculture, Nutrition, and Forestry, US Senate.

DEACON, R. T. (1978) 'A Demand Model for the Local Public Sector', *Review of Economics and Statistics*, 50, 184–92.

DOMHOFF, C. W. (1967) *Who Rules America?* (Englewood Cliffs, N.J.: Prentice-Hall).

DOMHOFF, C. W. (1970) *The Higher Circles* (New York: Random House).

DOMHOFF, C. W. (1974) 'State and Ruling Class in Corporate America', *Insurgent Sociologist*, 4, 3–16.

DOMHOFF, C. W. (1978) *Who Really Rules? New Haven and Community Power Reexamined* (Santa Monica, Calif.: Goodyear Publishing).

DOOLEY, PETER (1969) 'The Interlocking Directorate', *American Economic Review*, 59, 314–23.

DOUGLAS, PAUL (Chairman) (1968) *Report of the National Commission on Urban Problems* (Washington, DC: US Government Printing Office).

DOWNES, BRYAN T. (1970) 'A Critical Reexamination of the Social and Political Characteristics of Riot Cities', *Social Science Quarterly*, 51, 349–60.

DOWNS, ANTHONY (1971) *Who Are the Urban Poor?* (New York: Committee for Economic Development).

DUE, J. F. (1961) 'Studies of State–Local Tax Influences on the Location of Industry', *National Tax Journal*, 14, 163–73.

DUNCAN, OTIS DUDLEY, SCOTT, W. RICHARD, LIEBERSON, STANLEY, DUNCAN, BEVERLY and SINSBOROUGH, HAL W. (1960) *Metropolis and Region* (Baltimore: Johns Hopkins Press, Resources for the Future Inc.).

DYE, T. R. (1972) *Understanding Public Policy* (Englewood Cliffs N.J.: Prentice-Hall).

EARICKSON, R. A. (1974) 'The Regional Impact of Growth Firms: The Case of Boeing 1963–1968', *Land Economics*, 50, 127–36.

EARSY, ROBERT and COLTON, KEN (1974) 'Boston's New High-Rise Office Buildings: a Study of the Employees and their Housing Preferences', (Boston Redevelopment Authority, Research Department) July.

EDEL, MATTHEW (1971) 'Urban Renewal and Land Use Conflicts', *Review of Radical Political Economics*, 3, 76–89.

EDEL, MATTHEW (1972) 'Planning, Market or Warfare? – Recent Land Use Conflict in American Cities', in Matthew Edel and Jerome Rotherberg (eds), *Readings in Urban Economics* (New York: Macmillan).

EDEL, MATTHEW and SCLAR, ELLIOT (1974) 'Taxes, Spending and Property Values: Supply Adjustment in a Tiebout–Oates Model', *Journal of Political Economy*, 82.

EDGAR, RICHARD E. (1970) *Urban Power and Social Welfare* (Beverly Hills, Calif.: Sage).

EISINGER, PETER (1973) 'The Conditions of Protest Behavior in American Cities', *American Political Science Review*, 67, 11–28.

EPSTEIN, EDWIN M. (1969) *The Corporation in American Politics* (Englewood Cliffs, N.J.: Prentice-Hall).

ERIE, STEVEN P. and BROWN, MICHAEL K. (1979) 'Social Policy and the Emergence of the Black Social Welfare Economy', unpublished (SUNY: Department of Political Science).

FARLEY, REYNOLDS (1977) 'Trends in Racial Inequalities: Have the Gains of the 1960's Disappeared in the 1970's?', *American Sociological Review*, 42 (2), April, 189–207.

FEAGIN, JOE R. and HAHN, HARLAN (1973) *Ghetto Revolts* (New York: Macmillan).

FITCH, ROBERT and OPPENHEIMER, MARY (1970) 'Who Rules the Corporation?', *Socialist Revolution*, 1, 73–107; 5, 61–114; 6, 33–94.

FOARD, ASHLEY and FEFFERMAN, HILBERT (1966) 'Federal Urban Renewal Legislation', in Wilson (ed.), *Urban Renewal*, 71–125.

FOGELSON, R. M. (1971) *Violence as Protest: a Study of Riots and Ghettos* (Garden City, N.Y.: Anchor Books).

FORBES, J. D. (1972) 'Central Place Theory – An Analytical Framework for Retail Structure', *Land Economics*, 48, 1.

FORD FOUNDATION (1963) 'American Community Development', preliminary reports by Directors of Projects assisted by the Ford Foundation in four cities and a state (presented at the Twenty-Ninth Annual Conference of National Association of Housing and Redevelopment Officials, Denver, Colorado).

FORM, WILLIAM H. and MILLER, DELBERT (1960) *Industry, Labor and Community* (New York: Harper & Row).

FOX, DOUGLAS (1972) *The New Urban Politics* (Pacific Palisades: Goodyear).

FREEMAN, CLINTON C., FARARO, THOMAS J., BLOOMBERG JR, WARNER and SUNSHINE, MORRISH M. (1963) 'Locating Leaders in Local Communities: a Comparison of Some Alternative Approaches', *American Sociological Review*, 28, October, 791–8.

FREMON, CHARLOTTE (1970) *Central City and Suburban Employment Growth, 1965–1967* (Washington, DC: Urban Institute).

FRENCH, ROBERT MILLS (1970) 'Economic Change and Community Power Structure: Transition in Cornucopia', in Michael Aiken and Paul E. Mott (eds), *The Structure of Community Power* (New York: Random House) 181–92.

FRIED, JOSEPH (1971) *Housing Crisis – USA* (New York: Praeger).

FRIED, R. C. (1975) 'Comparative Urban Performance', in F. I. Greenstein and N. W. Polsby (eds), *Handbook of Political Science*, vol. 6 (Reading, Mass.: Addison-Wesley).

FRIEDLAND, ROGER (1977) 'Class Power and the Central City: the Contradictions of Urban Growth' (unpublished Ph.D. dissertation, University of Wisconsin).

FRIEDLAND, ROGER and DUMONT, MARY (forthcoming) 'Corporate Headquarter Relocation, 1960–1975', unpublished paper.

FRIEDLAND, ROGER, PIVEN. FRANCES FOX and ALFORD, ROBERT R. (1977) 'Political Conflict, Urban Structure and the Fiscal Crisis', *International Journal of Urban and Regional Research*, 1, 3, 447–51.

FRIEDMAN, JUDITH (1973), 'Variations in the Level of Central Business District Retail Activity Among Large U.S. Cities: 1954 and 1967', *Land Economics*, 49, 3, 329–35.

FRIEDMAN, JUDITH (1977a) 'Community Action on Water Pollution', *Human Ecology*, 5, 4, 329–53.

FRIEDMAN, JUDITH (1977b) 'Central Business District and Residential Urban Renewal: Response to Undesired Change?', *Social Science Quarterly*, 58, 45–59, June.

FRIEDMAN, LAWRENCE (1968) *Government and Slum Housing – a Century of Frustration* (Chicago: Rand McNally).

FRY, B. R. and WINTERS, R. F. (1970) 'The Politics of Redistribution', *American Political Science Review*, 64, 508–22.

FUCHS, V. R. (1967) 'Differentials in Hourly Earnings by Region and City Size, 1959', Occasional Paper no. 101 (New York: National Bureau of Economic Research).

GALASKIEWICZ, JOSEPH (1976) 'Social Networks and Community Decision-Making: a Study of Corporate Actors', Ph.D. dissertation (University of Chicago).

GAMSON, WILLIAM A. (1975) *The Strategy of Social Protest* (Homewood, Ill.: Dorsey Press).

GANNON, JAMES P. (1967) 'Divided Unions', *The Wall Street Journal* 6 July, 1.

GANZ, ALEXANDER (1972) *Our Large Cities: New Light on their Recent Transformation* (Cambridge, Mass.: MIT Laboratory for Environmental Studies).

GARDINER, JOHN and OLSON, DAVID J. (1974) *Theft of the City* (Bloomington, Indiana: Indiana University Press).

GINZBERG, ELI *et al.* (1975) *The High Service Metropolis Project*, Conservation of Human Resources Project (New York: Columbia University).

GLAZER, NATHAN (1965) 'Why are the Poor Still With Us? Paradoxes of American Poverty', *Public Interest*, 71–81.

GODDARD, J. B. (1973) *Office Linkages and Location: a Study of Communications and Spatial Patterns in Central London* (Oxford: Pergamon Press).

GODDARD, J. B. (1975) *Office Location in Urban and Regional Development* (London: Oxford University Press).

GODDARD, J. B. and MORRIS, D. (1975) *The Communication Factor in Office Decentralization* (Oxford: Pergamon Press).

GOLDBERG, M. A. (1970) 'An Economic Model of Intrametropolitan Industrial Location', *Journal of Regional Science*, 10, 75–9.

GOODING, B. (1972) 'Roadblocks Ahead for the Great Corporate Move Out', *Fortune*, 86, 78–83.

GOODWIN, W. (1965) 'The Management Centre in the United States', *Geographical Review*, 55, 5–6.

GORDON, DAVID (1977) 'Capitalism and the Roots of Urban Crisis', in Roger Alcaly and David Mermelstein (eds), *The Fiscal Crisis of American Cities* (New York: Vintage) 82–112.

GOTTMANN, JEAN (1961) *Megalopolis* (Cambridge, Mass.: MIT Press).

GRAMLICH, EDWARD M. and GALPER, HARVEY (1973) 'State and Local Fiscal Behavior and Federal Grant Policy', *Brookings Papers on Economic Activity* (Washington, DC: Brookings Institution) 1, 15–58.

GRAY, KENNETH E. and GREENSTONE, J. DAVID (1961) 'Organized Labor in City Politics', in Edward Banfield (ed.), *Urban Government* (Glencoe: Free Press) 368–78.

GREENBERG, STANLEY (1974) *Politics and Poverty* (New York: Wiley).

GREENSTEIN, FRED (1963) *The American Party System and the American People* (Englewood Cliffs, N.J.: Prentice-Hall).

GREENSTONE, J. DAVID (1970) *Labor in American Politics* (New York: Vintage Books).

GREENSTONE, DAVID and PETERSON, PAUL (1970) 'Reformers, Machines and the War on Poverty', in James Q. Wilson (ed.), *City Politics and Public Policy* (New York: Wiley) 267–91.

GREENSTONE, J. D. and PETERSON, P. E. (1973) *Race and Authority in Urban Politics: Community Participation and the War on Poverty* (University of Chicago Press).

GRIMES, MICHAEL D., BONJEAN, CHARLES M., LEON, J. LARRY and LINEBERRY, ROBERT L. (1976) 'Community Structure and Leadership Arrangements: a Multidimensional Analysis', *American Sociological Review*, 41, August, 706–25.

GURR, TED (1968) 'Urban Disorder: Perspectives from the Comparative Study of Civil Strife', in Louis H. Masotti and Dan Bowen (ed), *Riots and Rebellion* (Beverly Hills, Calif.: Sage) 51–67.

GURR, TED (1971) 'A Causal Model of Strife', in James C. Davies (ed.), *When Men Revolt and Why* (New York: Glencoe Free Press).

HAMBERG, JILL and SMITH, DAVID (1972) 'The Urban Coalition in Action', in Perrow (1972).

HAMILTON, RICHARD (1972) *Class and Politics in the United States* (New York: Wiley).

HANSEN, NILES (1965) 'Municipal Investment Requirements in a Growing Agglomeration', *Land Economics*, 41, 1, February, 49–56.

HARRISON, BENNETT (1974) *Urban Economic Development* (Washington, DC: Urban Institute).

HARTMAN, CHESTER (1967) 'The Housing of Relocated Families', in James Q. Wilson (ed.), *Urban Renewal: the Record and the Controversy* (Cambridge, Mass.: MIT Press) 293–335.

HARTMAN, CHESTER (1974) *Yerba Buena: Land Grab and Community Resistance in San Francisco* (San Francisco: Glide Publications).

HARVEY, DAVID (1975) 'The Political Economy of Urbanization in Advanced Capitalist Societies – the Case of the United States', *Urban Affairs Annual Review* (Beverly Hills, Calif.: Sage).

HAWLEY, AMOS (1971) *Urban Society: an Ecological Approach* (New York: Ronald).

HAWLEY, AMOS (1963) 'Community Power and Urban Renewal Success', *American Journal of Sociology*, 68, 422–31.

HAYES, EDWARD (1972) *Power Structure and Urban Policy* (New York: McGraw-Hill).

HAYS, SAMUEL (1969) 'The Politics of Reform in Municipal Government in the Progressive Era', in Alexander B. Collow (ed.), *American Urban History* (New York: Oxford University Press).

HEILBRUN, JAMES (1974) *Urban Economics and Public Policy* (New York: St Martin's Press).

HENDERSON, J. VERNON (1977) *Economic Theory and the Cities*, (New York: Academic Press).

HICKS, ALEXANDER, FRIEDLAND, ROGER and JOHNSON, EDWIN (1975) 'Class Power and State Policy: the Case of Large Business Corporations and Governmental Redistribution in the American States', *American Sociological Review*, June, 302–15.

HILL, RICHARD CHILD (1973) 'Urban Income Inequality' (unpublished Ph.D. dissertation from the Department of Sociology, University of Wisconsin, Madison).

HILL, RICHARD CHILD (1974) 'Separate and Unequal: Governmental Inequality in the Metropolis', *American Political Science Review*, December.

HILL, RICHARD CHILD (1976) 'Black Struggle and the Urban Fiscal Crisis', *Kapitalistate*, 4.

HIRSCH, WERNER Z., VINCENT, PHILLIP E., TERRELL, HARRY S., SHOUP, DONALD O. and ROSETT, ARTHUR (1971) *Fiscal Pressures on the Central City: The Impact of Commuters, Nonwhites, and Overlapping Governments* (New York: Praeger).

HOCH, I. (1972) 'Income and City Size', *Urban Studies*, 9, October, 294–328.

HOFFERBERT, R. I. (1972) 'State and Community Policy Studies: a Review of Comparative Input–Output Analyses', in J. A. Robinson (ed), *Political Science Annual: an International Review*, vol. 3 (Indianapolis: Bobbs-Merrill) 3–72.

HOLLAND, DEMPSTER K. and WENDEL, GEORGE D. (1973) 'Development of Industrial Parks in St. Louis County, Missouri', A Working Note (Santa Monica, Calif.: RAND Corporation).

HOLLAND, STUART (1976) *Capital versus the Regions* (New York: St Martin's Press).

HOLLINGSWORTH, J. R. (1973) 'The Impact of Electoral Behavior on Public Policy' (unpublished paper, University of Wisconsin).

HOWELL, JAMES M. and STAMM, CHARLES F. (1979) *Urban Fiscal Stress* (Lexington, Mass.: Lexington Books).

HUNTER, FLOYD (1953) *Community Power Structure: a Study of Decision Makers* (Chapel Hill: University of North Carolina Press).

HUNTINGTON, SAMUEL (1968) *Political Order in Changing Societies* (New Haven: Yale University Press).

JANKOVIC, IVAN (1977a) 'Punishment and Post-Industrial Society: a Study of Unemployment, Crime and Imprisonment in the United States', Ph.D. dissertation (Santa Barbara: University of California).

JANKOVIC, IVAN (1977b) 'Labor Market and Imprisonment', *Crime and Social Justice*, 8, 17–31.

JENNINGS, EDWARD T. JR. (1978) 'Urban Riots and Welfare Policy Change: a Test of the Priven–Cloward Theory' (paper delivered at the 1979 Annual Meeting of the American Political Science Association, New York, September).

KAIN, JOHN F. (1962) 'The Journey-To-Work as a Determinant of Residential Location', *Papers and Proceedings of the Regional Science Association*, 9, 137–60.

KAIN, JOHN F. (1968) 'The Distribution and Movement of Jobs and Industry', in James Q. Wilson (ed.), *The Metropolitan Enigma* (Cambridge, Mass.: Harvard University Press).

KAIN, JOHN F. (1975) *Essays on Urban Spatial Structure* (Cambridge, Mass.: Ballinger).

KALACHECK, EDWARD and GOERING, JOHN (1970) *Transportation and Central City Unemployment* (St Louis: Institute for Urban and Regional Studies, Washington University).

KAPLAN, HAROLD (1966) *Urban Renewal Politics* (New York: Columbia University Press).

KASARDA, JOHN (1972) 'The Impact of Suburban Population Growth on Central City Service Functions', *American Journal of Sociology*, 77, 6, 1111–24.

KASARDA, JOHN (1979) 'Population and Economic Base Changes in Metropolitan Areas: Apropos Urban Policy Research' (paper presented at the NSF Conference on Comparative Urban Policy Research, Chicago) April.

KATZNELSON, IRA (1975) 'The Crisis of the Capitalist City: Urban Politics and Social Control', in W. Hawley and M. Lipsky (eds), *Theoretical Perspectives on Urban Politics* (Englewood Cliffs, N.J.: Prentice-Hall).

KATZNELSON, IRA and KESSELMAN, MARK (1975) *The Politics of Power* (New York: Harcourt Brace Jovanovich).

KEITH, NATHANIEL (1973) *Politics and the Housing Crisis Since 1930* (New York: Universe Books).

KESSLER, ROBERT P. (1973) 'Regional Background to YBC Development' (unpublished paper, University of California, Berkeley).

KESSLER, ROBERT and HARTMAN, CHESTER W. (1973) 'The Illusions and the Reality of Urban Renewal: A Case Study of San Francisco's Yerba Buena Center', *Land Economics*, November, 440–53.

KRAMER, R. M. (1969) *Participation of the Poor: Comparative Community Case Studies in the War on Poverty* (Englewood Cliffs, N.J.: Prentice-Hall).

KRUMME, G. and HAYTER, R. (1975) 'Implications of Corporate Strategies and Product Cycle Adjustments for Regional Employment Changes', in L. Collins and D. F. Walker (eds), *The Dynamics of Manufacturing Activity* (New York: John Wiley) 325–56.

LAUMANN, EDWARD O., GALASKIEWICZ, JOSEPH and MARSDEN, PETER V., (1978) 'Community Structure as Interorganizational Linkages', *Annual Review of Sociology*, 4, 455–84.

LeGATES, RICHARD T. (1972) 'Can the Federal Welfare Bureaucracies Control Their Programs: the Case of HUD and Urban Renewal', Working Paper No. 172 (Institute of Urban and Regional Development, University of California, Berkeley).

LIEBERSON, STANLEY and SILVERMAN, ARNOLD (1965) 'The Precipitants and Underlying Conditions of Race Riots', *American Sociological Review*, 30, 887–98.

LIEBERT, ROLAND (1974) 'Municipal Functions, Structure and Expenditures: A Reanalysis of Recent Research', *Social Science Quarterly*, 54, March, 765–84.

LIEBERT, ROLAND J. and IMERSHEIM, ALLEN W. (eds) (1977) *Power, Paradigms and Community Research*, (Berverly Hills, Calif.: Sage Studies in International Sociology, 9).

LINCOLN, JAMES R. (1976) 'Power and Mobilization in the Urban Community: Reconsidering the Ecological Approach', *American Sociological Review*, 41, 1, 1–15.

LINCOLN, JAMES R. (1977) 'Organizational Dominance and Community Structure', in Roland Liebert and Allen W. Imersheim (eds), *Power, Paradigms and Community Research* (Beverly Hills, Calif.: Sage).

LINCOLN, JAMES R. (1978) 'The Urban Distribution of Headquarters and Branch Plants in Manufacturing: Mechanisms of Metropolitan Dominance, *Demography*, 15 (2), May, 213–22.

LINCOLN, JAMES R. and FRIEDLAND, ROGER (1978) 'Metropolitan Accessibility and Socioeconomic Differentiation in Non-metropolitan Areas', *Social Forces*, 57, 2, December, 688–96.

LINEBERRY, ROBERT L. (1977) 'Equity, Public Policy and Public Service: The Underclass Hypothesis and the Limits to Equality', *Policy and Politics*.

LINEBERRY, ROBERT L. and FOWLER, EDMUND P. (1967) 'Reformism and Public Policies in American Cities', *American Political Science Review*, 61, 701–16.

LISTON, LINDA (1970) 'Proliferating Industrial Parks Spark Plant Location Revolution', *Industrial Development*, March–April, 7–11.

LOGAN, JOHN (1976) 'Industrialization and the Stratification of Cities in Suburban Regions', *American Journal of Sociology*, 82, September, 333–48.

LOGAN, JOHN (1978) 'Growth, Politics and the Stratification of Place', *American Journal of Sociology*, 84, September, 404–16.

LOGAN, JOHN and SCHNEIDER, MARK (1979) 'Governmental Organization and Changing City–Suburb Income Inequality: 1960–1970' (paper presented at the American Sociological Association) August.

LOWE, JEANNE (1967) *Cities in a Race with Time* (New York: Random House).

LOWI, THEODORE (1967) 'Machine Politics Old and New', *The Public Interest*, 9, 83–92.

McKEE, JAMES B. (1953) 'Status and Power in the Industrial Community: a Comment on Drucker's Thesis', *American Journal of Sociology*, January.

McLAUGHLIN, EDMUND M. (1975) 'The Power Network in Phoenix: an Application of Smallest Space Analysis', *Insurgent Sociologist*, 5, 185–95.

McWATTERS, ANN ROBERTSON (1979) 'Financing Capital Formation for Local Governments' (Berkeley, Calif.: Institute of Governmental Studies) Research Report No. 79–3.

MANNERS, GERALD (1974) 'The Office in Metropolis: an Opportunity for Shaping Metropolitan America', *Economic Geography*, 50, 2, April, 93–110.

MARCUSE, PETER (1980) 'Public Crisis for Private Profit: On the Usefulness of the Urban Fiscal Crisis' (Papers in Planning, no. 20, Columbia University).

MARSDEN, PETER V. and LAUMANN, EDWARD O. (1977) 'Collective Action in a Community Elite: Exchange, Influence Resources, and Issue Resolution', in Liebert and Imersheim (1977: 199–250).

MASOTTI, LOUIS H. (1974) 'Private/Public Partnerships: the Only Game in Town', (Center for Urban Affairs, Northwestern University) January.

MASTERS, NICHOLAS (1962) 'The Organized Labor Bureaucracy as a Base of Support for the Democratic Party', *Law and Contemporary Problems*, 27.

MILLER, DELBERT (1958) 'Decision-Making Cliques in Community Power Structure: a Comparative Study of an American and an English City', *American Journal of Sociology*, 64, November, 299–310.

MILLS, C. WRIGHT and ULMER, MELVILLE (1970) 'Small Business and Civil Welfare', in Michael Aiken and Paul E. Mott (eds), *The Structure of Community Power* (New York: Random House) 124–54.

MOLLENKOPF, JOHN (1973) 'On the Causes and Consequences of Neighborhood Mobilization' (paper delivered at the 1973 American Political Science Association Meeting, New Orleans).

MOLLENKOPF, JOHN (1976) 'The Post-War Politics of Urban Development', *Politics and Society*, 247–295.

MOLLENKOPF, JOHN (1979) 'Paths Toward the Post-Industrial Service City: the Northeast and Southwest' (Conference on Municipal Fiscal Stress – Problems and Potentials, Department of Housing and Urban Development, Miami Beach) March.

MOLOTCH, HARVEY (1976) 'The City as a Growth Machine: Towards a Political Economy of Place', *American Journal of Sociology*, 82, 2, 309–31.

MORGAN, W. E. (1967) 'Taxes and the Location of Industry', University of Colorado Studies Series in Economics, no. 4 (Boulder: University of Colorado Press).

MORGAN, W. R. and CLARK, T. N. (1973) 'The Causes of Racial Disorders: a Grievance-Level Explanation', *American Sociological Review*, 38, 611–24.

MORLOCK, LAURA (1974) 'Business Interests, Countervailing Groups and the Balance of Influence in 91 Cities', in Willis Hawley and Frederick Wirt (eds), *The Search for Community Power*, 2nd edn (Englewood Cliffs, N.J.: Prentice-Hall).

MOSES, L. N. and WILLIAMSON, H. F. JR. (1967) 'The Location of Economic Activities in Cities', *American Economic Review*, 57, 211–21.

MOTT, PAUL E. (1970) 'The Role of the Absentee-owned Corporation in the Changing Community', in Michael Aikin and Paul E. Mott (eds), *The Structure of Community Power* (New York: Random House) 170–80.

MOYNIHAN, DANIEL PATRICK (1969) *Maximum Feasible Misunderstanding* (New York: Free Press).

MUELLER, WILLARD F. (1970) 'The Spreading Imprint of the Conglomerate', *AFL–CIO American Federationist*, August.

MUELLER, WILLARD F. (1972) 'The Impact of Changing Industrial Organization on Community Development' (paper presented at the American Agricultural Economics Association) August.

MULLER, THOMAS (1975a) *Growing and Declining Urban Areas: a Fiscal Comparison* (Washington, DC: Urban Institute) November.

MULLER, THOMAS (1975b) *Impacts of Land Development* (Washington, DC: Urban Institute).

MULLER, THOMAS and DAWSON, GRACE (1972) *The Fiscal Impact of Residential and Commercial Development: A Case Study* (Washington, DC: Urban Institute).

MULLER, THOMAS, NEEDS, KEVIN, TILNEY, JOHN and DAWSON, GRACE (1978) *The Impact of Beltways in Central Business Districts: A Case Study of Richmond* (Washington, DC: Urban Institute).

MUNGER, FRANK (1961) 'Power Structure and its Study', in Roscoe Martin *et al.* (eds), *Decisions in Syracuse* (Bloomington: University of Indiana Press).

MURPHY, R. E. and VANCE, J. E. (1954) 'Delimiting the CBD', *Economic Geography*, 30, 189–222.

MUSHKIN, SELMA and COTTON, JOHN F. (1969) *Sharing Federal Funds for State and Local Needs* (New York: Praeger).

NADER, RALPH and GREEN, MARK J. (1973) *Corporate Power in America* (New York: Grossman).

NATIONAL COMMISSION ON URBAN PROBLEMS (1968) *Building the American City* (Washington, DC: US Government Printing Office).

NIEDERCORN, JOHN H. and HEARLE, EDWARD F. R. (1964) 'Recent Land-use Trends in Forty-eight Large American Cities', *Land Economics*, XL (1), February, 105–9.

NOLAND, E. WILLIAM (1962) 'The Roles of Top Business Executives in Urban Development', in Stuart Chapin and Shirley Weiss (eds), *Urban Growth Dynamics* (New York: Wiley) 226–59.

NOLL, ROGER (1970) 'Metropolitan Employment and Population Distributions and the Conditions of the Urban Poor', in John Crecine (ed.), *Financing the Metropolis* (Beverly Hills, Calif.: Sage) 481–514.

NORTHAM, RAY (1971) 'Vacant Urban Land in the American City', *Land Economics*, XLVII, 4, November, 345–55.

OATES, WALLACE E. (1972) *Fiscal Federalism* (New York: Harcourt Brace Jovanovich).

O'CONNOR, JAMES (1973) *The Fiscal Crisis of the State* (New York: St Martin's Press).

PAIGE, J. M. (1971) 'Political Orientation and Riot Participation', *American Sociological Review*, 36, 810–20.

PARK, ROBERT (1936) 'Human Ecology', *American Journal of Sociology*, XLII, July, 1–15.

PELLEGRIN, ROLAND J. and COATES, CHARLES H. (1956) 'Absentee-owned Corporations and Community Power Structure', *American Journal of Sociology*, 61, 413 and 419.

PERROW, CHARLES (1972) *The Radical Attack on Business* (New York: Harcourt Brace Jovanovich).

PERRUCCI, ROBERT and PILISUK, MARC (1970) 'Leaders and Ruling Elites: the Interorganizational Bases of Community Power', *American Sociological Review*, 35, December, 1040–57.

PETERSON, GEORGE E. (1978) 'Capital Spending and Capital Obsolescence – The Outlook for Cities', in Roy Bahl (ed.), *The Fiscal Outlook for Cities* (University of Syracuse Press) 49–74.

PETERSON, PAUL (1979) 'A Unitary Model of Local Taxation and Expenditure Policies in the United States', British Journal of Political Science, 9, 281–314.

PHELAN, JAMES and POZEN, ROBERT (1973) *The Company State* (New York: Grossman).

PHILLIPS, BRUCE A. (1979) 'A Time-Series Analysis of Local Highway Expenditures' (Warren, Michigan: General Motors Research Laboratories) July.

PIVEN, FRANCES FOX (1975) 'The Urban Crisis: Who Got What and Why?', in Frances Fox Piven and Richard Cloward, *The Politics of Turmoil: Essays on Poverty, Race and the Urban Crisis* (New York, Pantheon).

PIVEN, FRANCES FOX and CLOWARD, RICHARD A. (1971) *Regulating the Poor* (New York: Vintage).

PIVEN, FRANCES FOX and CLOWARD, RICHARD A. (1977) *Poor People's Movements* (New York: Pantheon).

PIVEN, FRANCES FOX and CLOWARD, RICHARD A. (1979) 'Electoral Instability, Civil Disorder and Relief Rises: a Reply to Albritton', *American Political Science Review*, 73, 1012–19.

PIVEN, FRANCES FOX and FRIEDLAND, ROGER (1981) 'Public Choice and Private Power: the Origins of Urban Fiscal Strain', (unpublished paper).

POLSBY, NELSON (1963) *Community Power and Political Theory* (New Haven: Yale University Press).

POWLEDGE, FRED (1970) *Model City* (New York: Simon & Schuster).

PRED, ALLAN (1977) *City-Systems in Advanced Economies* (New York: Wiley).

QUINNEY, RICHARD (1977) *Class, State and Crime* (New York: McKay).

RATCLIFF, RICHARD E. (1980) 'Declining Cities and Capitalist Class Structure', in G. William Domhoff, (ed.), *Power Structure Research* (Beverly Hills, Calif.: Sage) 115–38.

REICH, MICHAEL (1973) 'Racial Discrimination and the White Income Distribution' (unpublished Ph.D. dissertation, Department of Economics, Harvard University).

RICHARDSON, HARRY (1978) *Urban Economics* (Hinsdale, Illinois: Dryden Press).

ROKKAN, STEIN (1970) *Citizens, Elections, Parties: Approaches to the Comparative Study of the Processes of Development* (New York: McKay).

ROSETT, ARTHUR and CRESSEY, DONALD R. (1976) *Justice by Consent: Plea Bargains in the American Court-House* (Philadelphia: Lippencott).

ROSSI, PETER, BERK, RICHARD and EIDSON, BETTYE (1974) *The Riots of Urban Discontent* (New York: Wiley).

RUSHING, W. A. (1967) 'The Effects of Industry Size and Division of Labor on Administration', *Administrative Science Quarterly*, 12, 273–95.

SALISBURY, ROBERT H. (1960) 'St Louis Politics: Relationships Among Interests, Parties and Governmental Structure', *Western Political Quarterly*, 13, 498–507.

SPUR (San Francisco Planning and Urban Renewal Association) (1975) 'Impact of Intensive High-Rise Development on San Francisco', (San Francisco).

SCHULZE, ROBERT O. (1958) 'The Role of Economic Dominants in Community Power Structure', *American Sociological Review*, 23, 3–9.

SCHUMAKER, P., (1974) 'Protest Groups, Environmental Characteristics and Policy Responsiveness' (presented at Annual Meeting of the Midwest Political Science Association, Chicago).

SEARS, DAVID and McCANAHAY, JOHN (1973) *The Politics of Violence* (Boston: Houghton Mifflin).

SEILER, LAUREN H. (1975) 'Community Verticalization: On the Interface between Corporate Influence and the Horizontal Community', (paper presented at the Annual Meetings of the American Sociological Association, San Francisco) August.

SEMPLE, KEITH (1973) 'Recent Trends in the Spatial Concentration of Corporate Headquarters', *Economic Geography*, 49, 4, October, 309–18.

SIMMEL, GEORG (1950) *The Sociology of Georg Simmel*, edited by Kurt Wolff (New York: Free Press).

SINGELMANN. J. (1978) 'Sectoral Transformation of the Labor Force in Seven Industrialized Countries: 1920-1970', *American Journal of Sociology*, 85(5), 1224-34.

SKOLNICK, JEROME (1969) *The Politics of Protest: Violent Aspects of Protest and Confrontation* (Washington, DC: US Government Printing Office).

SLAYTON, WILLIAM L. (1966) 'The Operation and Achievements of the Urban Renewal Program', in Wilson (1966).

SMITH, JOE, BROMLEY, DAVID and MANTON, KENNETH (1979) 'Changes in the Coincidence of the Boundaries and Populations of Central Cities', *Social Forces*, 57 (3), March, 931–51.

SMITH, LARRY (1961) 'Space for CBD's Functions', *Journal of the American Institute of Planners*, XXVII, 6, February.

SMITH, RICHARD A. (1976) 'Community Power and Decision-Making: a Replication and Extension of Hawley', *American Sociological Review*, 41, August, 676–90.

SPILERMAN, SEYMOUR (1970) 'The Causes of Racial Disturbances: a Comparison of Alternative Explanations', *American Sociological Review*, 35, 627–49.

SPILERMAN, SEYMOUR (1971) 'The Causes of Racial Disturbances: Tests of an Explanation', *American Sociological Review*, 36, 427–42.

SPILERMAN, SEYMOUR (1974) 'Structural Characteristics of Cities and the Severity of Racial Disorders' (Institute for Research on Poverty, discussion papers, Madison, Wisconsin) February.

STANBACK, THOMAS M. JR, and KNIGHT, RICHARD V. (1976) *Suburbanization and the City* (Montclair, N.J.: Allanhead, Osmun & Co.).

STEISS, ALAN WALTER (1975) *Local Government Finance: Capital Facilities Planning and Debt Administration* (Lexington, Mass.: Lexington).

STERNLIEB, GEORGE and HUGHES, JAMES W. (1977) 'Metropolitan Decline and Inter-Regional Job Shifts', in Alcaly and Mermelstein, (eds), *The Fiscal Crisis of American Cities* (New York: Vintage) 145–64.

STEWART, R. (1967) *Managers and their Jobs* (London: Macmillan).

STINCHCOMBE, JEAN L. (1968) *Reform and Reaction* (Belmont, Calif.: Wadsworth Publishing).

STONE, CLARENCE N. (1976) *Economic Growth and Neighborhood Discontent* (Chapel Hill: University of North Carolina Press).

STONE, CLARENCE N. (1980) 'Systemic Power in Community Decision-Making: a Restatement of Stratification Theory', *American Political Science Review*, 74, 4, December, 978–90.

STRAUS, NATHAN (1944) *Seven Myths of Public Housing* (New York: Alfred A. Knopf).

STUART, A. W. (1968) 'The Suburbanization of Manufacturing in Small Metropolitan Areas: a Case Study of Roanoke', *The Southeastern Geographer*, 8, 30–9.

STRUYK, R. J. (1977) 'Need for Local Flexibility in United States Housing Policy', *Policy Analysis*, 3 (4).

SUTHERLAND, EDWIN H. and CRESSEY, DONALD P. (1978) *Criminology*, 10th edn. (Philadelphia, Pa.: Lippincott).

THOMPSON, WILBUR (1965) *A Preface to Urban Economics* (Baltimore: The Johns Hopkins University Press).

TIEBOUT, CHARLES M. (1956) 'A Pure Theory of Local Expenditures', *Journal of Political Economy*, 64, 416–24.

TIGER, LIONEL (1974) 'Is this Trip Necessary? The Heavy Human Costs of Moving Executives Around', *Fortune*, September, 139–41.

TILLY, CHARLES (1978) *From Mobilization to Revolution* (Reading, Mass.: Addison-Wesley).

TILLY, CHARLES, TILLY, LOUISE and TILLY, RICHARD (1975) *The Rebellious Century, 1830–1930* (Cambridge, Mass.: Harvard University Press).

TURK, HERMAN (1970) 'Interorganizational Networks in Urban Society', *American Sociological Review*, 35, 1–19.

TURK, HERMAN (1973a) 'Interorganizational Activation in Urban Communities: Deductions From the Concept of System', ASA Rose Monograph (Washington, DC, American Sociological Association).

TURK, HERMAN (1973b) 'Comparative Urban Structure From an Interorganizational Perspective', *Administrative Science Quarterly*, 18, 37–55.

UDELL, JON G. (1969) 'Social and Economic Consequences of the Merger Movement' (Madison, Wisconsin: Graduate School of Business, University of Wisconsin).

URQUHART, HEATHER J. (1974) 'The Ford Foundation and the Origins of the War on Poverty' (unpublished senior essay for sociology, for William Domhoff, U.C. Santa Cruz) June.

USEEM, MICHAEL (1979) 'The Social Organization of the American Business Elite and Participation of Corporation Directors in the Governance of American Institutions', *American Sociological Review*, 44, August, 553–72.

USEEM, MICHAEL (1980) 'Which Business Leaders Help Govern?', in William G. Donhoff (ed.), *Power Structure Research* (Beverly Hills, Calif.: Sage) 199–225.

US CHAMBER OF COMMERCE (1951) *Creating Better Cities* (Washington, D.C.).

US DEPARTMENT OF COMMERCE (1972) *Statistical Abstract of the United States*, 93rd annual edn (Washington, D.C.: US Government Printing Office).

US DEPARTMENT OF HOUSING AND URBAN DEVELOPMENT (1966) *Urban Renewal Project Characteristics* (Washington, DC: US Government Printing Office).

US HOUSE OF REPRESENTATIVES, BANKING AND CURRENCY COMMITTEE (1973) *Housing in the Seventies*, 93rd Congress (Washington, DC: US Government Printing Office). (Reprinted in edited form by US Department of Housing and Urban Development, 1974, under the same title.)

US OFFICE OF ECONOMIC OPPORTUNITY (1966) *Information Book as of June 30, 1966* (Washington, DC: US Government Printing Office).

US SENATE, COMMITTEE ON BANKING AND CURRENCY (1973) *The Central City Problem*, 93rd Congress (Washington, DC: US Government Printing Office).

VANNEMAN, REEVE D. and PETTIGREW, THOMAS F. (1972) 'Race and Relative Deprivation in the United States', *Race*, XIII, 461–86.

VERNON, RAYMOND (1959) *The Changing Economic Function of the Central City* (New York: Committee for Economic Development).

VERNON, RAYMOND (1967) *The Myth and Reality of Our Urban Problems* (Cambridge, Mass.: Harvard University Press).

WALLACE, DAVID A. (1968) 'The Conceptualizing of Urban Renewal', *University of Toronto Law Journal*, 18 (3), 248–58.

WALTON, JOHN (1967) 'The Vertical Axis of Community Organization and the Structure of Power', *Social Science Quarterly*, 48, 353–68.

WALTON, JOHN (1970) 'A Systematic Survey of Community Power Research', in Michael Aiken and Paul E. Mott (eds), *The Structure of Community Power* (New York: Random House).

WALTON, JOHN (1973) 'The Structural Bases of Political Change in Urban Communities', *Sociological Inquiry*, 43, 174ff.

WARREN, ROLAND L. (1963) *The Community in America* (Chicago: Rand McNally).

WARREN, ROLAND (1967) 'A Note on Walton's Analysis of Power Structure and Vertical Ties', *Social Science Quarterly*, 48, 369–72.

WARREN, ROLAND L. (1969) 'Model Cities First Round: Politics, Planning and Participation', *Journal of American Institute of Planners*, 35.

WEBER, MAX (1968) *Economy and Society*, vol. 1, edited by Guether Roth and Claus Wittich (New York: Bedminster Press).

WEICHER, JOHN C. (1972) 'The Effects of Urban Renewal on Municipal Service Expenditures', *Journal of Political Economy*, 80, 86–101.

WEICHER, JOHN C. (1976) 'The Fiscal Profitability of Urban Renewal Under Matching Grants and Revenue Sharing', *Journal of Urban Economics*, 3, 193–208.

WEISS, MARC A. (1980) 'The Origins and Legacy of Urban Renewal', in Pierre Clavel, John Forester and William W. Goldsmith (eds), *Planning in Age of Austerity* (New York: Pergamon Press) 53–80.

WELCH, SUSAN (1975) 'The Impact of Urban Riots on Urban Expenditures', *American Journal of Political Science*, XIX, 4, November, 741–61.

WELCH, SUSAN and KARNIG, ALBERT K. (1978) 'The Impact of Black Elected Officials on Urban Expenditures and Intergovernmental Revenue' (paper delivered at 1978 American Political Science Association meetings) September.

WHITT, J. ALLEN (1979) 'Toward a Class-Dialectical Model of Power: an Empirical Assessment of Three Competing Models of Political Power', *American Sociological Review*, 44, February, 81–100.

WHITT, J. ALLEN (1981) *The Politics of Contradiction: Public Transportation and the Ruling Class* (N.J.: Princeton University Press).

WILLIAMS, W. V. (1967) 'A Measure of the Impact of State and Local Taxes on Industrial Location', *Journal of Regional Science*, 7, 49–60.

WILLIAMS, JOHN A. and ZIMMERMAN, ERWIN (1979) 'Business Organizations and Redistributive Interests in American Cities' (unpublished paper).

WILLIAMS, OLIVER P. and ADRIAN, CHARLES R. (1963) *Four Cities: a Study in Comparative Policy Making* (Philadelphia: University of Pennsylvania Press).

WILSON, JAMES Q. (ed.) (1966) *Urban Renewal: the Record and the Controversy* (Cambridge, Mass.: MIT Press).

WOLMAN, HAROLD L. and THOMAS, N. C. (1970) 'Black Interests, Black Groups and Black Influence in the Federal Policy Process: The Cases of Housing and Education', *Journal of Politics*, 32, 875–97.

YINGER, JOHN (1977) 'The Capitalizations of Transportation Costs, Neighborhood Amenities and Local Fiscal Variables', Discussion Paper D77–16 (Harvard University Urban Planning, Policy Analysis and Administration).

ZEITLIN, MAURICE (1974) 'Corporate Ownership and Control: the Large Corporation and the Capitalist Class', *American Journal of Sociology*, 79, 1073–1119.

ZIMMER, BASIL (1964) *Rebuilding Cities: the Effects of Displacement and Relocation on Small Business* (Chicago: Quadrangle Books).

ZIMMERMAN. D. (1975) 'On the Relationship Between Public Goods Theory and Expenditure Determinant Studies', *National Tax Journal*, 28, 277–89.

Interviews

In the course of this research project, interviews were carried out with a variety of corporate executives, developers, and other informants. In order to protect the confidentiality of some of the information and its source, I will only list the organizational affiliations of those individuals I interviewed. In a few cases, I have decided not to name even the organizational affiliation of the informant. All of the interviews were carried out in 1973 and 1974.

American Cyanamid; Wayne, New Jersey
Bank of America; San Francisco, California
Collins Radio; Dallas, Texas
Continental Airlines; Los Angeles, California
Department of Housing and Urban Development; Washington, DC
Evans Products; Portland, Oregon
Exxon; Houston, Texas
Magnovox; Ft Wayne, Indiana
Mattel; Hawthorne, California
National Conference of Mayors
National Urban Coalition
Oscar Mayer; Madison, Wisconsin
RAND Corporation; Santa Monica, California
Shell; Houston, Texas
Tenneco; Houston, Texas
Whirlpool; Benton Harbor, Michigan

Author Index

Subject Index